LEICESTER
IN THE TWENTIETH CENTURY

EDITED BY DAVID NASH AND DAVID REEDER
WITH PETER JONES AND RICHARD RODGER

ALAN SUTTON
LEICESTER CITY COUNCIL

First published in the United Kingdom in 1993
Alan Sutton Publishing · Phoenix Mill · Far Thrupp · Stroud · Gloucestershire
in association with Leicester City Council

First published in the United States of America in 1993
Alan Sutton Publishing Inc · 83 Washington Street · Dover · NH 03820

British Library Cataloguing in Publication Data

Leicester in the Twentieth Century
  I. Nash, David
  942. 542082

  ISBN 0–7509–0487–9

Library of Congress Cataloging-in-Publication Data applied for

Typeset in 10/13 Plantin Light.
Typesetting and origination by
Alan Sutton Publishing Limited.
Printed in Great Britain by
The Bath Press, Avon.

CONTENTS

LIST OF EDITORS AND CONTRIBUTORS

Introduction: written by David Reeder with a contribution from David Nash.

Chapter One: The Built Environment: written by Richard Rodger. The material provided by Ned Newitt on inter-war housing and by Alan Strachan on the evolution of park provision is gratefully acknowledged, as is information supplied by John Dean regarding recent planning developments. Marilyn Palmer and Peter Neaverson provided information on North Evington, and Tim Brindley, Michael Miller, Richard Gill, David Nash, Roy Stuttard, Phil Smillie and various local history groups also generously made material available for inclusion, and often provided the audience as various ideas were tried out upon them.

Chapter Two: The Local Economy: written by David Reeder with Clive Harrison, who supplied the draft on the post-war economy, and with contributions from Peter Jones and Ned Newitt on the pre-1944 economy.

Chapter Three: Politics: written by Peter Jones, with contributions from Stuart Ball on local and parliamentary elections, David Nash on early Leicester Labour politics and Ned Newitt on pre- and post-war Labour politics.

Chapter Four: Municipal Provision: Education, Health and Housing Development: written by David Reeder with Cynthia Brown, who contributed the section on pre-1944 public health, Ned Newitt who wrote on pre-1944 housing policy and John Dean who contributed material on post-1944 town planning and redevelopment.

Chapter Five: Organizational and Associational Life: written by David Nash with additional contributions; Cynthia Brown contributed material on working men's clubs and allotment societies, Roy Stuttard was responsible for material on the co-operative movement and co-operative housing, Harriet Bradley wrote the material on women's factory culture, Frances Pollard wrote on the WEA and adult education, Alan Strachan and Joan Strachan provided the material on the development of immigrant communities in Leicester, Aubrey Newman and Nina Martschenko contributed more detailed information on the Jewish and the Ukrainian communities.

Chapter Six: Leisure and Consumption: written by David Nash with additional contributions; Ivan Waddington provided material on Leicester street disorder, Pat Murphy contributed a substantial piece on the organizational history of Leicester City Football Club, Helen Leacroft wrote on the history of Leicester Theatre and Music Hall, Philip Thornton provided information relating to the development of cinema in Leicester, Chris Tarrant assisted with the provision of many of the charts used in the text, and Jean Jackman generously provided work in progress on leisure in Leicester during the Second World War.

FOREWORD

Like many cities in recent years, Leicester has been grappling with the challenge of how it can meet the demands of the future without compromising the best of its past. The many splendid buildings – and indeed the design of the City itself – are a proud and permanent reminder of the way in which our City has developed and grown over the years. It is an inheritance which we must cherish and for which we shall be forever grateful.

But the true challenge is found beyond the City's fine architecture and innovative approach to planning. For it is to the *people* of Leicester that we owe our greatest debt of gratitude – those who, over the centuries, have made the City what it is today. These men and women had the vision to see not only how their ideas would benefit the City in their own time, but how the citizens of Leicester would profit from them in the years to come. That is the gauntlet that has been thrown down for us today. It is a heavy responsibility, yet one which the City Council has embraced eagerly and enthusiastically.

Leicester in the Twentieth Century seeks to bring our heritage to life. It is the product of a partnership of local historians, led by the University of Leicester's Centre for Urban History and supported by Leicester City Council. The book has drawn exclusively from the work of many people who are investigating aspects of Leicester's recent past. Without their specialist knowledge this publication would not have been possible.

We have been overwhelmed by the enthusiasm and commitment which these contributors have shown for the project. It is therefore a great pleasure for us, through this book, to help make it possible for them to share their knowledge with a wider audience.

The people of Leicester are proud of their city. I hope that this book will enrich their understanding of the developments which have made Leicester the city it is today.

Councillor Peter Soulsby
Leader, Leicester City Council

ACKNOWLEDGEMENTS

The editors would like to thank the following for their kind co-operation and involvement in the work of the 'Leicester in the Twentieth Century Project'.

The *Leicester Mercury* and its photographic library assisted in providing many of the photographs for this publication. Almost all of the remaining pictures were provided by the Leicestershire County Record Office and Museums Service. Leicester City Council and many of its officers have also been heavily involved in the project, and particularly we would like to thank Graham Chapman and Jo Dungey for their assistance and encouragement. In addition to this, Leicestershire County Cricket Club, Leicester City Football Club, Leicester Labour Party, Leicester Sketch Club, and Leicester Women's Art Club all provided valuable material which aided the publication of this book, and the editors would like to acknowledge this debt.

The editors would particularly like to acknowledge the help of the Director of the Centre for Urban History, Professor Peter Clark, who has provided constant help and editorial advice throughout the project. The numerous speakers at our yearly workshops: Mel Read MEP, Malcolm Fox, Satish Kapur, Mohammed Bashir, Rita Patel, Pete Loman, Paul Winstone, Jeremy Crump and Brian Jenkinson also stimulated interest in the project and provided the editors with much material to work with. David Alexander, Shirley Aucott, Su Barton, Alan Bennett, Nikki Dandeker, Dev Diwana, Pauline Fisher, John Goodacre, Chris Hasluck, Mike Huk, Kathy Jessop, Peter Neaverson, Marilyn Palmer, Laurie Potter, Anthony Sutcliffe, Kate Thompson, Katherine Towsey, Mike Turner (senior), Jo Vivian and Deryck Wills all provided assistance and advice that contributed to the formulation and ultimate success of the project, and of this publication in particular.

Introduction

For that acerbic local historian W.G. Hoskins, Leicester was 'at first sight a wholly uninteresting Midland city'. The judgement echoed that of the writer J.B. Priestley in 1936, who found the city bright and clean but 'lacking in character'. But as Hoskins himself recognized, and this book will demonstrate, looks are deceptive.

Since Roman times Leicester has been an important economic and strategic point in the East Midlands – as a market town in the Middle Ages, as a garrison town besieged in the Civil War, as the cradle of the hosiery industry in the eighteenth century, as a rapidly growing industrial city with a strong nonconformist and individualistic ethos in the Victorian age, and as a vibrant and prosperous manufacturing city for much of the present century.

Leicester in the twentieth century – the home of C.P. Snow, Joe Orton, Sue Townsend and other British writers – has a complex and fascinating story to tell in its own right. It is a story of how social life and politics were forged and reshaped by local tradition and circumstance, and of how the city came to represent a twentieth-century modernity in its buildings and housing developments as in its social and economic life. But it is a story also of how one provincial city responded to changes in national policy (not always beneficial), the disturbances of war and other international upheavals, the impact of technological change, new social priorities and lifestyles, and the problems that arose in the post-war period when the economic climate started to deteriorate and the city's housing stock began to age. Relating this story is to provide insights on the changing quality of modern urban life.

This is a book, then, which sets out to show how Leicester evolved during the twentieth century as a place in which to work, play and live. It deals with alterations in the physical appearance of the city as well as its social character, describes economic trends and political movements, traces the development of municipal policies, particularly as regards housing, education and social welfare, and discusses the wider organizational and associational life of the city, and the changing pattern of leisure. The history of these aspects of urban development is brought up to the end of the 1980s, when they have only just ceased to be contemporary. Hence the book touches on matters that are still important issues in the city – debates over the levels of employment and economic activity, the role of the municipality in housing and community development, planning strategies, the extent of participation in cultural and sporting life, and the way that Leicester's ethnic communities have contributed to its economy and culture.

A good part of the history in this book will be within the living memory of older residents, and many will be familiar still with the names of the leading figures in the life of the city, particularly during the inter-war years – the business leaders, philanthropists and councillors, such as Fielding Johnson, Percy Gee, Sir Jonathan North, Charles Keene, and Emily Fortey, to name but a few of those who have been commemorated in the city's educational institutions. References will be made to the contribution of this and later generations of city leaders in the following pages, but in the context of the larger scenario of urban change – a scenario that embraces the great variety of movements, trends, structures, conditions and images associated with the growth of a modern city.

In recent years town history has been very much in vogue. This is due to the remarkable growth of urban and local history since the 1960s along with increasing community recognition of the value of having a fresh record of the history of individual towns. A number of city councils in England and Scotland are currently associated with urban historical projects and some have actively sponsored research and publications. In this way a tradition of town history, which last reached a climax in the late Victorian and Edwardian period, is being continually revived and renewed.

Yet the historic transformation of town and city life in the twentieth century, as revolutionary as any of the changes in earlier times, has received surprisingly little attention in published studies. There are relatively few precedents for a volume which deals only with the period since 1900. In the case of Leicester, while there are numerous books on its early history and several distinguished contributions to the history of the Victorian city, work on the present century has been more patchy and often inaccessible to local readers. Jack Simmons has provided the only overview of key developments in Leicester from 1860 in a study that conveys, in typically elegant manner, one historian's view of the distinctive characteristics of the modern city. The present volume in contrast brings together a variety of historical expertise with the aim of providing an informed account of urban change since the close of the nineteenth century.

In this way the book updates the older inter-war accounts of the making of the modern city as well as extending the work of an earlier generation of scholars on particular aspects of twentieth-century Leicester life – as, for example, the previous studies by historians of local politics, housing developments and the growth of Leicester, the analysis which geographers have made of the social and demographic patterns of the city based on the censuses of 1971 and 1981, the contributions of geographers and economists to our understanding of the local economy and the development of Greater Leicester as a sub-regional unit. More recently studies have been made of the cultural experiences of Leicester people, in reconstructions of the experiences of factory women for example, and of the way that Asian immigrants settled in the city. There are also several more specialized studies now available on a wide range of other matters, from education and the policing of Leicester to community development and the experiences of the Afro-Caribbean and Asian communities in the city.

The Mayor Samuel Lennard and the Mayoress Annie Lennard welcome Leicester's citizens to the new century

The book also seeks to reflect the lively popular interest in the recent past. In Leicester, as in other British towns, this is manifested in the commercial publication of books of photographs, the support given to local history societies, the writings of local historians about Leicester streets, buildings and personalities, numerous town trails, and the development of an oral history archive during the 1980s. All of these activities should be stimulated further by the 1992 initiative of the city council in setting up a Living History Unit within the City Leisure Department to save and protect the non-official records of Leicester's recent history through the collection and exhibition of photographs, documents, and recollections on tape, and to advise on and sponsor local history publications and projects.

While the present book makes no claims to be a community history as such, it draws on available sources of oral testimony, where relevant, and is illustrated with a selection of old photographs, mainly from the collections held by the *Leicester Mercury* and the County Record Office. These photographs, of buildings, street scenes, municipal services, business and political figures, many of them published for the first time, are documents of a kind. They recover the history of Leicester embodied in its public face as well as evoking memories of the way we lived then.

The preparation of the book also provided an opportunity to bring together academic and local historians in a programme of new research. The idea of undertaking the project came initially from the Centre for Urban History at the University of Leicester. It was readily taken up by the Leicester City Council who agreed to finance a research officer and support publication, establishing a partnership with the university. From the first the research officer, David Nash, sought to activate local interest in the project and draw local historians, teachers and representatives of community groups into it. A series of one-day workshops took place over the three years of the project, dealing with local politics and municipal policy, and such aspects of urban life as leisure and work. Three of these gatherings were held in the historically charged surroundings of the city council chamber in the Town Hall. Over the three years of the project nearly fifty people from the city have been actively involved in it.

Planned as a collaborative effort, the responsibility for most of the writing as well as the editing of the six chapters was given to four members of the larger research group. The scope of each chapter is necessarily dependent on the work and interests of the principal authors and the research and contributions available to them as well as constraints of time and space. Inevitably much has had to be left out but it was thought preferable to deal with a limited range of subjects thoroughly, drawing on new work wherever possible, than to paint a broader canvas superficially. We hope very much that publishing this book will stimulate further research to make good the gaps and omissions in the text and to elaborate on the subjects with which they deal. To this end the research officer has provided a guide to the primary holdings of records, covering the twentieth century, relating to published and documentary material held in the County Record Office and the former Local Studies Library in Bishop Street, moved in 1993 to the Leicestershire Record Office at Wigston. This guide is available from the Centre for Urban History, Leicester University. It is in itself a testimony to the abundance of materials already available for studying the history of Leicester in the twentieth century, of which only a very limited selection of basic sources is cited at the end of the chapters in this volume.

When Jack Simmons was writing about modern Leicester in the mid-1970s one of his main concerns was to emphasize the historical continuities in the evolution of the city. For him, the most important thing about Leicester was the way that an industrial city had been grafted on to an older market town – 'the largest market town in England'. He thought that to a degree unusual for a modern industrial city it was the product of a long evolution: 'It was fortunate to escape large scale change in wartime, and in its physical landscape as in its social life its story has been one of steady continuous adaptation to changing circumstances and opportunities.' This emphasis on evolution and adaptation was the more significant perhaps because Simmons was writing in a period when changes were taking place in the city that threatened a definite break with the past, as he was well aware. With the advantage of a further twenty years or so, it is becoming clearer that the period from, say, the early 1960s to the late 1970s was a watershed in the city's twentieth-century history, during which its character and image began to be radically transformed from that 'small town homeliness', 'solid, Victorian, brickbuilt and prosaic', which W.G. Hoskins had recalled in 1957. Leicester seems in many ways a different place now from what it had been in the 1950s, or what it had attempted to be in the 1930s, although it can be argued still, as the first chapter in this volume maintains, that change within continuity has persisted as the distinctive hallmark of the evolution of Leicester's built environment.

Nevertheless, the 1960s and 1970s undoubtedly saw an acceleration of changes affecting the central area of Leicester as represented by such developments as the creation of the southern underpass, the reconstruction of parts of the inner city with high-rise buildings, the new office buildings, and the increasing congestion of the city road system with the growth of motor traffic. The later 1970s also saw changes in the character of the shops in the centre of the city, now pedestrianized, and the first of the shopping centre precincts. Many of these developments were seen at the time as initiating a new phase in the history of modern Leicester, refurbishing the longstanding image of the city as a prosperous and progressive place – an image which can be traced back to the inter-war years. From the 1920s council publications and city guide books repeatedly projected a picture of the 'new Leicester'. As early as 1921 one official handbook announced that the city was making history in its workshops and factories, conveying a picture of a go-ahead light industrial city of the future: those who are 'induced to make a closer acquaintance with Leicester', the guide book proclaimed, 'will soon share that civic pride which characterizes its inhabitants, a pride based on thriving industries, efficient local government, residential amenities of a high order and attractive shops'. Commentators in the 1920s expressed admiration for the electric trams and how Leicester was being surrounded by attractive residential districts and parks. The activities of the municipal council were frequently promoted as representative of the new Leicester: its town planning and council housing estates, the tramways and gas undertakings, the Derwent valley water scheme, new health department and school reorganization scheme, the maternity clinics and special schools, and even the city crematorium and municipal farm. 'Leicester: progressive city and county' was the headline of a *Daily Telegraph* survey in 1936.

The image of Leicester as a prosperous city has been especially potent. Moreover this has been almost invariably explained by reference to the innovative character of the local economy and the ingenuity of its workforce, which seemed to demonstrate more than most provincial cities the economic virtues of small-scale enterprise. Although the city was not immune from the unemployment and distress of the depression years, as will be shown, the average level of household incomes by 1936 was such as to give it the reputation of being the 'second most prosperous city in Europe'. This judgement was still being invoked thirty years on, as revealed in Sir Robert Mark's biography of his period as Chief Constable in Leicester, where he remarks that he arrived in 'a town which was then, in terms of income per family, the second wealthiest in Europe'.

It was in the buoyant and expansive period of economic growth in the years following the Second World War that Leicester's image of prosperity was most justified. As the conclusion to the *Victoria County History* explained, the Leicester of 1955 was 'wealthy, healthy and bustling'. It had acquired a character that was 'marked by a high level of industrial and commercial activity, by a high general standard of living, and by the absence of any extreme or distinctive movement in politics, religion, or culture'. But as Chapter Two in this volume argues, the apparent economic success of Leicester disguised fundamental underlying structural problems that a change in the economic climate during the 1970s, as the long post-war boom came to an end, began to expose. Since then investigations of the social and economic condition of British and European cities have provided indicators which can be used to show that in the early 1970s Leicester was relatively problem free and still rated quite highly among European cities, but that from about 1975 its economic health worsened and the city deteriorated *vis-à-vis* other cities in Britain and Europe in respect of income, levels of employment, housing and other social problems. During this period the role of manufacturing in the local economy became more problematical and it came under further pressure during the 1980s. As a consequence, more effort went into promoting the image of the city as a regional shopping centre, and, with the development of the M1/M69 business park, as the hub of a widespread regional trading distribution network.

But it might well be claimed that the boom years of the 1960s rather than the economic downturn of the mid-1970s marked the more important turning point for the city. The decline of the local footwear industry in this decade and the way that many city based companies in the prosperous trades were swallowed up by national and international concerns had important social as well as economic implications. When Jack Simmons wrote about the 1960s as dealing a death blow to the old Leicester, he was not thinking about the physical changes affecting the expanding city, so much as the declining significance of the old dynastic family firms. In the inter-war years the characteristic pattern of Leicester industry and commerce was that of the family business, on a relatively small scale, and although that pattern was greatly modified after the Second World War, it still exercised a profound influence in maintaining a close knit middle-class society. The tone of Leicester society reflected bourgeois values which made it seem a rather dull place from a metropolitan perspective. But this kind of society began to change with the emergence of large concerns in the local economy, the decline in the numbers of small businessmen and the growth of a managerial and professional class. The suburban development of the city in the post-war years was also important as new middle-class suburbs were formed outside the city boundary. These grew away from the city, acquiring their own institutions and loyalties.

It was from the ranks of the family business dynasties too that Leicester's social leaders had been mainly drawn prior to the 1960s, as a long tradition of philanthropic activity in the city testifies. Although the representation of business interests on the council had gone down in the post-war period, the city still maintained many aspects of nineteenth-century civic life up to the 1960s, and several of the local civic officers as well as the leading city fathers represented Leicester families and interests of some antiquity. The *Leicester Mercury* constituted an important element in this world. It had absorbed other newspapers such as the

Chronicle and *Evening Mail* to become the premier newspaper in the city by the 1960s. The editors have never been outsiders, and more often than not reinforced the role and outlook of the Leicester establishment in cultivating a strong sense of the history and distinctive identity of the city.

One of the themes in the chapter on the politics of the city concerns the declining influence of an older generation of city fathers in the post-war years and the growing importance of party political concerns in the conduct of municipal affairs. The reconstitution of the local Labour group on the council, and a change in the tempo and character of civic life can be dated from the 1970s, which this chapter identifies as the watershed decade.

However, if we think of the growth of municipal responsibilities then it may be that the entire twentieth century up to the late 1980s perhaps can be regarded as a watershed in the development of the city. The steady accretion of municipal responsibilities has given the city council a much more active role than in the nineteenth century in shaping the character of the city, and to an extent the quality of urban life. In this book considerable attention is paid to the involvement of the council in supplying housing accommodation and to its role, among with external agencies, in post-war inner city redevelopment. But the chapter on municipal provision also draws attention to Leicester's role in pioneering ideas of preventative health care and in the growth of welfare services. These kinds of activity all had their own distinctive cycles of evolution as shaped basically by changes in national legislation and policy. Despite this, what has impressed us in researching the Leicester story has been the continuing scope for local autonomy as exercised through the leading officers of the council. The record of the inter-war years as described here seems to have been especially important from that point of view. The strong sense of civic accomplishment in the city was set back by the reorganization of local government in 1974, although it might be argued that ultimately it was the more gradual erosion of local responsibilities for such areas as housing provision and education, which set in during the later 1980s and early 1990s, that will be seen by a later generation as marking the turning point in the history of municipal provision in this country.

Not only the changing patterns of provision but also the underlying problems which they were intended to combat had their distinctive cycles over the twentieth century. One kind of cycle referred to in Chapter Four was the changing pattern of mortality and of the incidence of disease, which are of course fundamental to such matters in any study of city life. It was Leicester's exceptionally high infant mortality rates during the Edwardian years, for which it had an unenviable national reputation in medical circles, that lay behind the pioneering of many clinic based services in the fields of maternity and infant welfare in the city. But since the 1970s a greater concern in Leicester, as in other cities, has been the ageing of the population and the impact on adult mortality rates of what have become known as the diseases of civilization – which in Leicester is exacerbated by the vulnerability of some ethnic groups to particular types of disease. But in an altogether wider sense the cycles of growth and decay are also apparent in the evolution of the city itself in the twentieth century. With the ageing of the housing stock, older neighbourhoods began to figure in league tables of physical and social deprivation during the 1970s and 1980s.

Furthermore, over the last thirty years or so councillors and officers have had to contend with an increasingly complex set of issues, some of which have been extremely contentious. During the inter-war years the city had gained the reputation for moderation in its political outlook: political life was generally intense but it was rarely violent. This reputation was maintained in the post-war years but seemed for a time in the 1970s to be in danger as difficult local issues, not least the battle over comprehensive schooling and the furore over the way that the sudden influx of new migrants was handled, created new tensions in council politics and among the people of the city. However, the raising of the political temperature in the 1970s proved to be a temporary phase. Despite the problems that migration on the scale of the 1970s brought, Leicester's reputation as a welcoming city for immigrants was eventually reinforced – and its schools have had a particularly important part to play in this.

What has to be borne in mind here is the long history of migration into the city. It had been a reception area for different European groups of migrants since the First World War when it became the home for a number of Belgian refugees. This was continued in the years immediately following the Second World War when Poles, Yugoslavians and Ukrainians found a home in the city, as did the Hungarian refugees in 1956. So the arrival of the Ugandan refugees in the 1970s came in a long tradition, although for this group as for other groups coming to the city, such as the earlier influxes of Caribbean and Asian peoples, Leicester's reputation as a thriving economy was the magnet that drew them.

Before the 1960s and '70s, however, and still to some extent thereafter, the overall social character of the city was set by its indigenous working-class factory population. With so many women factory workers, it shared some of the characteristics of the older manufacturing textile centres of the north. The involvement of working women in the culture of the factory and the lifestyle this encouraged in the pre- and post-war years forms one aspect of the discussion of changing lifestyles in Chapter Five.

To complain, as some commentators have done in the past, that the city lacked character is to overlook the growth of a working-class community life based on the pub and the club as much as the community centre, despite the wholesale transference over the years of large sections of working-class people to the new housing estates on the periphery. One manifestation of this has been Leicester's reputation as a sporting city – a reputation which not only derived from a long pedigree of successful performance in a variety of sports but also the involvement of many individuals in city-wide competitive sport. In the pre- and post-war years many Leicester firms had their own works teams in sports such as football, cricket and hockey, with the last of these being particularly popular among women workers. The very number of sports pitches marked out on Victoria Park and other suburban spaces is testimony to the level of participation in organized sport that the city has fostered, quite apart from the table tennis leagues and the unrecorded darts matches and pub quizzes. Yet in these activities as in other aspects of Leicester's leisure life, for example the popularity of dance halls and the cinema, the 1950s may seem in retrospect to have been the climax of an era. Particularly in the last twenty years the consumption of public entertainment and the level of active participation in sport and leisure, although still evident, seems to have dwindled for a variety of reasons that say more about how we live as a nation than it does about Leicester. At the same time efforts have been made in Leicester as elsewhere to encourage greater participation in sport through the provision of more accessible leisure services and sports centres where team, and previously restricted individual sports such as squash and swimming can be enjoyed.

The level of new provision has also been important in other areas of Leicester life in the post-war period, with the spread of opportunities to gain access to education, library services, welfare services, the arts and other community inspired organizations. Chapter Five describes the various styles and forms of intervention in the community life of the city since the early twentieth century, from the activities of such voluntary organizations as the Charity Organization Society to the growth of community and cultural provision on the part of the city council. The latter has been a feature of Leicester life in recent years that has done a good deal to mitigate its rather lacklustre reputation as a cultural centre.

In fact as the relevant chapter in this volume shows, the level of cultural activity in the city has gone through various phases over the years. During the 1930s for instance the city was recognized as a strong centre for music with several choral societies, the Philharmonic Society and the Symphony Orchestra. The latter was formed in 1922 by Malcolm Sargent and it brought Leicester to the fore musically, with the De Montfort Hall an important provincial venue both for new and established works. But by the late 1950s contemporary newspapers gave a distinct sense of a loss of cultural vitality, not so much in terms of music as in the decline of theatre-going, with the closure of the last of the city theatres. The 1970s in contrast saw a marked revival in the city's cultural life, with the establishment of the Haymarket Theatre and on a wider cultural front the beginnings of Radio Leicester, the first of the local broadcasting stations.

During the post-war years Leicester's town centre appeared to exude a kind of dogged provincialism which often seemed to prefer isolation from the worst, and, it has been sometimes said the best, that metropolitan culture could offer. Yet the later 1960s in some respects put the city on the cultural map. While the idea of a 'swinging Leicester' would be misleading, the city did gain some notoriety in this decade from its association with several cult figures and a successful popular music group. In the 1970s and 1980s the contribution of the city to the world of popular music and its gallery of Leicester-born or Leicester-based sporting heroes and novelists were all elements in conveying that sense of provincial rebellion in the face of metropolitan culture which Liverpool had pioneered. But what has most distinguished Leicester in recent years has been the developing cultural diversity of the city which stems from the colonization of various neighbourhoods by different ethnic groups. The impact of the migrations of the 1970s on the city's cultural life has been profound, as Leicester became one of a group of British cities endeavouring to work out in quite pragmatic terms how to facilitate the making of a composedly multi-racial society.

Thus earlier and rather simplistic images of Leicester no longer do justice to the multi-faceted character of its urban life, if ever they did. Many of the older images of the city were at best halftruths. We hope this volume will help Leicester people to go beyond these to understand more clearly the way their city has changed over the years. By reviewing various aspects of urban development over a period of nearly one hundred years, it seeks to offer an historical perspective on what has been happening to Leicester and, by implication, to other provincial towns and cities in twentieth-century Britain.

Further Reading

Brown, A.E., ed., *The Growth of Leicester* (1972)
Howe, Charles, *Leicester: its civic, industrial, institutional and social life* (1929)
The Leicester Economic Study (1974)
Marrett, Valerie, *Immigrants Settling in the City* (1989)
Pye, Norman, ed., *Leicester and its Region* (1972)
Simmons, Jack, *Leicester Past and Present*, vol. 2 (1974)
Victoria County History of Leicestershire, vol. 4 (1958)
Waddington, A.J., *The Making of a Modern City* (1931)

Chapter One

THE BUILT ENVIRONMENT

More than anything else, buildings and the spaces around them capture the identity of a city. The scale of offices, grandeur of historic buildings, congested streets, parks, pitches and playgrounds, just like pubs influence the way citizens relate to Leicester. Our mental maps – of childhood street games, romantic encounters, of VE-Day celebrations and jubilee street parties in 1977 – like more mundane daily activities associated with the journey to work, 'signing-on', and the position of particular market stalls, leisure and other facilities are heavily influenced by the built environment inherited from previous generations.

Yet this legacy of buildings and open spaces is not static. Though there are continuities in the physical fabric, for example in the façades of individual buildings, or groups of them, like the Town Hall, Grand Hotel, London Road railway station and the Coleman Road estate, and in the position of particular thoroughfares like Market Street, Aylestone Road or leafy Spencefield Lane, most have experienced the process of change as system building, glass-fronted multiple stores, and the attentions of DIY enthusiasts and keen gardeners have altered the built environment. Alterations have been wrought at the micro level through changing the purpose of shops, in-filling plots of land between existing houses, and by altering internally single family dwellings to provide multiple occupancy for nursing homes. At a medium scale, entire districts have been demolished and their character altered, as for example in the St Matthew's and Haymarket developments, or in a less conscious though still pervasive way, through the substitution of steel-framed structures for warm midland brick buildings, as in Vaughan Way. This has altered fundamentally the colour and texture of buildings. Visually the refurbishment of East Park and Belgrave in the 1980s and the construction of the Shires and Fosse Park shopping developments in the 1990s represent something of a reaction to the soulless functionalism of 1950s and 1960s architecture. The transformation has also been wrought in a deliberate way, through policy instruments. Planning, both on a grand scale, as with the Beaumont Leys estate and the business park in the M1/M69 triangle, and, more modestly, at the street level by creating pedestrian precincts, altering traffic flows, providing grants for replacement railings, and through the 'greening' of the city by planting kerbside trees and developing green 'wedges' of parkland or natural areas as at Aylestone Meadows, has aimed consciously at creating a living environment distinctive to Leicester.

A Victorian and Edwardian Legacy

Continuity in the present-day urban landscape owes much to the durability of the stock of housing. Leicester has retained important elements of its late nineteenth and early twentieth-century identity. As an industrial late developer, in the sense that the transition from workshop to factory in both hosiery and footwear was much later than in the textile towns of northern England or the metal-working industries of the west Midlands, the pronounced population expansion – it rose by 140 per cent between 1871 and 1911 – was accompanied by the construction of about thirty-five thousand new houses. The quality of these houses was significantly better than in earlier decades for two reasons: first, the town council enforced tighter building regulations relating to water supply, sanitary provisions, ventilation, and the density of new building construction; secondly, and more importantly, an increasing proportion of skilled manual and white collar workers was able to afford a high standard of accommodation. This was reinforced by high and reasonably stable levels of household income in Leicester compared to the West Midlands and other English boroughs, since both husband and wife could often find jobs in complementary industries. On the eve of the First World War, the average family size in Leicester was well below that for England, and had fallen by about 50 per cent between 1870 and 1910. Crucially, the pre-1914 built environment in Leicester was heavily influenced by the fact that 65 per cent of all Leicester families lived in

Highfields: St Peter's Road and Melbourne Hall

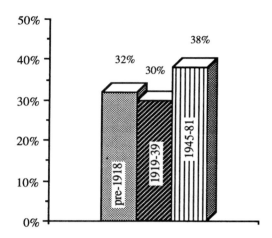

Age distribution of Leicester housing in 1992

houses with six or more rooms, which compared very favourably to the 31 per cent for English county boroughs as a whole; less than 1 per cent of dwellings contained more than one family; and there were only twelve blocks of flats with a mere fifty-one families living in them. So in 1911 the number of persons per room in Leicester was only 80 per cent of the average for the larger English boroughs.

The durability of the housing stock can be illustrated by the fact that, in 1981, almost a third of all houses in Leicester had been built before 1918 (though less than 1 per cent date from before 1870); approximately 30 per cent were built between the wars; and only 38 per cent (or just two in five) of the present stock of houses has been built since 1945. The compression of the principal expansionary phase of nineteenth-century building development into the four decades before the First World War has therefore left an indelible mark on the Leicester landscape of the 1990s. This can be seen in two forms – the architectural and the spatial.

Visually, areas such as Clarendon Park, Aylestone Park and Gipsy Lane owed much to the concerted efforts of a handful of developers and landowners within the space of relatively few years. For example, the Clarendon Park Land Company developed the area south of Victoria Park from the 1890s, and the Revd F. A. Burnaby and Arthur Wakerley, who were heavily involved in the development of the Spinney Hills and North Evington areas from the mid-1880s, did so in an integrated way so that styles, materials and architectural details, though varied, did not conflict. While 70 per cent of all Leicester housebuilding projects involved the construction of five or fewer houses, there were some larger firms – Isaac Harrison in the Newfoundpool area and Orson Wright in Knighton Fields both completed 200–300 houses in the 1880s – which provided a unifying appearance in particular neighbourhoods. This visual uniformity was neither mean nor oppressive, as was often the case in other English boroughs, and stylistically owed something to an English vernacular revival. Architects, including Stockdale Harrison, Samuel Perkins Pick, Langley and Baines, H. H. Thompson and a rising group of their contemporaries, were responsible for significant numbers of brick-built houses, constructed for an emerging professional class and for hosiery and other manufacturers in Stoneygate, the Manor Road area of Oadby, and on the fringes of Charnwood Forest at Swithland. Rendered in roughcast with asymmetrical elevations, projecting eaves and bay windows, and with elegant detailing both inside and out, these high-status dwellings generated considerable repair, maintenance and domestic service work before the First World War. Though there was an active corps of Leicester architects designing detached villas, only in the more modest details of ornamental tiling and terracotta could their ideas offset the rigidity of the geometrical street plans superimposed on working-class housing by developers.

Commercial and public architecture of a high standard was also undertaken in the years before the First World War. Examples include Charles Kempson's Unitarian church (now Elim Pentecostal) on Narborough Road, and his Hopewell's shop on the edge of St Nicholas Circle; Goddard's News Reading Room (Granby and Belvoir Streets); Cecil Ogden and Amos Hall's Grand Hotel (Granby Street); Hall's Silver Arcade; Everard and Pick's National Westminster bank (St Martin's), and Chatwin & Son (Birmingham) who built Lloyd's bank (High Street). Wakerley's Singer Building and Harrison's Grand Clothing Hall in the 1902 reconstruction of the High Street are Edwardian examples of architectural excellence and individuality that distinguish the central business district of present-day Leicester. Commercial architecture, such as that in Horsefair Street and on the corner of Braunstone Gate

Lewis's Store (1935–6) in Humberstone Gate

Turkey Café, Granby Street (1900–1) with Oriental arches and Doulton tiles. Arthur Wakerley was the architect.

Marquess of Wellington, London Road

and Narborough Road, the half-timbered shop by Frank Jones for Gadsby's, Wakerley's Turkey Café in Granby Street, and a number of pubs – the Saracen's Head, Durham Ox, Marquis of Wellington, and the Tudor – illustrate the flair of many turn-of-the-century architects, some of whom incorporated Arts and Crafts influences and an easy-going rusticity. These and other notable buildings, like the pavilion on the former County Cricket Ground (Aylestone Road), the Arcadia Electric Theatre (High Street) and the De Montfort Hall are a collage of *fin de siècle* Leicester without which the contemporary urban scene would lose meaning; our visual reference points would be dislocated, and what we recognize implicitly as Leicester would be dislodged.

The spatial patterning which resulted from pre-1914 building developments have also remained persistent. Though the built-up area and social geography of Leicester changed little between 1870 and the mid-1880s, over the next thirty years the south-eastern drift was pronounced. The initial dispersal of population along Aylestone, Evington, Belgrave, Humberstone and Hinckley Roads was a practical response to suburbanizing influences – the need to have sewer, gas and transport connections determined these as the principal directions of early ribbon development. Infill between the spokes of this radiating network of access roads followed later. This process also led to a hierarchy of housing quality, the areas of greatest attraction being in the Knighton–Stoneygate area, with Highfields losing its appeal as the middle-class preference for privacy and a garden was compromised by the more restricted plots of the Highfields area. The south-eastern orientation to suburbanization was reinforced by two further factors. Firstly, a systematic flood prevention and sewage control scheme was completed only in 1891. Before this project there had been no road bridge for a distance of about $2\frac{1}{2}$ miles between the West Bridge and Aylestone, and this had restricted east–west communications. The rebuilding of the West and Braunstone Gate bridges and the addition of three new bridges opened up new areas, notably the Westcotes estate, which had been sold in 1886, to large-scale building development. Only in small pockets, as at Western Park, was middle-class exclusivity feasible amid the rapidly developing west bank of the Soar. Secondly, the triangle formed by the river and the two railway lines to the east and north of the city had already become associated with cheap, low quality housing, and this, too, constrained the suburbanizing process on the north side of the city.

The expansion and relative prosperity of the city before 1914 enabled a subtle social differentiation to take place. 'Slums' in the central area formed the base of a housing pyramid; solidly working-class areas included Newfoundpool, south Belgrave, and Spinney Hills; Clarendon Park, north Belgrave and south Westcotes were populated with a skilled artisan class; and the south-eastern wedge formed the apex of the social pyramid with high status villas. Of course this is an over-simplification; there were variations within and between streets. But to a considerable extent the social and physical template of twentieth-century Leicester was laid down in the three or four decades before the First World War.

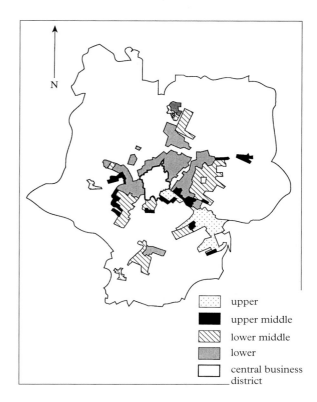

The social geography of Leicester by residential areas, 1911

upper

upper middle

lower middle

lower

central business district

Alternative Housing Strategies

City-wide, overcrowding levels were low compared to the rest of urban England. Only 1.1 per cent of the population of Leicester lived in overcrowded housing, defined as more than two persons per room, compared to an average of 7.4 per cent in English provincial towns. Leicester topped the housing league in the sense that no other borough of the 102 listed in the 1911 census had a lower level of overcrowding. While new flood control and sewage pumping facilities to Beaumont Leys eased some of the worst environmental problems, there remained districts where the provision of running water, sanitation and sinks in houses was either shared or non-existent.

Two unconnected strategies were pursued, both with a view to improving the quality of workers' accommodation. One initiative, an integrated industrial community in North Evington designed by the architect Arthur Wakerley, was an extension of the private enterprise building developments undertaken before the First World War. From 1885, when Wakerley bought 5 acres of brick pits for redevelopment, to 1914, when a total of 212 acres with twenty-eight factories employing over 5,000 workers had been developed, Wakerley nurtured the idea of North Evington as a self-contained suburb. Its independent aspirations were demonstrated by the construction of a market hall, surgery, police and fire stations, and a temperance hotel, together with many types of shops. Though Wakerley himself undertook the construction of some fine houses – on Wood Hill, East Park, and St Saviour's Roads – local contractors, such as Alfred Woodcock who built Asfordby and Baggrave Streets, were responsible for most of the building work. Distinctive features of this urban landscape were the small backyard workshops for outworkers in the hosiery and shoe trades, and arches between houses to ease the passage of carts to the larger workshops and stables behind terraced housing. This integration of housing and industry was developed on a grander scale with the Park Vale works of Smith, Faire and Co., and Gent's Faraday Works, but more typically on St Saviour's Road East, where houses and a cluster of shoe factories faced one another across the street. North Evington never quite functioned as conceived, mainly because the development of electric trams linking it to Leicester made this the most heavily used route in the city in 1906. However, the red-brick landscape of houses and factories remains largely intact.

Another strategy, based on an alliance of co-operative and temperance interests, also sought to improve workers' housing. The initiative grew out of the Anchor Boot and Shoe Co-operative Society – a workers' co-partnership which shared 'trading surpluses'. From basic educational instruction and classes on history, politics and physical health, it was not a giant step to consider the principle of mutuality in the context of an industrial village. Anchor Tenants, founded in 1902, used their savings to purchase land at Humberstone and to make instalment payments to develop the site. The first houses were occupied in 1908, and by 1915 there were ninety-four gabled cottages, roughcast, with shrubs in the gardens, and streets (Lilac and Chestnut Avenues, Laburnum Road, Fern Rise, and Keyham Lane) laid out on principles derived from Letchworth Garden Suburb. By 1939 there were 143 houses, and the community ideas remained robust with shops, a church, five hole golf course, open-air swimming pool and tennis courts providing integrated community facilities conspicuously lacking in later housing developments. Justifiably, the Humberstone Garden Suburb became a nationally recognized example of housing co-operation.

Homes Fit for Heroes? – Housing in the Inter-war Years

Lloyd George's election pledge 'Homes Fit for Heroes' was not the origin of council housing. Liverpool and Glasgow councillors had initiated such programmes fifty years earlier in the 1860s, and even in Leicester, three-storey council house blocks with forty-two dwellings had been built in 1900. More likely, the police and miners' strikes and the demobilization of soldiers combined to prompt what Lloyd George described in Cabinet as an 'insurance premium', the finance for municipal housing to counteract the risk of social unrest.

Locally, the climate was favourable towards the introduction of council housing after the war. Secularist and Fabian councillors such as F. J. Gould and Herbert Hallam embraced town planning and municipal housebuilding ideas on the eve of the First World War when the ILP held the balance of political power in the council chamber. Hallam noted the links between housing, health and profits by observing '. . . that in St Margaret's children died three times as fast as the children of Spinney Hill ward'. Though tenants on Red Clydeside gained national attention in 1915 through public demonstrations to oppose landlords' rental increases, Leicester possessed an equivalent organization, the newly formed Tenants' Protection League, which protested against 'the unpatriotic action of local landlords in raising rents during a time of national crisis'. The suspension of war-time house building, rising rentals, and an increasing number of shared dwellings meant that Leicester planned, for its own reasons, to build about ten thousand houses in the national house-building programme begun in the wake of Lloyd George's election victory in 1919. From over 1,800 councils to present plans to Whitehall, Leicester was in the leading group of fifty-two local authorities.

Though at the forefront of housing initiatives in 1919, by 1923 Leicester councillors were accused of a poor performance in the provision of new housing by Ministry officials in London and their regional representatives in Nottingham. Indeed, Leicester was 20 per cent below the average number of houses built per head of population compared to other English boroughs. Although there was some justification for the criticisms by central government, delayed Ministry approval for the first housing proposal at Coleman Road was compounded by contractual delays with builders over site access, materials and rising wage costs. The council departed

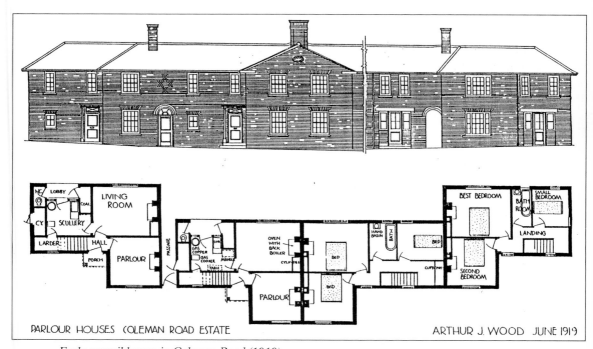

PARLOUR HOUSES COLEMAN ROAD ESTATE   ARTHUR J. WOOD JUNE 1919

Early council houses in Coleman Road (1919)

from Ministry approved designs, insisted on parlours in houses against the wish of Whitehall, and undertook several smaller projects simultaneously on Narborough Road, Gipsy Lane and Halsbury Street, all factors which involved additional contractual supervision and resulted in procedural delays. Whereas, nationally, the average project was for forty council houses, in Leicester it was for thirty-four houses.

In the deteriorating international economic situation after 1921, the government sought to contain public expenditure. But while the threat of unrest remained, the housing programme could only be curtailed, not abandoned. Pressure was put on all local authorities to economize, and though the minimum housing standards approved by the Ministry represented a quantum leap for some councils in comparison to their nineteenth-century housing stock, this was not so in Leicester. The Housing Committee found that the Ministry either delayed approval or requested alternative proposals; specifications approved in January 1921 were revised downwards and rejected yet again on six further occasions. Eventual approval for houses costing £433 – less than half those originally approved in 1910 – meant very high rents, and a 'Wakerley' design resulted, a particularly distinctive and affectionately regarded Leicester housing type still apparent in Herrick and Harrison Roads (Knighton) and Rushey Fields. Economies in lead and brickwork, together with a ground-floor third bedroom which doubled as a parlour, brought Wakerley's design down to £299, about a third of the price of the first Coleman

The 'Wakerley' designed council houses, 1922

Road houses, though this cut builders' margins to a minimum and several went bankrupt as a result. There was, then, considerable friction between an independently minded council and the centralizing authority. Furthermore, without a direct works department, council house-building projects had to compete with the private sector for both building labour and materials, both of which remained in short supply after the war.

Quality and diversity were the twin objectives of early council housing projects. Overall the Housing Committee anticipated the addition of about ten thousand houses. Yet the early financial inducements from central government were quickly curtailed in 1921, and when re-introduced in 1923 councils throughout the country were hamstrung by the need to prove that private builders were incapable of fulfilling housing needs. Bureaucracy and very limited subsidies meant relatively few houses were built under the provisions of the 1919 and 1923 Acts; in Leicester, 1,384 houses costing £1.1 million were built under the terms of these government grants. Even the most consolidated project at Coleman Road took some years to complete, and with building work scattered among twenty-one other sites, the council's housing efforts were not particularly conspicuous. Criticisms of the council's housing achievements, especially in a campaign mounted by the *Mercury*, led to an examination of alternative materials, specifically concrete; the Housing Committee was accused of ill-founded prejudice and compared unfavourably to Leeds. A building workers' strike in 1924, the expert views of the Institute of Structural Engineers, and an abrupt shift of preference by the Ministry for alternative materials, together with the *Mercury*'s campaign – 'concrete stands the test of time' – forced the Housing Committee to adopt new materials. If local builders were less than enthusiastic over the pared terms of the Wakerley contracts, the successful tendering by the Sheffield based firm of Henry Boot and Sons for concrete houses left them both without much work and also discontented since the final prices agreed, far from being lower, were some 25–32 per cent above those of traditional brick-built houses.

The nature of central government housing finance had shaped the way building plans were executed in the early 1920s. The Leicester Housing Committee's preference for parlour houses had produced tensions with the Ministry and its officials. However, the emphasis that Leicester councillors had placed upon local preferences coincided with the terms of the Housing Act proposed by the new Labour administration in 1924. The cumbersome Ministry approval apparatus was dismantled; local authorities could build as they saw fit so long as they contributed 50 per cent of housing costs from the rates. As a result a series of new estates was developed, phased to overlap and thus sustain momentum towards the 10,000 new houses which Hallam predicted would be required by 1930.

The Park or Saffron Lane estate was given particular impetus by the new climate of central and local government relations. Garden suburb principles were invoked: curves and natural contours were used, and straight streets rejected; northern or southern aspects determined the room layout so that parlours and larders were on

Saffron Lane housing estate, 1920s

the north, living rooms on the south; detailing differed on chimneys and windows, and a variety of coloured roughcast finishes and roof shapes was used. But infrastructural provisions diverged markedly from a plan which promised a new shopping centre, library, institute, railway station, three churches, schools and playgrounds for the 2,000 new houses split equally between brick and concrete construction. The London, Midland and Scottish Railway Company was never interested in building a station; the Working Men's club was built only in 1935 and the 'pork pie' library at Southfields in 1939; the lack of shops meant tenants used their houses to sell bread and groceries and thus risked eviction; and despite frequent polls in favour of pubs on the estate, the residents' views were resolutely rejected by the temperance interests in the council. It was the lack of these amenities that concerned tenants' association meetings, but defective structural standards were immediately obvious too. Cracks in the concrete foundations were evident as early as 1925, and since reinforcing rods ran not down the centre of the support columns but to their outside, the resulting rusting fractured surfaces even before the guarantee from Henry Boot and Co. had expired. Over 2,000 houses were completed in a brief period of three years from late summer 1924, and though this represented a major achievement in improving the housing supply in Leicester, the short and long term consequences of the design and materials used were considerable, and claims of defective workmanship on the estate were common from the outset.

As a new settlement with a mixture of personalities and nationalities, 'Chinatown', as the Saffron Lane estate was called initially, produced a degree of amazement among its residents. Some thought of it as 'heaven' and others referred to it as 'paradise', mainly 'because they had a bath, and the children could have a separate bedroom', and another tenant commented that 'only those that have lived in two rooms can really know what I'm talking about'. One resident 'couldn't get over the fact that I didn't have to go very far, other than to a tap in the house, to get water'. But the sense of isolation and anonymity was also present: '. . . when we moved in we knew nobody, and we had been there nearly a fortnight before I spoke to a next door neighbour. She asked me if my stove had arrived. I said "no" and we had to cook on a fire. It took about six weeks for the stove to come.'

Just outside the city boundary 1,200 acres of the Braunstone estate were compulsorily purchased in 1925. In 1927 the first residents moved in; by 1931 over 2,500 houses in ten phases of development had been built. As on the Saffron Lane development concrete was used, though only for the first 500 houses, and Garden Suburb ideas also were embraced. The City's Assistant Architect, J.S. Fyfe, was mainly responsible for the design, which featured protected open space, wide verges, low building densities, and a series of gracefully curving roads with interconnecting crescent-shaped streets. Stylistically, half-pitched roofs, dormer and bay windows, rustic features including genuine half-timbering and sash windows added quality and visual variety, and cavity walls provided insulation against cold and damp. Bungalows for the aged indicated that the council had acknowledged the need for diversity when building new estates.

Together the development of the Saffron Lane and Braunstone estates modified the pre-existing nineteenth-century urban landscape in a significant way. Despite the best of garden suburb intentions, these consolidated building programmes produced a degree of uniformity which was unavoidable, though in Leicester they compared very favourably with the drabness and mean floor space of housing estates in Leeds, Manchester, or many Scottish burghs. Rather like the buildings, the age and social composition of the residents lacked the diversity of established Victorian communities, and daily patterns of sociability, shopping and journeys to work were altered abruptly. Though new homes proved attractive to most, in the absence of amenities tenants' lives became more introspective and compartmentalized. The contrast between the built environment of North Evington and Saffron Lane, which straddled just thirty years, was marked.

The peak of new council house-building in Leicester was registered in 1927, and long before the completion of the Braunstone estate in 1931 the local and national economic and political climate had moved decisively from additions to the general stock of housing to more focused, qualitative changes based on slum clearance and 'de-crowding'. Owner-occupiers became the focus of additions to the housing stock, since interest rates, released from exchange rate considerations in 1931, remained at a new low of 2 per cent from 1932 until the Second World War. Wider availability and cheaper mortgages gave the private sector an unprecedented boost; the spread of semi-detached suburban villas was the result.

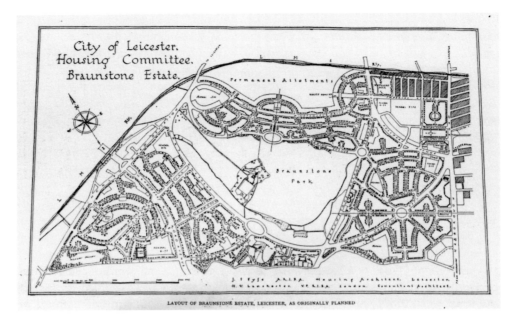

LAYOUT OF BRAUNSTONE ESTATE, LEICESTER, AS ORIGINALLY PLANNED

Garden city influences on council housing estate: Braunstone estate layout, 1926, and houses off Narborough Road 1929–30

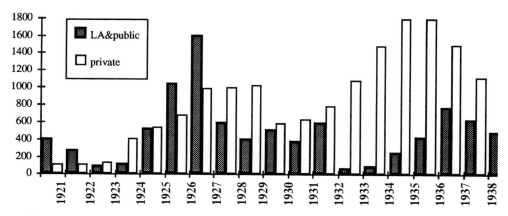

Public and private sector housebuilding, 1921–39

Council house-building in the 1930s did not cease, but was redirected towards replacement dwellings for those inner city residents displaced by the programme of demolitions. Poor council staffing levels, and a County Court sympathetic to property owners' appeals against demolition slowed the clearance of city-centre sites initially. Cheaper, meaner in floor area, plain in design and more densely built, Tailby (1932–3), Freake's Ground (1934–5), and the two larger estates of Northfields (1935–9) and North Braunstone (1936–9) together comprised 2,800 new houses for inhabitants of demolished city-centre Victorian properties. Areas adjacent to Green and Sandacre Streets in St Margaret's ward were first to be demolished, followed by Thornton and Bakehouse Lanes and Redcross Street. Residents of Britannia, Wharf, Upper Hill, St Mark's and Grove Streets were relocated in Northfields; others displaced from Bedford, Wharf, Dover, and Calais Streets, and Sanvey Gate and Burley's Lane went to North Braunstone. By fumigating their furniture and obliging residents to move *en bloc*, Tailby, Northfields and North Braunstone estates were labelled and consigned to the relegation zone in the league table of housing estates. The concentration of needy families by the Housing Committee was both ill-considered and difficult to reverse, and the colloquial name 'Dodge City' reflected the fact that North Braunstone housed one of the highest concentrations of debtors in the Midlands. This produced contrasting reactions, as the daughter of one family re-housed to North Braunstone in 1938 commented: the house 'was champion, six rooms, light, water on hand', while others remarked on the lack of amenities:

> There was nothing, no bus stops or bus services. Actually I can remember we used to be lost. There was nothing to do all of a sudden. Everything was new and shiny. You couldn't make a chock and play marbles in the street. There was one big advantage – you had a big garden. But the men took a big pride in them . . . and we weren't allowed on them. As regards entertainment there was nothing.

Transformation in the landscape. Residents whose houses were cleared from Wharf Street (above) and areas in the city centre in the 1930s were relocated in non-parlour houses with steel-framed windows in Northfields, and others in North Braunstone (below)

To Corporation Tenants!!

ARE YOU COMPETING
FOR THE
Challenge Cups & Valuable Prizes
OFFERED AT THE
Braunstone Tenants' Association
3rd Annual ROYAL INFIRMARY

Garden Competition

Week Ending, Saturday, July 18th.

Competition Secretary: Mr. J. L. B. SHERWIN, 37 Hamelin Road.

Rules and Conditions.

(1) That this Competition shall be called "The Braunstone Tenants' Association ROYAL INFIRMARY Garden Competition."

(2) The Competition shall be open to Council House Tenants resident upon the Braunstone Estate, upon payment of ONE SHILLING Entrance Fee, of which sum 50 per cent. shall be remitted to the Leicester Royal Infirmary.

(3) The Gardens of Competitors to be judged during week ending July 18th, 1936.

(4) Entries to close on Saturday, July 4th, 1936.

(5) Competitors must stipulate on Entry Form whether they are entering under Class A or B.

(6) No special points awarded for contents of Glasshouses and Frames.

(7) The whole of the Garden attached to dwelling of the Competitor to be judged.

The Competition will be judged in two Classes as follows:—

Class A.—MIXED GARDEN ... ... 30 points
Arrangement and Cleanliness ... ... 20 points

1st Prize: Braunstone Tenants' Association Challenge Cup.

Class B.—FLOWER GARDEN ... ... 30 points
Arrangement and Cleanliness ... ... 20 points

1st Prize: Leicester "Evening Mail" Challenge Cup.

Maximum Points: 50 in each Class.

Other Valuable Prizes for each Class will be given.

Send your Entries to any of the following :—Mr. J. H. Bell, 27 Hamelin Road ; Mr. A. E Hall, 145 Winstanley Drive ; Mr. E. Paragreen, 18 Camville Road ; Mr. B. Shenton, 10 Winton Avenue ; Mr. F. Haggis, 369 Narborough Road ; Mr. W. King, 6 Segrave Road ; Mr W A. Smith, 52 Hallam Crescent East : Mr. Dickson, 6 Newfields Avenue ; Mr. Taylor, 17 Wynthorpe Rise or the Secretary, 37 Hamelin Road.

ENTRY FORM.

I wish to enter the Braunstone Tenants' Association Royal Infirmary Garden Competition, and agree to abide by the conditions and enclose 1/- entrance fee.

Name ....

Address ....

Class A ....

Class B ....

Place a X against the Class you wish to enter. To be handed in to any member of Committee before July 4th.

THE ENTRANCE FEE (1/-) MUST ACCOMPANY THIS FORM.

Have you joined the BRAUNSTONE TENANTS' ASSOCIATION ?

H. GAMBLE, Printer, 10½ Flint Street, Leicester. T.U.

Handbills encouraged tenants' participation in political and leisure activities

By 1939 approximately 12 per cent of the housing stock was publicly owned, and 35 per cent of all new housebuilding during the inter-war years was undertaken by the public sector – a little higher than the English average. While the Victorian legacy in terms of the street plan and social geography remained largely intact, new zones on the edge of the city, and the transport routes which served them, ensured a degree of reorientation. Both through its semis and its estates the urban landscape altered appreciably in the twenty years after the First World War.

The extent of this re-orientation can be seen from the map on p. 33. Not only do the new council estates show up clearly as solid areas, so too do areas of private building. The 'way' roads – Byway, Romway, Trueway, Broadway, New Way, Highway, Homeway, Kingsway and Midway – were typical of areas in the 1930s of concentrated middle-class development, assisted by mortagage interest rates reductions which from their 1920s plateau of 6 per cent fell to 4.5 per cent by 1936. for those in work, rising real incomes, falling building costs and declining mortgage repayments proved an attractive prospect, and it was this combination which generated the buoyant conditions for private housebuilders in the inter-war years in Leicester.

For a down payment of £20, and an outlay of 11s 3d per week, a plain fronted semi-detached house built by Sherriff and Co. was available on the Humberstone Park estate in the mid-1930s. 'Leicester's leading house builder', Sherriff and Co., had their works off Gipsy Lane, and according to their publicity, 'sold more houses that any other builder in the City'. Between Scraptoft Lane and Uppingham Road, and 'only five minutes' walk from the tram terminus and frequent buses from Humberstone Gate', 575 houses of 'varied and distinctive design' were offered by the company in the mid-1930s. Sherriff's pattern book and show homes offered another ten styles, including some bungalows, and the top of the range detached

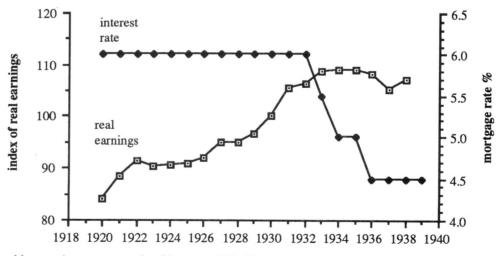

Mortgage interest rates and real incomes, 1920–39

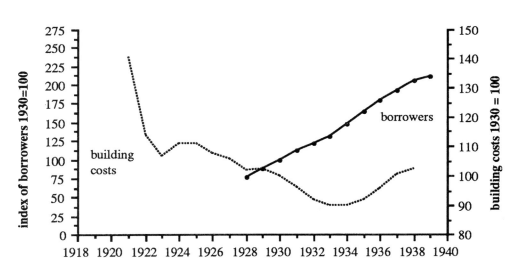

Private housing developments, 1920–39

house with garage cost £750. More modestly, the plain fronted three-bedroom, semi-detached house of 850 sq. ft with living room and front room, oak floors, 'glide-easy curtain fittings', and colour decoration according to the purchaser's choice, cost £395 (£405 with a separate scullery) which together with a plot of land priced at £50, brought the total purchase price up to £445. In construction costs, this was comparable with the £433 for early council housing designs at Kimberley Road, and roughly equivalent to the costs of council housing on Saffron Lane, Tailby, Gwendolen Road and at Knighton Fields, which ranged from £340 to £470 for houses with slightly more generous floor areas than the basic Sherriff house. In conjunction with the Leicester Permanent Builing society, mortgage finance at 4.5 per cent was available so that after a down payment of £20, mortgage costs at 11*s* 3*d* were not so far adrift of the rentals of 8*s*–10*s* payable by Saffron Lane tenants in the 1920s, though with the addition of rates at about 3*s* per week, total weekly expenditure rose to approximately 14*s* 3*d*, too high to be affordable for a family reliant upon the average male worker's weekly wage of £3 in 1936. By comparison, middle class non-manual incomes averaged £5 per week, and so with rent and rates accounting for about 15 per cent of this, there were opportunities to spend on furniture and soft furnishings, radios, electrical goods and household equipment, and cars, the price of which were for the most part falling during the decade.

Post-war Reconstruction

Overcrowding had edged upwards during the inter-war years, and though Leicester experienced little war damage, the interruption to housing supply and minimal wartime maintenance combined with an increased number of households and higher post-war expectations to produce a housing shortage. In January 1946 the Housing

ILLUSTRATED LEICESTER CHRONICLE

No. 1395 New Series   REGISTERED AS A NEWSPAPER   SATURDAY, AUGUST 25, 1951   ESTABLISHED 1810   TWOPENCE

LEICESTER'S BLACK SPOTS

Most of the householders in the slum areas have to share an outside water tap—the only source of supply—with neighbours. As many as six houses share one communal tap. The houses are without sinks, pantries or coppers. Mrs. F. Squires, Mrs. Flanagan and Mrs. Creighton are seen queuing for water by their homes in Wheat Street. Alternative accommodation has been sought by many of the families. Mrs. Flanagan has been waiting for another house for eight years.

Above: A picture which speaks for itself. This house is occupied by eleven people. Below: This bedroom at the two-roomed house of Mr. and Mrs. Frank Smith, 22, Warrington Street, is occupied by five. In the bed on the right sleep a girl aged 14, one aged nine, and a boy aged 11.

LAST WEEK'S front page of the Illustrated Leicester Chronicle presented Leicester as a city of flowers. This week we show the other side of the picture.

Hundreds of Leicester people are living in conditions of appalling squalor through no fault of their own.

A tour of some of the worst houses—in St. Margaret's Ward—produces sights and smells to turn the stomach. It is high time the conscience of Leicester City Council was pricked about this filthy blot on the name of the city.

There are many frightful instances of overcrowding. In one house eight people occupy the only bedroom.

One lavatory frequently serves three houses; sometimes a lavatory has to do duty for many more. Many of these lavatories are derelict, leaning at a precarious angle.

FELL THROUGH FLOOR

People living in Leicester's slums supplied these answers to a questionnaire put by St. Margaret's councillors: "Front door falling off"; "lavatory tumbling down"; "no drains—water runs down yard"; "heavy rain brings pools of water in children's bedroom"; "walls patched up with cardboard"; "all doors hanging off"; "boy 14 boarding out owing to conditions"; "boy aged 14 occupying same bedroom as schoolgirls."

A child fell through the bedroom floor on to a table below at one house. Another house is between two empty houses, both of which have become dumps for all kinds of refuse. Beds have had to be put on boards to prevent them falling through the living room ceiling.

In other houses, walls bulge, stairs are broken down and propped up with bricks. Hundreds of windows are smashed, many window frames are perished, and many "windows" are merely gaping holes.

A CLEAN CITY?

Mice, ants, cockroaches are common pests. Yards are full of indescribable collections of rubble and rubbish. Pools of stagnant water collect about drains. Living room floors are rough, broken bricks.

Citizens know Leicester as a clean city proud of that reputation. These revelations will come to them as a shock. We make no apology for showing pictures of frightful dwelling conditions. They must be shown in their true ugliness before they can be righted.

Post-war housing problems publicized

'Washday blues' was the Leicester Mercury's *caption for this scene, typical of many in Leicester's worst slum housing areas after the Second World War*

Department informed the Labour Council that 2,000 houses still lacked an internal water supply, that 8,000 applications for council housing had been received from tenants in the private rented sector alone, and thus 10,000 houses were needed immediately. In the longer term possibly as many as 56,000 houses might be required. Throughout the 1950s, Leicester's housing black spots could still make front page news.

The pattern of inter-war years housing development was reproduced after 1945: initial emphasis was placed on quantity or 'volume' housing in the form of extensive new estates around the edge of the city, to be followed later in turn by a strategy of slum clearance and then by one of qualitative improvements – repairs and rehabilitation to older properties.

Extensions to the built-up area were accompanied by new structures and designs. Initially some 572 'prefabs' altered the appearance of sections of the Braunstone and New Parks estates along Hinckley and Wykes Roads, and also on Ambassador Road and Hughenden Drive. The erection of 500 steel-framed houses at New Parks eased immediate shortages, and John Laing's 'Easiform' system for poured concrete walls also provided non-traditional housing, albeit with conventional external features.

'Comfy and compact and a roof over our head': prefabs parked in Hinckley Road eased the post-war housing shortage, and transformed the landscape for longer than planned

Adaptations to the military camp huts at Braunstone Park, and a further suspension of slum clearances relieved some of the immediate housing pressure. But a transformation in the Leicester landscape resulted from a major new building programme which produced 13,000 houses between 1946 and 1959. Almost 25 per cent of them were built at New Parks, approximately 10 per cent at both Stocking Farm and Mowmacre Hill, and others at Thurnby Lodge (13 per cent) and Eyres Monsell (20 per cent) where the city and county were both involved in house-building projects.

Including prefabs, over 7,050 houses were built in eight post-war years (1946–53), two-fifths of them at New Parks. The record compared favourably to 9,250 houses built during twenty inter-war years. Yet the scale of development and a continuing preference for housing design and street layouts similar to those of the garden suburb estates of the 1930s meant extensive land purchases and infrastructural investment were required. Since the most urgent housing priority was for families, the construction of three-bedroom type accommodation produced what the Housing Committee called 'unbalanced' neighbourhoods – dwellings of uniform size and appearance for communities with roughly similar age distributions. So the success of an experiment with flats in 1951 at Aikman Avenue, the availability of new materials and mass-produced house-building techniques, and the persistent Ministry attempts to prune building costs and subsidies, meant new ideas about architectural design and building methods were adopted. The resumption of slum clearance programmes added a degree of urgency to produce new housing for those displaced from Warrington Street, Abbey Gate and many other inner areas.

New Parks estate, 1950

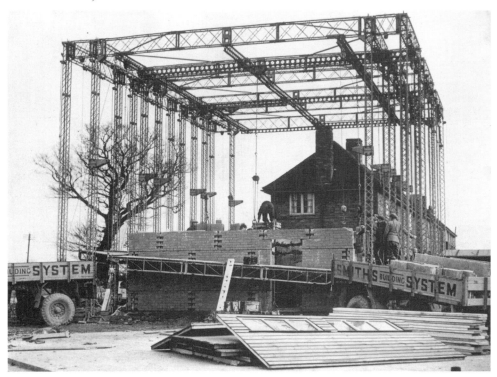

The post-war housing programme and the age of mass housing: Mowmacre Hill houses, 1954

*A resumption of slum clearance
programmes: Warrington Street
(1958) (left) and Abbey Gate (1964)
(below)*

A limited experiment: Leicester's multi-storey blocks at Rowlatt's Hill

The redevelopment of St Matthew's

From 1958 fundamentally different housing solutions resulted, as can be seen at St Mark's, St Matthew's, St Peter's and at Rowlatts Hill. High-rise, high-density structures dominated the skyline: two twenty-two-storey slab blocks of flats on the prominent Crown Hills ridge (Rowlatts Hill 1964–7) and two twenty-four-storey, steel-framed beige blocks at St Matthew's (1965–8). In the St Matthew's case, the majority of building was in a series of four-storey blocks of flats and maisonettes, which formed an almost continuous wall around the estate, connected by concrete balconies. The fortress appearance of the development was reinforced by the extensive central area. Flat roofs and cantilevered projections were particularly intrusive in the Leicester townscape. Architectural 'brutalism' enjoyed a period of ascendancy.

Renovation, Re-settlement and Immigration

Though there was some overlap in the chronology, three stages of immigration – the period of male migration in the 1950s; family reunions in the 1960s; and the arrival of East African Asians in the 1970s – have had a profound effect on the social geography of Leicester and on the character of specific neighbourhoods. A sixfold increase in immigration during the 1950s, mainly from the Punjab, Gujarat and Pakistan but also including a significant number of Kenyan-born Asians, obtained accommodation not in council properties, where they had a low priority, but in the private rented sector along the principal access routes such as Narborough and Uppingham Roads, with their access to textile and other employment opportunities. Smaller concentrations of Asians were to be found in Spinney Hill, Wycliffe, Westcotes and Charnwood, where larger turn-of-the-century houses provided cheap lodgings and possibilities for multiple occupancy and subdivisions. Initial segregation was mainly voluntary, with little inter-ethnic conflict.

The second phase of immigration during the 1960s coincided with a period of promising employment opportunities and a low official unemployment rate of around 3 per cent. The increase in family migration produced a more balanced age composition in the ethnic communities and was in part an attempt to anticipate the restrictions contained in the Immigration Act of 1962. The effect on the spatial structure of the city was pronounced. Most obviously, the arrival of families meant a demand for more permanent accommodation, but it also contributed to a cultural revival in which religious practices and social interaction were dependent on proximity to like-minded ethnic members. Immigrants moved rapidly from rented housing to owner occupancy, the process accelerated by the low purchase price of dilapidated housing vacated by a white population relocated on new council and private estates. Three wards, Spinney Hills, Westcotes and Charnwood contained 65 per cent of Asians by 1969, though Latimer and Belgrave wards also attracted some immigrants. The combined effects of chain migration and housing concentration were the primary forces for the emergence of specialist shops, services and places of worship, and these in turn bound communities together and attracted subsequent new arrivals. The preponderance of Asian settlement to the east of the city itself reflected the age distribution of the housing stock and echoed the late Victorian and Edwardian developments in these areas. Planning blight associated with the Eastern Relief Road affected Belgrave, and demolitions both there and in Highfields caused house prices to plummet, and fostered uncertainty among whites in the late 1960s and early 1970s. The resulting vacuum proved attractive to Asians and the resulting dense settlement in Belgrave, together with a review of traffic needs by City and County planners, led to the abandonment of the proposed road. Precarious links between immigrants and whites were severed as a complex network of kin and friendship links produced a social exclusivity paralleled by a desire for spatial separation.

From 1968–78 more than 20,000 displaced East African families arrived in Leicester – more than anywhere else in the UK. This third wave of immigrants also affected the spatial character of the city. Entire families, sometimes comprising three generations, arrived as refugees bringing their life savings with them. These financial resources, coupled with a trading background and some knowledge of English, were used both to move quickly from rented to privately-owned property and to set up businesses and specialist services. Though Highfields attracted some Gujaratis, Belgrave was transformed into a thriving residential and shopping area, with a lively business community able to finance moves to larger and more prestigious housing in Rushey Mead, Crown Hills and Evington. Since the majority of Ugandan, Kenyan and Tanzanian immigrants were Hindu, their social organizations, ethnic institutions and religious facilities were also reflected in the built environment of Belgrave. Conversely, Pakistani Muslims mostly have avoided the area; mosques are found only in Highfields.

Racially distinct areas have thus developed, reinforced by the allocation of residential space through the operations of Asian estate agents, financiers, and solicitors dealing essentially with their own ethnic sub-group. Individual East African homeowners' refusal to sell property except to members of their ethnic group has resulted in an exclusivity and social segregation normally associated with whites' attempts to protect socially exclusive residential zones. So voluntary segregation by some has meant obligatory segregation for others.

An emerging trend during the 1980s was the residential dispersal of Asians. In part this was due to their improved access to peripheral local authority estates. But it was also due to an enhanced occupational status, the acquisition of wealth, and a pioneer's willingness to abandon the protective environment of their own community in favour of the many private sector estates which developed in the 1980s. The resistance of a suburban or county white population was an insufficient deterrent for many Asians who sought improved housing in most city wards, while maintaining a measure of cultural continuity with former neighbourhoods through increased car ownership.

Private sector efforts, often energized by the Asian community, contributed to the rehabilitation of inner city areas in the 1970s. These efforts were complemented by public initiatives in which the demolition programme, recommenced in the 1950s and extended into the 1960s, was reversed in favour of a strategy for the renovation and renewal of buildings. The initiative gained initial impetus in Clarendon Park where

*Guru Nanak Gurdwara in Holy Bones
(near Vaughan College): an example of
changing landmarks and altered property
use in this former factory complex*

more than a decade earlier a demonstration of housing improvement sponsored jointly
with the Ministry of Housing had attracted 17,000 visitors. However, the objective, to
encourage landlords to improve their properties, was regarded as an 'utter failure' by
the council in 1957. A change of priorities and the funding of General Improvement
Areas and Housing Action Areas assumed a new momentum from the mid-1970s. The
Urban Programme re-emphasized the importance of environmental improvements by
making central government grants available to councils prepared to contribute 25 per
cent of the cost of renewal projects.

Improvements in the physical fabric also resulted from the activities of about twenty
separate housing associations in Leicester. Some associations were stimulated by a
slump in demand for offices in the 1970s, which enabled them to acquire prime sites at
favourable prices; new housing, as in the Dover Street/Calais Hill and de Montfort
Housing Society's Oxford Street areas resulted. Other organizations, for example
Coventry Churches Housing Association, converted office blocks, such as Midland
House in Charles Street, and properties above shops for use as dwellings in the 1980s.
Just as important have been those housing associations which have played a prominent
part in the upgrading programmes for estates such St Peter's and St Matthew's, and
others, such as ASRA (Asian Sheltered Residential Accommodation) which provide
sheltered accommodation for the elderly.

The transformation of the built environment was spearheaded, however, by the Council's own housing renewal strategy. Launched in 1976 to revamp 14,000 houses, the programme acted as a major channel of resources to Leicester's inner city neighbourhoods through an elaborate system of improvement grants. Completed grant work indicates a rate of housing improvement better than that achieved nationally; the modest degree of housing disrepair continues to be the envy of most other English councils. However, it was precisely the underlying success of the improvement programme which from 1983 was seen by planners as threatening the longer term process of clearance, new building and redevelopment. Indeed, members of Leicester's Housing Strategy Team were involved at a national level in reviewing the housing improvement strategy, and the demolition programme proposed for the Grand Union Housing Action Area in Belgrave was a local test case of an emerging national policy. Two Asian councillors took a central role in this 'fundamental clash of outlook and values between the grassroots and the town hall'. Though opposed by the Labour chairman of the Housing Committee who endorsed the clearance proposals, the councillors were able to obtain the support of the local MP. Though their concerted efforts as 'middlemen' were not without personal and party costs, since elements of the Asian community were antagonized and the Labour party was split over the issue, after a protracted struggle the proposed demolition of fifty predominantly Asian owned terraced houses was scaled down to only ten houses. This Labour policy U-turn, undertaken at a time of impending local elections and a disinclination to antagonize the Asian vote, registered a victory for housing improvement over housing clearance.

This clash of values in the early 1980s contained the hallmarks of conflict which characterized the slum clearance eras of the 1930s and the 1950s: a confrontation between the official, orthodox view of the inner city – decaying houses and substandard environments – and the grassroots or popular version of the inner city – cheap but adequate housing and convenient, supportive neighbourhoods. For environmental professionals, the ideology of progress through physical change remained the central rationale; for business interests, new building was where the main profits lay. In the renewed call for demolition in the 1980s, professional and business interests conflicted with those of local residents.

Plans, Planning and Beaumont Leys

New houses, slum clearance, urban renewal and immigration combined, after 1945, to provide a unique spatial mixture, the character of which contributes to the identity of Leicester. To these initiatives was added a more integrated, consciously planned development.

Bomb damage and inner city disrepair together formed powerful forces for a comprehensive approach to post-war planning in many British cities. So although war damage was slight in Leicester, the city was obliged, like all others, to set out its intentions for development under the terms of the Town and Country Planning Act,

1947. A planning blue-print based on ideas set out by professionals in surveying, engineering and architecture produced rather inflexible development plans with no obligation to involve the public. This consensus among planning professionals rested on the continued acceptance of slum clearance and a redistribution of population. The Leicester Plan, 1952, embraced these principles, which were largely intact when, preceded only by Newcastle, the city established a City Planning Department under Konrad Smigielski in 1962. Smigielski's view – 'the only solution is complete clearance and redevelopment' – echoed this post-war consensus, but the 'motor revolution' during the 1950s prompted him to develop a new plan – the Leicester Traffic Plan, 1964. This considered not only the implications of changing transport patterns but also addressed the inter-connected issues of population change, employment patterns and housing requirements. Extensive questionnaires, transport models and computer analyses aroused national interest, techniques which Smigielski considered 'removed town planning from the vague field of intuition and put it on a firm quantitative basis'.

The City Council never approved the Traffic Plan in full. Instead, and in conjunction with Leicestershire County Council, a sub-regional study was undertaken between 1966 and 1969, which was again innovative since it was one of the first of its kind, and because it adopted a more flexible concept of planning: 'the plan is not a "master plan" but a programme of recommended changes'. Flexibility became the planning keynote. Overall objectives were amended in the light of changing circumstances, and in response to public participation in the planning process. The Town and Country Planning Acts, 1968 and 1971, officially encouraged a flexibility which, to an extent, Leicester had already embraced.

The largest single tract of land in or near the city became available for development when, after seventy-five years of operations, the sewage treatment works at Beaumont Leys was replaced in 1966 by a new plant at Wanlip. The 1967 master plan for Beaumont Leys was the brainchild of the City Planning Department. However, responsibility for the release of land was in the hands of the Estates Committee, and this division between planning and finance proved to be the subject of considerable tension between them. As the scale and phasing of site development costs for Beaumont Leys grew so the leverage of the Estates Committee increased, since the project had profound implications for the Council's finances. The implementation of the plan and the technical expertise of the planners were constrained by financial considerations, as a subsequent memo from the City Estates Surveyor to the Chief Planning Officer made clear: '. . . in the initial stages we shall have to rely upon the disposal of industrial sites and the Town Centre Super-Store site to raise capital. It follows therefore that before the residential developments can commence, the industrial and commercial element must be well under way.'

The central influence on the design of Beaumont Leys was the motor car, or rather its absence. The enthusiasm of the City Surveyor's and the Planning

The separation of pedestrians and cars was a key design feature of Beaumont Leys

Departments for the separation of pedestrians and vehicles, both heavily influenced by Smigielski's previous award-winning designs in London, together with national projections for car ownership, proved decisive factors. So, too, did a modified American city planning layout of the 1920s – the 'Radburn' design. Used in Wrexham in 1952, and subsequently in Northampton, Sheffield, Cumbernauld and other second generation New Towns in the 1960s, the Radburn layout was adopted for Beaumont Leys. The main Radburn characteristic was the segregation of people and cars using over and underpasses, neighbourhood parks, and housing designed to give open views from living rooms. It also justified higher density building, claiming that close family and neighbourly ties were important, and that living densities were offset by nearby public open areas. In reality, financial considerations were prominent in determining housing densities. There were, too, some landscaping advantages: garages, tarmac and kerbside parking need not disfigure the entire estate, but could be clustered together leaving a unified landscape of footpaths, trees and informal open spaces. The Rowlatt's Hill estate (1964–7) provided an early version of the layout, and by 1967 the Radburn design principles had become widely accepted. The original master plan for Beaumont Leys involved a linear system of open spaces which formed the backbone or green spine to the new development, along which ran a cycle track, an elevated monorail, and a pedestrian promenade. Linked to the backbone were green wedges containing pedestrian footpaths that divided the residential areas, which together would eventually accommodate 40,000 people. Footpaths linked shopping facilities and schools without reference to the road system so that 'a child walking to school need never meet a car'. The road network was based on a main loop, from which ran access roads and culs-de-sac.

The construction phase of the pilot area began in 1971. But by 1973, and under the newly appointed City Planning Officer, John Dean, the principle of pedestrian/vehicle separation came under review. A revised plan, the Abbey District Plan (1977) incorporated a flexible approach to town planning and compromises were sought – subways became optional and pavements alongside roads were acceptable. Planning came to be regarded as a process, requiring constant review and updating, though with well-defined objectives, and as a result strict adherence to the Radburn principles was rejected. This coincided with the dislike of Radburn design features as expressed by private builders who preferred conventional housing – the rhythm of work on walls, garages and the fittings of individual dwellings was familiar to them. Private landlords and developers also disliked the stigma associated with the communal Radburn layout since this was identified with working-class housing. As one observer noted: 'class consciousness is the Englishman's most persistent vice, and so long as municipalities continue to provide subsidized housing, the speculators will find it necessary to build estates which are visibly different from the municipal product'. The opposition of the private sector was completed by private owners, who opposed rented housing in their neighbourhood as it was thought to have a depressing influence on property values.

Social segregation was perpetuated at Beaumont Leys as the 1981 census data showed. In Phase I of the development, 76 per cent of residents in the pilot area belonged to social classes I–III(M) (professional, intermediate, non-manual, and skilled manual occupations); in Barleycroft it was 44 per cent, and Dudley Meadow, 40 per cent in groups I–III(M). The loss of the social mix ran counter to planners' wishes, but the imperative of first a Labour (1974–6) and then a Conservative (1976–9) Housing Committee was to build 1,000 houses a year, a target which was only feasible by allocating large tracts of land to the south of Krefeld Way.

Nor were residents always glowing in their praise. Complaints were directed at open-plan floor plans, curved and thus indirect footpaths, access by car to the rear, and confusing road networks which disorientated inhabitants. Underpasses and landscaped shrubbery contributed to an embattled, threatened feeling among residents. So subsequent phases of development, for example at Heatherbrook, Astill and Beaumont Lodges, incorporated pavements and took some account of residents' complaints. Greater housing variety, diversity of materials and smaller concentrations of housing developments were among later devices used to overcome the monotony of earlier development, as was a more balanced distribution of housing tenures. In the 1980s the opening of the Beaumont Centre, the Tesco superstore and Leicester Leys Leisure Centre, together with the Bursom Industrial Park, added further elements in the spatial diversity of Beaumont Leys.

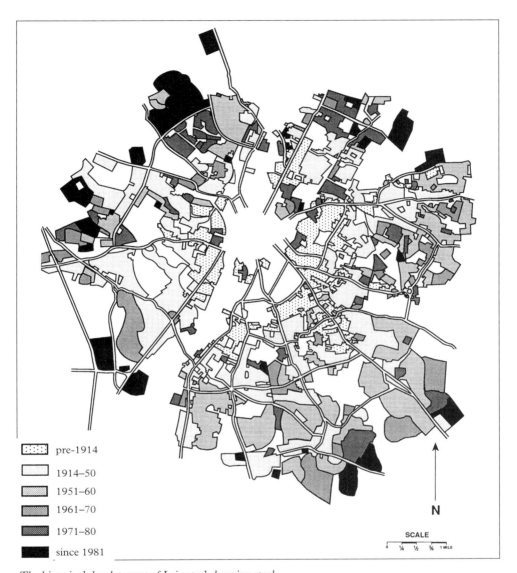

pre-1914

1914–50

1951–60

1961–70

1971–80

since 1981

N

SCALE

0   ¼   ½   ¾   1 MILE

The historical development of Leicester's housing stock

Parks, Amenities and the 'Greening' of the City

Public parks and gardens are an integral part of the built environment. They provide an insight into the social conditions and aspirations of the period during which they were created, and though their location and size has remained relatively constant, their character and facilities have not been unchanging.

Different phases can be identified in the development of open spaces in Leicester. Initially municipal policy was directed towards the provision not of parks but of open spaces, mainly for walking. On the fringe of the built-up area, St Margaret's Pasture and Victoria Park provided such opportunities, but the 'Southfield' or Welford Road Recreation Ground (now Mandela Park) was the council's first official attempt to allocate space by creating a recreation ground. The chains of private gardens and squares, such as New Walk, added public amenity too. In the second half of the nineteenth century the town council assumed further responsibilities for the built environment and adopted a more interventionist programme for the creation of large, landscaped parks with facilities for rest, relaxation and recreation. In keeping with the Victorian ideas of 'order' these parks and recreation areas were more formal in their design and were provided with higher standards of upkeep and levels of regulation through the appointment of park keepers. Four major urban parks, three recreation areas and a number of small neighbourhood parks and gardens were established during the last quarter of the nineteenth century. To foster civic identity and pride the town council, in addition to building the Town Hall, museum and art gallery, and library decided to establish a showpiece 'city' park. The Abbey Marsh (57 acres), purchased in 1877, was drained and landscaped to the highest ornamental standards with gardens, abbey grounds, boating lakes, river, grass enclosures and woodland, together with a cricket oval, bandstand and refreshment pavilions. Abbey Park continues to fulfil this central role in Leicester's park hierarchy, having gained many new facilities and conceded other functions as fashions and public demands have altered over the years. A number of secondary parks were also developed – the conversion of the race course to Victoria Park (1882: 69 acres); Spinney Hill Park (1885: 34 acres); and Western Park (1899: 78 acres). The original formal layout of these three parks, characterized by tree-lined pathways, gardens, expanses of grass, bandstands and pavilions, is still evident today, even if amended by the addition of a range of sports pitches and facilities together with specialist play and activity areas. A complementary municipal strategy, to establish recreation facilities – often little more than grass areas – in densely built-up districts such as at Cossington Street (1892: 12 acres) and Fosse Road (1897: 11 acres) added amenity to these neighbourhoods. Though hard court sports and expanded play areas have been developed, and baths and a sports hall added at Cossington Street, these Victorian open areas have remained important to local residents. Neighbourhood needs were also uppermost in the creation of ornamental gardens with grass areas at Humberstone.

By comparison with the years 1875–1900, the first two decades of the twentieth century were a period of relative inactivity in park development. Eventually, and in response to ratepayers' insistence that open space should be provided in the southern suburbs, the council acquired land at Aylestone (1902: 20 acres). Laid out mainly for football and cricket, and still intensively used, the recent addition of a sports hall, specialist play area and car parking have added greatly to Aylestone's status in the city's hierarchy of public parks. More modest population growth and war-time restrictions meant that the town council concentrated on developing facilities within existing parks, and, not without difficulty, on establishing small neighbourhood parks and gardens; new amenities were limited to ornamental gardens at the Castle, Westcotes and St George's church, two playgrounds at Taylor Street and Uppingham Road, and a small park at Westcotes.

Social, transport and institutional changes during the years 1920–50 altered radically the scale and nature of open space provision in Leicester. The suburban extensions of the built-up area reflected the combined effects of greater affluence, particularly among the middle classes, a shorter working week, the rising appeal of houses with gardens, improved public and private transport, and the introduction of council estates. At the same time the need to co-ordinate urban development gained acceptance, and the Town and Country Planning Acts of 1932 and 1947 gave expanded powers and responsibilities to local authorities in respect of open spaces planned on a comprehensive rather than piecemeal basis. Open space provision became a central element of urban planning, and the National Playing Fields Association devised guideline 'standards' which stated that a minimum of 6 acres of playing fields should be provided for every 1,000 population, excluding school playing fields and golf courses. This unofficial standard has persisted to the present day, with an additional element of l acre of parks and gardens per 1,000 advocated in a Ministry of Housing and Local Government Circular of 1956.

The result was an upsurge in the provision of all forms of public open space in Leicester. Four multi-purpose parks were created in the emerging suburbs to the south-west, south and east of the city, designed from the outset to include sports pitches, tennis courts and bowling greens in addition to the more traditional walking and gardens areas, seats and shelters. The largest, Braunstone (167 acres), was developed around the house and park purchased from the Winstanley family in 1925, and with its ornamental pond and extensive walking area formed the centrepiece and recreational focus of the council's large Braunstone garden suburb. This estate, like those at Elston Fields and Northfields, Tailby Avenue and Coleman Road, included a new type of urban open space – the amenity area – in the form of corner areas, squares and banking. This new type of provision contrasted with the three more traditional district parks established during this period at Humberstone (1928: 20 acres), Knighton Park (from 1937: 79 acres), and Evington (1949: 44 acres). Fortunately for future generations of park-goers the owners of these properties had resisted earlier overtures from land developers, thereby preserving substantial open spaces for park and sports facilities in areas already leap-frogged by suburban building.

Participation rates in sports increased after the First World War, and since existing playing field provision could not cope, two substantial new recreation areas were established, one in the north of the city at Rushey Mead (1921: 29 acres) and the other serving southern suburban needs at Aylestone Playing Fields (1946: 83 acres). In addition, several smaller parks were laid out within the various new council estates (102 acres) and contributed significantly to their amenities.

Since 1950 the traditional idea of parks as separate from housing has been gradually abandoned in favour of a more integrated design. Public open space has been valued as part of estate layout; pedestrians' legitimate claim on open space has also been recognized. Showpiece parks have given way to a profusion of small, unfenced neighbourhood spaces containing children's playground equipment and kick-about areas. Provisions have often taken the form of incidental amenity areas. A few larger open spaces, Netherhall (1953: 32 acres), Thurncourt (1958: 28 acres) and Ingold (1970: 15 acres) were established on land unsuited to residential development, though their potential as neighbourhood parks has been realized only partially. Three recent developments have diversified recreational provisions in the city: the Leicester Arboretum (1970: 54 acres) on Shady Lane, Humberstone Heights golf course and pitch-and-putt (1975: 55 acres), and Beaumont Park (1985: 56 acres), with its grassy walking areas, sports pitches and a pitch-and-putt course.

A concerted effort has also been made over the past forty years to establish small parks and play areas within easy reach of all neighbourhoods. While these could be included as integral design features of all council estates, Leicester has been fortunate to acquire large houses and their associated grounds, or garden areas, at Humberstone, Aylestone, Evington and Belgrave, which provide attractive formal garden areas as well as play facilities. In addition to the creation of thirty small parks and recreation grounds between 1950 and 1990 which form an outer suburban ring, some 33 acres of amenity open space have been incorporated into fifteen council estates, and these provide a greater feeling of space. While most council estates do now possess formal and informal play areas, many still lack the recreational foci to meet the needs of all sections of the community.

Parks and gardens have been the creation, almost exclusively, of the city council. From a single city park, three district parks and handful of local play areas at the beginning of the century, the emphasis has shifted to the provision of many more local and neighbourhood parks. The park hierarchy now consists of one city, twelve district, twenty neighbourhood, and twenty-four local parks. As a consequence, there are 7.5 acres of open space per 1,000 population in 1990, a provision which compares favourably with other British cities, though the absence of a sizeable central park remains a serious limitation.

Riverside Park, a 12-mile linear park developed in several stages since 1974, stretches uninterrupted from Bluebank Lock on the Grand Union Canal in the south to the Watermead Country Park to the north of the city. These 2,400 acres incorporate 20 miles of walks, bridleways and cycle paths; rowing and narrow boat enthusiasts share the canal and River Soar with anglers. Access points for the disabled are provided along sections of the park. In a unique urban development combining ecological, historical and recreational interests, the linear Riverside Park provides an ambitious alternative to the city-centre park. This is partly because the industrial archaeology of Leicester is well represented – a medieval packhorse bridge, canal locks, Aylestone and Pingle coal wharves, gasworks and a pumping station, the site of Stephenson's Leicester-Swannington railway line, and mills such as Pex's West Bridge, Friar's, and Dunlop's St Mary's mill, Victorian mileposts and parish boundary posts, and innumerable graceful bridges. But the distinctive and qualitative contribution of Riverside Park is its emphasis on ecology. Wetland and wildlife provisions symbolize a civic commitment to enable all Leicester people to see for themselves the plant, marine and bird life, without the artificiality or expense of a zoo setting. Several new ponds have been dug, and thousands of native trees and shrubs planted with these aims in mind, and areas of former dereliction have been transformed into a positive amenity. An award, the European Nostra Award, was an explicit acknowledgement of an innovative environmental strategy as implemented in Leicester.

The 'greening' of the city has not been restricted to the riverside area, however. A city-wide Ecology Strategy was officially launched in 1989, though in effect a vigorous unofficial policy was in place throughout the 1980s. The Riverside Park was one element, but this and other efforts have relied to a considerable extent on advice from the Ecology Advisory Group, and on a comprehensive Leicester Habitat Study undertaken by the City Wildlife Project during 1983–7. This thorough assessment of open spaces provided an empirical base for subsequent environmental and greening policies. The survey identified the type, size, quality, location and concentrations of existing habitats in the city and the plants and animals which they support, and graded each site according to its ecological merit. The survey showed that 35 per cent of the land area of the city was undeveloped and provided a variety of wildlife habitats, as did 189 miles of canals, rivers, streams, railways, road verges and hedges. But it was the impressive local detail of the survey which ensured that an ecological dimension to open spaces could not be marginalized in Leicester. From the study it emerged that Welford Road cemetery supported over 130 species of wildflowers, and the gravestones alone sheltered twenty-five types of lichens; Western Park golf course retained the remnants of an ancient hay meadow; disused allotments at Blackmore Drive in Braunstone were the habitat of 125 different plant species. Stinging nettles, normally regarded as something of a nuisance, supported 107 species of insects, including colourful butterflies such as the Small Tortoiseshell and Peacock. The list of species found in Leicester is impressive: over 500 wild plants, more than 100 species of birds, 27 different mammals, and 23 butterfly species.

Yet Leicester, like other urban areas, presents a wide range of ecological stresses, including pollution, noise and damage to natural habitats. In the last century the number of ponds within the city has declined from 438 to 42, and since 1919 marshland plants, such as Marsh Bedstraw in Aylestone Meadows, have been superseded by those, such as Meadow Cranesbill, preferring drier habitats. Though the streets are lined with 24,000 trees, a significant number are diseased.

So for the education and enjoyment of its citizens, and for the protection of wildlife, nature conservation has assumed a central importance as part of land use planning and management. Ecological merit now informs developmental decisions, though several local plans initiated by the City Council itself will, if implemented, destroy a further 22 per cent of the undeveloped land area. Selectively, forty-two

*Environment City: Beaumont Woods is one
of many elements in the ecology strategy*

nature sites and ecology projects ranging from small ponds and nature areas in
restricted locations – for example in Prebend Street (close to the railway station) or
Rally Nature Garden (Tudor Road) – to more ambitious and extensive meadows
and woodlands – as at Piper Way (New Parks), Beaumont Wood, Knighton
Spinney and Watermead Ecological Park – provide new environmental
improvements. Revised park management strategies demonstrate that the greening
influences are more subtle. No longer are open areas routinely mowed on a regular
basis; woodland canopies are thinned to allow light to penetrate to the woodland
floor; hedgerows are managed to provide wide and dense growth at their base. The
enrichment of the flora and fauna is a direct consequence.

The eventual impact on plant and animal species, their survival and variety, is a
long term matter. However, few would quarrel with the motives, particularly when
these are complemented with educational projects. School Nature Areas in Leicester
(SNAIL) is one initiative which encourages the development of nature areas as part
of the school curriculum. The City Wildlife Project has assisted pupils at Montrose
School in the revitalization of a nearby flooded sandpit, and has provided 'site alert
maps' to advise local residents and councillors, and to warn developers, of the
ecological merits of particular areas.

In raising local consciousness regarding these issues, the City Council has
responded energetically to a national and international groundswell of

environmental opinion, and has sought locally to counteract the adverse effects of economic development on the built environment in which Leicester residents live. Designated as 'Environment City' by the Royal Society for Nature Conservation in 1992, Leicester received further international credit for its environmental strategies as the only UK city, and one of only twelve cities worldwide, nominated by the United Nations Conference on Environment and Development (UNCED) at the Earth Summit in Rio de Janeiro in 1992. The integration of conservation, ecology and recycling strategies, as well as the development of a social environment in which city centre safety, traffic and cultural provisions are given a high priority, has established Leicester as a city with a progressive vision of the urban environment. This has been acknowledged in various quarters: HRH Prince Charles observed 'the splendid progress in Leicester', and Sir David Attenborough commented that 'Leicester is pioneering [an approach] which should affect all aspects of environmental activity in the City'. Through its participation at the local level in strategies approved in Rio, Leicester's Agenda 2020 is a thirty-year strategy that seeks to build on acknowledged excellence in environmental planning.

Conservation

In the years after the Second World War, and once rebuilding and redevelopment were underway, it became apparent that the character of particular areas was under threat. Clearances, new streets and multi-storey buildings altered the built environment radically. The process of listing buildings, begun nationally in 1948, offered some measure of protection as the list of Leicester buildings surveyed by the Department of Environment was extended in the early 1970s, but it did little to protect an area with worthy, if not architecturally outstanding, buildings, trees and features that distinguished it from other neighbourhoods. Wider planning powers under the Civic Amenities Act, 1967 enabled the city council to designate New Walk, the Town Hall Square, Guildhall and cathedral, together with areas around the castle and its gardens, as the first conservation areas in 1969–70. In 1974–5, another six conservation areas were designated, including Old Humberstone, Market Place, and Belgrave Hall. Other areas have since been added, with a burst of activity in 1989 that included Market and High Streets, St George's, Evington village, Ashleigh Road and Westcotes Drive, so that in a twenty-year period a total of twenty-two conservation areas have been identified. Constraints on private actions to benefit public amenity formed the basis of this environmental strategy.

The preservation of older neighbourhoods reflects the growing awareness of late-Victorian buildings and their settings as valued elements in the contemporary townscape. Individual buildings have also been protected under the listing procedures of the Department of the Environment. About 363 Leicester buildings have now been listed – 8 Grade I, 32 Grade II* and 304 Grade II. Most, of course, are not twentieth-century properties; two-thirds are pre-1840 buildings, approximately 30 per cent are from the period 1840–1914, and there are a mere five

The Lutyens war memorial, Victoria Park, 1923

Kirby and West's diary, Eastern Boulevard

Liberty Works, Eastern Boulevard

entries for the post-1914 years – the Lutyens war memorial and its gates in Victoria Park, two telephone kiosks on London Road, and 78 and 80 Rutland Street.

Several twentieth-century industrial premises form distinctive landmarks for Leicester residents – Liberty Works (Eastern Boulevard); Corah's St Margaret Works (St John Street); Kirby and West's dairy (Western Boulevard); Equity Shoes (Western Road); Cherubs Ltd. (Charles Street); Co-op buildings (Knighton Fields

Leicester University's trio of high rise towers – Stirling's Engineering building, the Attenborough Tower and the Charles Wilson building

Road); Dunlop Works (Evington Valley Road); and, until it was demolished in 1992, Abbey Bakeries (Blackbird Road). The industrial premises of Harrison and Hayes (Deacon Street), Frisby Jarvis Mill (Frog Island), Farben Works (Slater Street), and Gimson's (Vulcan Road) are among other notable Leicester landmarks. Educational buildings such as Newarke Girls School (Imperial Avenue), Southfields College, and the Polytechnic's (now De Montfort University) Hawthorn and Clephan Buildings are other distinctive creations of the twentieth century, though perhaps most prominent are Leicester University's trio of high-rise towers – Stirling's Engineering building, the Attenborough Tower and the Charles Wilson building – which provide a unique skyline to the city and prompt mixed reactions as to their architectural merits.

As part of this continuous process of reformulation in the Leicester landscape, the mosques in Loughborough Road and Conduit Street, and the Jain Centre in Oxford Street, also add their distinctive form. Though considered in the course of planning proposals, these twentieth-century buildings remain unlisted. They are among a number of 'non-statutory' buildings, a form of waiting list for buildings of local interest that contribute significantly to the contemporary townscape. This non-statutory list includes many familiar buildings and landmarks: libraries in Cossington Street, Clarendon Park Road, Narborough and St Barnabas Roads; schools in Slater, Belper, Bruin, Gateway and Medway Streets; several churches such as St Guthlac's (Holbrook Road), St Ann's (Letchworth Road), St Michael's

New landmarks: the Jain Centre, Oxford Street

New landmarks: mosque, Conduit Street

(Melton Road), St Alban's (Harrison Road), the Church of the Martyrs (Westcotes Drive), and the Methodist churches (Fosse Road North and Narborough Road). Pubs such as the Old Black Lion (Humberstone Gate), and the Uppingham and Western Hotels also appear on the waiting list, as do many shops in Belgrave and Braunstone Gates. It is almost twenty years since a systematic listed buildings survey was undertaken in Leicester, and for some distinctive and distinguished properties, such as the Abbey Bakeries, it is already too late.

Monuments and Monumentality

Many twentieth-century buildings reflect a scale of construction unknown a century ago. New materials, principally concrete and reinforced steel frames, have contributed to a transformation of urban space in terms of colours, textures and designs. However, vertical terraces in the form of skyscraper blocks with adjacent landscaping have not replaced conventional horizontal terraces except in a few, limited areas of Leicester. Low-rise terraces and semi-detached housing, and modestly scaled commercial buildings distinguish Leicester from other provincial cities such as Leeds, Birmingham and Sheffield, where high-rise buildings have achieved a stronger hold. So although Leicester University's towers, Rowlatt's Hill, Elizabeth House, the City Council's New Walk Centre and the Post Office buildings (Charles Street), together with a few other premises, provide bulky and intrusive

*Functional architecture: the New Walk
Centre, a speculative office building designed
by Newman, Levinson, 1971–5, and now
Leicester City Council offices*

forms in the modern townscape, the housing supply and employment structure in
Leicester were never so dire as in many other British cities as to necessitate high rise
solutions or massive industrial plant developments during the 1950s and 1960s
when such buildings were in vogue. In the main, high rise development bypassed
Leicester.

However, if the city avoided the monumental scale of much twentieth-century
construction, to compensate it gained more than its fair share of drab, commercial
building. Vaughan Way and Burley's Way were littered with tedious commercial
units during the 1950s and 1960s, and the prime retailing site, the Haymarket
Centre (1971–3) offers a standard of mall shopping design inferior to most other
British cities. In more recent decades the crude functionalism of retail outlets – the
'tin sheds' of Queensway, MFI, Texas, B&Q on St Margaret's Way, St Peter's
Lane, St George's, and elsewhere – and of industrial premises such as at Freemen's
Common and Cannock Street, Thurmaston, have provided Leicester residents with
elements of visual monotony in the townscape. Though these stores create local
jobs, the multiples cannot afford in their retail wars to neglect a population
concentration the size of Leicester; minimal landscaping and planting concessions
have been made by them in their quest for prime sites. As it is, through their
corporate logos and colour schemes, Boots, Marks and Spencer, BHS, Tesco,
Sainsbury, Dixons, and a host of high street shoe and clothing outlets have had a
homogenizing effect on the built environment. Leicester has not escaped the trend.

Neon signs, plastics and building materials such as steel and concrete, together

The bland and inventive Haymarket Centre in Humberstone Gate (1971–3) was typical of much retail building in the 1970s

with a selective use of chrome, alloys and glass have amended the texture of the Leicester townscape, and its geographical extent has been extended significantly. The form of late 1980s and early 1990s commercial developments at the Shires shopping mall and the Royal Insurance office development on London Road have attempted to break down monolithic developments through much greater attention to architectural detailing than existed in the 1960s.

The twentieth-century revolution in motor transport has provided individuals and families with a wider orbit for their recreational and work opportunities. Another trend, towards entertainment in the home, in sequence through radio, TV and video, has also lessened Leicester citizens' dependence on the city centre and public entertainment. This introspection has strengthened individualism; it has altered the relationship between residents and the buildings and open spaces in the city.

To a degree the dominance of motor traffic since 1945 has been offset by various 'greening' strategies and qualitative changes in public thoroughfares in the 1980s. Pedestrian precincts such as St Martin's and bricked pavements like those around the Town Hall have been complemented with replicas of Victorian street lights, bollards, signs and flower baskets. Historical echoes abound in the shop frontages and paint colours in and around Loseby Lane, many facilitated by grant-aided work. In Egginton Street, an Asian supermarket has been restored with civic grants

*Post-modernist architecture in the city centre
(left) and commercial building in the London
Road (below) was part of a reaction to the
bland functionalism of the 1960s and 1970s*

Bollards, baskets and benches in Town Hall Square, Gallowtree Gate and other city centre thoroughfares have been part of an attempt to beautify the contemporary townscape

to resemble, externally, a turn-of-the-century shop. Though eyebrows may be raised at the replication and glorification of the essentially Victorian character of this new street furniture, the effect is much better than the alternative – neglect. The extensive relaying of central and suburban pavements has reflected a genuine commitment to improve disabled and wheelchair access. Roundabouts and parks have been planted with annuals and bulbs, and these reinforce seasonal differences, as do lighting for Diwali and Christmas, and the annual Leicester Show. A social conscience has informed a civic consciousness in the development of policies to improve the fabric of Leicester in the last two decades.

In these subtler ways the built environment has evolved. Social customs and national trends have been expressed with local Leicester variants. In this, private efforts and municipal initiatives have reshaped the physical surroundings to provide a distinctive identity to the city; Leicester could never be mistaken for Liverpool, Leeds or a London borough. Our grandparents would recognize the Leicester of the 1900s in the street patterning and by particular buildings and landmarks; our grandchildren will recognize the Leicester of 1990 for the same reasons, though with many distinctive twentieth-century contributions grafted on to the Victorian legacy. Change within continuity in the built environment, therefore, provides a set of reference points for the people of Leicester.

Further Reading

Leicester City Council, *Abbey District Plan*

Leicester City Council, *Renewal Strategy: Programme Report* (1976)

Leicester City Council, *Grand Union Housing Action Area* (1982–3)

Leicester City Council, *Leicester Ecology Strategy* (1989)

Leicester City Council, *The Quality of Leicester* (1993)

Newitt, N., 'From slums to semis: housing the people of Leicester 1919–39', unpublished M. Phil. thesis, University of Leicester (1993)

Pevsner, N., *The Buildings of England: Leicestershire and Rutland*, 2nd revised edition by E. Williamson (1992)

Phillips, D., 'The social and spatial segregation of Asians in Leicester' in P. Jackson and S. Smith, *Social Interaction and Ethnic Segregation* (1981)

Pritchard, R.M., *Housing and the Spatial Structure of the City* (1976)

Smigielski, K., *Leicester Traffic Plan* (1964)

Smigielski, K., *Leicester: Today and Tomorrow* (1968)

Stoker, G. and Brindley, T., 'Asian politics and housing renewal', *Policy and Politics*, 13, pp. 281–303 (1985)

Chapter Two

THE LOCAL ECONOMY

Inter-war Foundations

At first sight the development of Leicester's economy seems to have been a considerable success story at least until the 1970s. The origins of the city's reputation as a prosperous industrial centre dates from the inter-war years. Leicester had made the transition to a manufacturing economy in the late nineteenth century and by 1914 the two staple manufacturing industries of hosiery and footwear underpinned its economic role as a major exporter. During the 1920s Leicester came to be known internationally as the greatest boot and shoe distributing centre in Britain and the largest centre in the world for the production of knitted goods of every description. 'Leicester clothes the world from head to foot' was the proud boast of its Chamber of Commerce in 1924.

The years between the two World Wars were characterized by the consolidation of the two staples in the local economy, the development of related industries and the beginnings of diversification. In 1911 the Leicester Chamber of Commerce listed a total of sixty-two firms. By 1936 this number had grown nearly twenty-fold. Leicester was represented in commercial publications as a city of seventy-nine industries and more than a thousand allied trades. The range of job opportunities was frequently alluded to in the 1930s as an explanation for the relative prosperity of the local economy despite the depression.

Looked at in a longer timespan, however, the inter-war years were a transitional period in the process of diversification. In 1939 what might be called the traditional industries, including engineering – which emerged in the period before the First World War – still dominated the local economy in terms of employment. Out of a total of 135,000 factory workers, four sectors employed nearly two thirds: hosiery 34,000, boots and shoes 21,000, distributive trades 15,000 and engineering 13,000. It was in the period following the Second World War that the local economy really took off in terms of new enterprises and variety of products. From that point of view the inter-war years are best regarded as laying the foundations for the later period of explosive growth.

Economic Change, 1914–39

The First World War was an important stimulus, both to growth and new innovations. The city economy benefited from a general increase in demand for the town's staple manufactured goods and the impact of government orders for footwear and hosiery products. The establishment of new industries was also given an impetus by the war. The emergence of an engineering industry was a logical development of the growth of factory production in the town's staples, and closely associated initially with the making of hosiery and footwear machines. It was in the area of light engineering that a break with the old staples was first achieved, although advances were also made in the electrical and rubber industries through such firms as J.T. Gent and Co. (formed 1903) and the John Bull Rubber Co. which began in 1906. The growth of elastic web manufacture was an example of late nineteenth-century innovation.

The First World War acted as a pacemaker for Leicester industry, encouraging existing industries to innovate and diversify their product range, and also bringing in new firms to the town. Examples of product diversification included textile dyes (Oram Bros), shell components (Young Austen and Young) and propeller shaping and the making of aeroplane struts (on the part of A.J. Wadkins, the wood machinists). A shortage of war materials was one stimulus to innovation in the engineering industry by encouraging local tool-makers, for example, to adapt their machines to the war effort. Indeed tool-makers and drilling machine companies seem to have been able to take unique advantage of war requirements, none more successfully than the firm of Jones and Shipman.

An important development associated with the growth of new industry, anticipating modern trends, was the role of outside capital in the city's economy. The old staples had largely been fostered indigenously, providing opportunities for the self-made entrepreneurial capitalist – a typical figure in the late nineteenth-century business scene in Leicester. This was because the capital requirements of both hosiery and shoes were relatively small, although the claim that 'one room and a five pound note' were sufficient to start boot and shoe manufacturing was an exaggeration. In the new engineering fields, however, the levels of investment required were considerably greater. To meet this challenge the old and formerly independent family firm of Stibbe began to act as agents for American companies, adapting machines for British shoe manufacture and for Leicester's shoe industry in particular. An even more striking example of the importance of outside capital was provided by the British United Shoe Machinery Co. formed in 1899 by an amalgamation of the local engineering firm of Pearson and Bennion with the United Shoe Machinery Company of America. By 1900 the Union works and branch depots were producing two thirds of the shoe machines sold in Britain. Similarly, in light engineering, the American Thomas Gillette established his first razor blades factory in the city in 1905, and three years later the Imperial Typewriter Company established its main base in the city.

A bootmaker's workshop, c. *1912*

Nevertheless there were continuing opportunities for small-scale enterprise and local capital in all these industries during the inter-war years: the small-scale producer was not squeezed out by any means. The greatest number of firms in 1936 in Leicester were to be found in the hosiery and boot and shoe industries. In hosiery some 250 firms were engaged in the city and more than a hundred others in the surrounding country towns and districts, notably at Hinckley and Loughborough. There were 200 manufacturers of boots and shoes in the city and county. Moreover, the requirements of these industries had stimulated new enterprise in subsidiary trades, not only machine-making but also the production of thread (British Thread Mills Ltd) and the production and distribution of leather goods.

The hosiery industry continued to prosper in the inter-war years, and in consequence older firms such as J. Pick and Sons and Corah's were able to consolidate their position. The firm of Alfred Corah Ltd expanded its plant in 1919 and again in 1932 – developments that were greeted in the local press as typifying the progress of the hosiery trade in the city. In the 1930s there was also a new spate of company formations in knitwear and several notable Leicester firms (still going strong in the 1970s) date from this period, such as A. A. Manufacturing and C.W. Attenborough and Co. Ltd. Footwear manufacturing, however, suffered from a setback after the end of the war. The firms to come out best were those which specialized in particular products, as for example the firm of T. Roberts and Sons, founded by Thomas Roberts in 1872 and adopting limited liability in 1932. This

W.H. Allen's premises on Castle Street are typical of the small businesses that used to flourish in Leicester's textile trades

firm specialized in making women's footwear under the brand name of Portland. The difficulties which the shoe industry had in the 1920s seem to have affected most of those older manufacturers who had gone into retailing, such as Stead and Simpson and Hilton Shoes. However, both had regained their pre-war position by 1936, while other retail outlets such as the clothing wholesalers, Hart and Levy, a partnership formed in 1880, prospered in the inter-war years. Hart and Levy provides an example of how by 1936 older firms were beginning to outgrow family management, with the first non-family member appointed as Managing Director.

By 1936 the local engineering industry included firms engaged in making footwear machinery, many of them specializing in particular product areas, and firms making knitwear machinery, most of them founded by individuals or partnerships who had come to Leicester to live – for example John Bentley, who started the Bentley Engineering Co. in 1910. By 1939, 18 per cent of Leicester's workforce was employed in engineering, two thirds of which was given over to the production of hosiery and footwear machines.

In the remainder of the engineering industry, however, there was already evidence of considerable product variety, with the production of machine tools, pumps, lifts, cranes, road making and quarry plant, diesel engines, electric clocks and time recorders, and typewriters. There were specialist firms providing machinery for other industries besides the staples, and a number of bridge-building and constructional engineering firms. In heavy engineering Leicester based firms were establishing a strong position; firms dating from the early years of the century which continued to do well in the inter-war years included Richard's Engineering, Frederick Parker, Pochin's (subsequently Goodwin Barsby), and Gimson. In light engineering too there was still room for the small partnership to succeed, as shown by the Taylor Hobson optical firm and by Jones and Shipman in the machine tool industry. One of the best-known local firms was that of Wadkins, which as we have seen turned to metal-working from wood-working during the war.

The expansion of the city economy undoubtedly brought new opportunities for local enterprise. Thus the number of firms involved in electrical manufacture increased threefold from twenty-three in 1922 to sixty-three in 1932; as the *Trade Review* of 1936 commented, most of the engineering firms established in recent years were in one or other of the branches of electrical engineering. There were also new establishments which manufactured office equipment, paper, and carbon paper. The printing industry was well established in the city. Food processing was another area in which local enterprises flourished – Frears biscuits and Keene's meat pie works were notable examples, as was the firm of W.H. Dawson, which had moved from Great Yarmouth to Leicester in 1890. Another local firm to become famous in this area was the sweet manufacturer and wholesale grocer, W.R. Fox.

Cover of the Leicester Evening Mail *promoting the city's industry, 1939*

However, the growing popularity of the department store in the inter-war years brought in new outside capital, with the establishment of a branch of the Liverpool based firm of Lewis's Ltd at a cost of £¾ million.

A Prosperous City

The strength of the economy after the depression years seemed to be confirmed by the findings of the Bureau of Statistics of the League of Nations in 1936, which rated Leicester 'the second most prosperous city in Europe'. But this statistic related to the average level of household income rather than to the level of business wealth.

Nevertheless, the inter-war years seem to have been a period of remarkable stability for Leicester's business community, during which the older and most successful families consolidated their position. The value of estates left at death provides one yardstick of the kind of fortunes accumulated by these families. National figures suggest an assessment for probate purposes of £100,000 as indicative of substantial wealth in this period, but only a tiny handful of Leicester businessmen came into this category. The precedents had been set by Sir Israel Hart (d. 1911), and two boot and shoe manufacturers, Edward Wood (d. 1916) and Stephen Hilton (d. 1914), all of whom left more than £100,000, the former two estates approaching £200,000 each. In the first thirty-two years of the twentieth century, twenty-eight of the city's leading businessmen died leaving £50,000 or more, of whom seventeen left £100,000 or more. In the latter category were some very well-known names in Leicester's public life, such as T. Fielding Johnson, the worsted spinner (d. 1932), Charles Bennion, the shoe machinery manufacturer (d. 1929), Major William Freer, solicitor and clerk to the Council, and H. Simpson Gee. The last named was a leading figure in the retail shoe trade, the founder and for many years director of Stead and Simpson, and the first of the city's half-millionaires.

All told, this small group of top wealth holders included fourteen manufacturers, two builders and a timber merchant, and one tradesman. Of the remainder, five had no specified occupation and one, Christiana Viccars, was the daughter of T. Fielding Johnson. But there were in addition a further 163 probates in this period valued at £10,000 or more – which lends some support to the popular idea of Leicester as 'a city of many small fortunes'. It should be noted, however, that probates of this value represented only a tiny percentage of probated estates in any one year.

It was the general appearance of prosperity in the city during the 1930s that struck observers such as J.B. Priestley in 1936 and the authors of the Pilgrim Trust in 1938, who remarked that it certainly had 'the most prosperous air' of any of the places they had visited. This impression probably derived from the relatively high average level of household income, due to the contribution of Leicester's working wives and young people to the family budget. It was also the case that Leicester had managed to sustain economic buoyancy in the inter-war period in a way that would

A.H. Broughton's hosiery shop floor, photographed in 1928

have been the envy of the older industrial cities. During the depression Leicester's hosiery industry had fared better than most. As skirts became shorter, silk and rayon stockings replaced the older woollen styles and the number of men employed on the fine gauge full fashioned hosiery machines grew. In this highly skilled section workers were unionized and the best paid in the industry. Moreover, as pullovers and cardigans became more popular with both sexes, the demand for knitwear increased. Out of fourteen new hosiery factories opened in Britain in 1933, eight were in Leicester.

Nevertheless there was some unemployment during the inter-war years and, for those affected, periods of distress. Post-war unemployment in the city reached 7,419 in October 1921 – about 5 per cent of the workforce – and the situation in Leicester became tense as hungry men demonstrated against the Guardians in what became known as the Rupert Street revolt. By 1926 unemployment had risen again to 9,000, reaching 16,000 in 1932. In 1931–2 the unemployed also suffered from the financial pressures on the local Public Assistance Committee. Although this

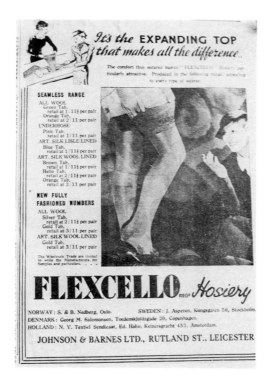

An advert for Leicester-made hosiery

committee was generally held to be more charitable than its counterpart in the county, the introduction of the means test meant that dole was stopped in 1,302 instances and reduced in another 698 between November 1931 and January 1932. These hardships gave the unemployed workers' movement a new impetus in Leicester as elsewhere.

Despite Leicester's subsequent reputation for prosperity, there were seldom fewer than 10,000 jobless in the city before the outbreak of the Second World War. There were also periods of short-time working in the footwear industry affected as early as the 1920s by foreign competition. By the 1930s non-unionized firms outside Leicester had begun to increase their share of the market. More generally, structural changes were beginning to affect the workforce as the semi-skilled were displaced by technological advance. Newer machinery simplified the work process and, as a result, lads were kept in work until they were eighteen or twenty-one and then turned out of a job unskilled. Their plight was concealed by the prevailing local prosperity, isolating them among wage earners bringing home good money. As the Pilgrim Trust Report of 1938 pointed out, what gave 'unemployment its special character in such a place as Leicester, is the contrast between the general prosperity and the man or the family, who is standing outside it, but witnessing it all day and every day . . .'. It was no accident, they went on, that 'the National Unemployed Workers' Movement should be mentioned more to us in Leicester than elsewhere'.

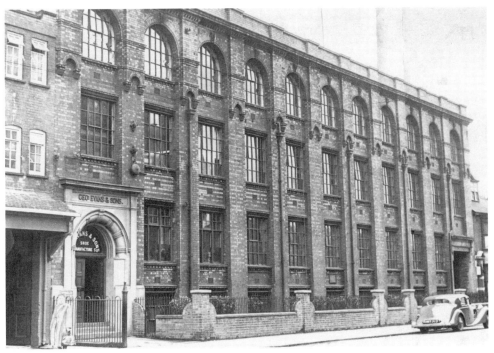

George Evans and Sons shoe factory in Belgrave Road

Economic Change since the Second World War: an Overview

Leicester came out of the depression years with its economy largely intact, and in the years after the Second World War the sustained growth of employment in many of its manufacturing industries gave the impression of a city that had acquired virtually an immunity from severe downturns in the trade cycle. Nor was Leicester subject to the structural problems of cities dependent on the older heavy industries of the nineteenth century. It was nearer in character to the boom towns of the west Midlands. Economic commentators laid emphasis on the diversity of its industrial structure and the role of its many small firms in contributing to this economic resilience. For most people, Leicester's economic strength and prosperity were based essentially on its strong, diverse, yet well integrated and outwardly buoyant manufacturing base.

These perceptions began to be seriously challenged in the 1970s, a decade which marks a major break in the post-war history of the economy, with the onset of a recession of a depth and extent previously unknown. While the economy seemed to pull out of this for a time in the early 1980s, a renewed contraction of economic activity set in during the later part of this decade, associated with accelerated rates of business failure. But even in the early 1970s the closure of a number of long-standing firms in traditional industries had affected the public consciousness and led to the first sustained analysis of the economy on the part of a group of economists at the former Polytechnic (now De Montfort University). Stage one of the report of the *Leicester Economic Study* challenged some of the more commonly held ideas about the city's economic success, suggesting that the time had come to 'reconsider views about Leicester's economy and to discard much of the popular mythology surrounding it; a mythology which is at best out-moded and at worst entirely erroneous'. The date of the publication of this report provides a convenient break in the following review of employment trends and industrial change in the city.

The Impact of the Second World War

There were clues to the way that Leicester's economy was to develop in the mixed fortunes of manufacturing industry during the Second World War. For the traditional industries of footwear and textiles, the war possibly marked the beginnings of trends that were to lead ultimately to the eclipse of both industries as the dominant employers in the area. A dramatic fall in numbers employed (as well as a loss of premises and machinery) was due to the demands of new munitions factories, compulsory recruitment to the armed services and pooling of labour. By 1944 employment in both industries had reached a low point with their respective shares of local manufacturing employment industry falling by over a half since the outbreak of the war. While numbers employed recovered immediately after the war to pre-war levels, neither industry regained its pre-eminent position in terms of local employment.

By contrast the duration of the war was a significant period of expansion for the engineering and related industries of the city because of the wartime need for production capacity to be fully utilized and expanded in the engineering, aircraft and vehicle industries. This was reflected in the employment figures, which reached post-war peaks and fell again immediately after the war. Much wartime expansion was temporary, but there were nevertheless permanent results. One was the accession of new firms to the city because of the wartime policy of industrial dispersal. Evacuated firms, mainly from the west Midlands, came to Leicester, taking up shared premises or settling in green field sites, as at Braunstone airfield and the villages of Whetstone and Desford. Many left after the war, but some remained and expanded – Tubes at Desford, BTH on the Melton Road and Reid and Sigrist. Other new entrants, especially in electrical engineering, were attracted by the availability of premises vacated by evacuated firms, but more especially by the large body of skilled male and female labour in the city.

Local firms also benefited from wartime expansion into munitions and moves into new premises and products were in some cases sustained after the war. The firm of Jones and Shipman for example took over the site of an evacuated munitions firm and expanded its products to become one of the leading and presently the largest remaining machine tool firms in Leicester. The development of new products by existing and new firms further diversified the engineering industry away from previously strong links with the textile and footwear industries into new markets. Of greater significance, perhaps, was the growth and diversification of the electrical engineering industry in the war as firms moved into electrical and electronic products or into specialized defence related products. A similar process of change occurred in other product sectors such as rubber products and precision instruments, where Taylor, Taylor Hobson became Rank Hobson. Most of these developments had a part in laying the foundations of Leicester's economic prosperity in the post-war period.

Growth and Expansion, 1948–74

The years from 1948 to 1974 must be regarded in retrospect as the most important period of growth in the city economy during the twentieth century. Most commentators regard it as a period marked by a high degree of diversification in terms both of new industries and new products. In consequence employment opportunities expanded, enabling the city to absorb the influx of migrants during the 1950s and '60s. Throughout the period unemployment levels were low, consistently lower than the national figure, and any fluctuations were small and short-lived. Most underlying unemployment was attributable to that arising from the normal turnover of labour or unemployability rather than structural change. This was a situation that began to change quite dramatically during the 1970s.

In the halcyon years of the 1960s many of Leicester's older family firms were caught up in the surge of capital that flowed into the city from outside investors. They found themselves vulnerable to larger predators as Leicester industry, in common with industry in other cities, was affected by takeovers and mergers on the part of conglomerates and international investment companies. This did not mean the end of the small firm, however, as will be seen. While many small firms went out of business – especially in the footwear industry which had already begun to decline – the diversification of the economy was associated with fresh waves of small business enterprise as well as the expansion of the larger and older established companies. During most of this period, certainly through to the late 1960s, Leicester's main economic problem was that of over employment with shortages of labour at all skill levels in most industries and services. In the textile industry, for example, there was a persistent shortage of female workers, aggravated by changes in demographic patterns relating to marriage and childbirth, and a break with the traditional practice of daughters following their mothers into the industry. To meet this shortage many firms sought to establish branch factories in surrounding villages and towns with localized pools of labour, or bussed labour in, or resorted to the traditional use of outworkers. More desperate methods included monetary inducements to employees who brought friends or relations into the firm, and even the use of sandwich-board men to advertise jobs. Responses to shortages of skilled labour in the engineering industry included the internal upgrading of semi-skilled workers to skilled status, and greater use of subcontracting of mainly routine work –

a situation that in itself provided a stimulus to the formation of small firms. Bussing was also adopted by some firms to extend the labour catchment area – the English Electric Co. at one time operated a network of over thirty bus routes throughout Greater Leicester and beyond. Despite overall decline even the footwear industry suffered from labour shortages, particularly female workers. In part this was a result of the departure of workers from the industry. When news of the closure of a footwear firm was pending, rival firms would be at the factory gates to tout for workers.

This employment situation tended to work against the city, inhibiting the physical expansion of major firms because of national policy for the location of industrial growth, the main thrust of which was to direct new factory building to 'development' or 'assisted areas', where the decline of the major industries was taking place and unemployment was running at high levels. In places like Leicester any industrial expansion, even to existing premises, beyond a prescribed level, could not be carried out without an Industrial Development Certificate from the Department of Trade and Industry. This was needed before planning permission could be granted for the development. The operation of the system could be so strict that when the Stibbe Company moved from their base at the corner of Vaughan Way and Highcross Street to new premises on the Braunstone Industrial Estate, the older premises were, in planning terms, taken out of use.

The late development of industrial growth in the late nineteenth century and early decades of the present century, to which reference was made earlier, gave Leicester a legacy of a relatively high concentration of industrial premises both in and immediately around the central area of the city, possibly greater than many other industrial cities. Despite redevelopment after the Second World War there remained a relatively high stock of such premises still fully utilized. Nevertheless a process of decentralization had begun during the inter-war years with the development of new industrial areas on the edge of the built-up area to the north and west of the city, and this was accelerated as we have seen during the war period. After the war the location of industrial areas was subject to planning policies and in particular to green belt policy. But most of the wartime sites on the fringes of the urban area became the basis for either individual firms or industrial estates such as the New Parks/Braunstone Frith development, which was also next to major new council housing areas. The other major industrial development was in the Barkby Road area, mostly former brickworks sites. These areas were variously occupied by existing Leicester firms seeking to expand from older inner but cramped sites, or who had lost premises through post-war slum clearance and redevelopment, or by new firms (i.e. new formations or inward entrants). Similar industrial estates were developed outside the city in Wigston, Oadby, Groby, and on a smaller scale in adjacent villages.

Such developments continued throughout the 1960s and into the 1970s. But there was no massive decentralization of industry, and firms such as Corah, Rowleys, Cherub and many others remained in the inner areas, in part because of their central location with regard to labour supply. A major problem for the city was the growing shortage of industrial land. The largest area to become available was at Beaumont Leys, the cornerstone of much of the new industrial growth along with developments in the Barkby Road area (Troon Way), and further development at Braunstone Frith. Within the inner city a number of small industrial areas were formed mainly on redeveloped land, for example Hastings Road.

The Changing Pattern of Employment, 1948–74

Employment statistics for the period show that despite the importance of manufacturing industry, the growth of a service sector was also providing employment opportunities. In 1955 about two thirds of workers in employment were engaged in manufacture compared with only one third in the service industries. But during the succeeding period there was a gradual increase in the proportion employed in the service sector, bringing this roughly into balance with manufacturing by 1972. The balance tilted in favour of the service sector during the next three years. Employment in service industries had grown consistently between 1955 and 1967, when there was a temporary break followed by recovery and a faster rate of growth from 1972. However, the change in the balance of employment in favour of this sector was also due to a contraction in manufacturing employment in the later part of the period. Even in the period up to 1967 the figures show that manufacturing employment had grown at a slower rate than in the service sector, and after a slight recovery in 1971 and 1972 they reveal a marked and continuing fall, reflecting the onset of recession in the local manufacturing economy.

There were also changes in the relative positions of the main industrial groups within the overall pattern of employment in this period, as reflected in local employment statistics. These employment trends need to be related to the economic fortunes and organizational changes in each of Leicester's main industrial groups (plus the service industries) to 1974.

Footwear Industry

As already noted, the most striking feature of Leicester's post-war economy was the decline of the footwear industry as a major employer. After recovery from the war years both actual employment and share of employment progressively declined, with only a slight but temporary recovery in 1951–2. By 1964 employment in the industry had fallen by 38 per cent to 12,521 employees, and share of employment from just under 20 per cent in 1948 to about 11 per cent in 1964. Employment by 1974 was only about 7,000. The persistence of this trend since means that, contrary to a still widespread belief, Leicester is no longer, in terms of manufacturing, a major footwear centre. Countless numbers of footwear firms, many of them with well-known trade names, have now disappeared – for example, the only relic of the well-known but deceased firm of Liberty is the statue on its former factory.

An advert for the British United Shoe Machinery Company

The decline of footwear manufacture had implications for the related footwear machinery industry, with many small firms, often specializing in particular product areas, either disappearing or diversifying. However, the largest firm in this field, the British United Shoe Machinery Corporation was in a strong position as part of a large American combine. With a virtual monopoly it had a key role within the footwear manufacturing industry. The BU was one of the largest employers in the city until the 1980s, as well as having links directly or indirectly with other firms that in some cases had themselves been involved in footwear but had subsequently diversified. The most important of those with a Leicester headquarters was the adhesives manufacturer, Bostick (previously the Boston Blacking Co. or BB Chemical), which had itself originated in the USA.

The decline of footwear manufacture in Leicester was related to the increasing levels of imported footwear, mainly from the Far East but also from Italy, which has to a large degree taken over from British firms not only the manufacture but also the design of footwear especially in the women's sector, which formed the basis of the industry in Leicester. But there were also other influences of importance.

One was the pace of technological change, with the introduction of new machinery and materials, notably the substitution of traditional materials by plastics in the manufacture of footwear components – a development which provided a stimulus to the growth of plastics and related tooling industries. The city still retains

Freeman, Hardy and Willis's works on Rutland Street, early 1960s

a substantial interest in these component and equipment trades. Another major factor to influence this industry was the rationalization and restructuring of footwear distribution. Traditionally a number of footwear manufacturers had been engaged in retailing, as in the case of such well-known names as Stead and Simpson, Brevitts, Freeman, Hardy and Willis. But the late 1950s saw the merger by aggressive take-over of several large and hitherto independent retailers – Saxone, Lilley and Skinner, Freeman Hardy and Willis, Dolcis and Curtess – to form the British Shoe Corporation. The formation of this company as part of the empire of the Sears group was connected with the meteoric rise of the financier Charles Clore, who from the late 1940s had been consolidating his hold over some of Leicester's traditional businesses. Based in Leicester, BSC became the largest footwear retail organization, controlling at one time something like 40 per cent of outlets, and owning a substantial manufacturing sector, BSC Footwear, whose units were retained until the late 1980s. There has been considerable debate among older former footwear men over the business policies of BSC in its early years, especially over the pricing policy of the firm, and whether this helped to trigger off the decline of the industry.

A number of other mergers have taken place over the years and other large groups have emerged, such as Oliver Group (George Oliver and Timpson) and

Tandem. Thus Leicester has seen the emergence of major footwear retailing groups that through market share and buying power effectively determined the fortunes of manufacturers. Many of these firms are still located in the Leicester area: the city might no longer be a footwear manufacturing centre but it still has an important role in the distribution field.

Knitted Textiles

In contrast to footwear manufacture, the knitted textile industry maintained its dominant role within both the manufacturing economy and the local economy more generally. In 1948 this industry employed 31,964 workers. However, the figures show that after a swift post-war recovery, employment levels varied up and down in a roughly five-year cyclical pattern. More importantly, there was a decline in the overall employment level over the period to 1974, although not at such a catastrophic level as in the footwear industry. The industry's share of local employment also declined a little but without disturbing its position as the largest employer, except for a brief period in the early 1970s when the engineering industry took over this position. The industry retained its dominant share of employment in the local manufacturing economy: 32.5 per cent in 1950, 29 per cent in 1964 and 28 per cent in 1974.

In retrospect the pattern of employment in this period suggests underlying trends that were eventually to give rise to concern about the future of the industry. But in this period the outward buoyancy of the industry, with its ability to cope with minor booms and recessions, masked longer term problems. Such resilience can in part be explained by the way that different product sectors, such as stockings, socks, outerwear and knitted fabric, tended to go through particular cycles at different times, and thus a fall-off in one sector tended to be offset by a boom in another.

The rate of formation of new firms, which was very high, reflected the buoyancy of this industry. Relative ease of entry remained a distinctive feature. Some operatives were able to make the transition to entrepreneur quite easily, with ready access to machinery and equipment particularly through the second-hand trade and by starting in low cost premises, which might initially be a shed or garage. Also, despite the skill element, textile manufacture remained essentially a craft more than a high technology industry. However, it was just as easy to fail, especially when there was dependence on commission, subcontract work or scarce female labour. Despite this a significant number of small firms established in the immediate post-war period did survive, possibly because they remained small and flexible.

At the same time it was possibly the presence of larger and longer established firms that in reality sustained the smaller ones through the training of operatives, provision of commission work and sales of discarded equipment. During this period there was considerable expansion of these larger firms through internal growth as well as merger and take-over activity, leading to the formation of a number of large groups. Corah grew largely through internal growth, for example, employing at its peak about 2,500–3,000 at its Leicester factories, but also establishing branch plants

Corah's hosiery works on Burley's Way

in the county and beyond. Courtaulds also established a major presence but largely through take-overs of previously independent firms that continued under their original names. A man-made yarn processing firm, its control over firms engaged in textile machinery, packaging and wholesaling (mainly lingerie) enabled it to make forward linkages. In the late 1960s Courtaulds controlled thirteen firms in the Greater Leicester area, and another yarn firm, that of Coats, also established ownership links, its most notable Leicester subsidiaries being Byfords and Wolsey. Other mergers tended to be more modest and locally based. Although these big groups were collectively powerful in employment terms, the knitted textile industry, and thus the local economy in general, cannot be said to have been dominated by them.

Perhaps the most powerful influence on the structure and performance of the textile industry was the rise of the large clothing retailers and mail order groups during the 1960s and '70s. This development tended to shift the centre of gravity in the relationships between manufacturers and retailers, mainly as a consequence of the buying power of the large retailers and the way they operated. The large retail groups initiated two processes – known as 'specification buying' and 'distribution shift' – which have continued with increased intensity through to the present decade, being given a particular twist in the late 1980s with the growth of firms such as Next and Burton Group. The pioneer of such a development was Marks and Spencer in the late 1950s. The way this firm required manufacturers to conform

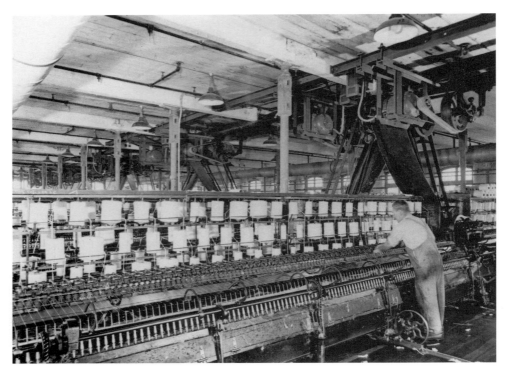

A view of the interior of Fielding Johnson's Bond Street Spinning Works

exactly to its specifications and insisted on the availability of stocks at specific times and quantities, clearly made it the dominant partner. One effect of this in the longer term was to undermine the independence of textile firms, with the gradual loss of marketing and design capability.

In Leicester, the firm of Nottingham Manufacturing had early links with Marks and Spencer, and Corah became a major supplier developing a close relationship. But other firms consciously sought to avoid such links, not without problems, especially in specialist clothing sectors. On the whole, local industry tended to look suspiciously at the activities of large retailers, and strongly criticized buying policies that seemed to encourage the import of clothing at cheap prices.

The high level of imported clothing has been a persistent issue for the Leicester textile industry, as elsewhere, and the industry has had to be particularly vigilant with regard to the arrangement known as the Multi Fibre Agreement, which was intended to restrict imports. This was a subject on which the industry has been united. Another persistent issue has been that of skilled labour shortages, as already noticed in referring to the strategies adopted to deal with the problem. Longer term responses were inhibited by two features of the knitted textile industry. One was the nature of technological improvements, which essentially involved new applications to an unchanged basic technology. The processes in which labour shortages

The Frisby Jarvis clothing factory on Frog Island

persisted remained labour intensive. It was also the case that certain major advances, for example in fabric cutting, were beyond the scope financially as well as operationally of all but the largest firms. The existence of so many small firms was also an inhibiting factor in the development of training opportunities, the small firms unable as well as reluctant to participate in training programmes, leaving this to the larger firms. The problem of small firms in this respect was eventually to be a factor in the early demise of the training board for the industry set up with other such boards in the late 1960s. On the other hand there are many who would argue that the strength of the textile industry in this period lay in the proliferation of small firms operated by ruggedly independent owners.

Engineering: Mechanical and General

The employment series for the engineering industry shows a steep fall at the end of the war followed by consistent growth from 1945 to 1965, when it reached its highest level of just over 34,000 workers, and briefly took over as the leading employment sector. Thereafter the picture is more variable, with a sharp collapse followed by recovery to almost the previous level in 1969, and a more severe and long term decline thereafter. Overall, the share of manufacturing employment grew modestly: 24.6 per cent in 1945, 23.5 per cent in 1956, rising to 26.2 per cent in

The shop floor at Wadkin Ltd, manufacturers of woodworking machinery, pictured in 1967

1964 and 28.4 per cent in 1971. However, this is a sector made up of a varied range of processes and products. Although vehicle products and instrument engineering are not included in the employment figures, this still leaves the two main traditional sectors of textile and footwear machinery and such sectors as typewriter manufacture, machine tools and heavy engineering products, all of which in terms of their historical origins can be regarded as traditional. Some of these sectors enjoyed virtually uninterrupted growth and success during the period until 1974.

This was the case, for example, with the heavy engineering sector, a diverse sector (stone-crushing machinery, foundry equipment, construction metal products, and, at the lighter end, cement mixers). Most of the firms dated back to the early years of the century, and some were associated with Leicester's oldest industrial families. The only significant development in this period was diversification into the manufacture of finished engineering products. By 1964 the sector had acquired a 10 per cent share of local engineering employment (2,970 workers) and reached 12 per cent in 1971 (with 3,820 workers).

The exception to the engineering success story was the footwear machinery industry whose fortunes, as we have seen, were closely intertwined with the footwear industry. Although employment figures for this sector cannot be separated out, other evidence indicates a significant decline in size and importance over the period. The loss of firms left it dominated by two major concerns, BUSM and Standard Engineering, which also specialized in footwear repairing machinery. There were

The Stibbe textile machine factory at the junction of Highcross Street and Vaughan Way, 1964

also a number of smaller firms concentrating on a narrow range of specialist machines (such as Livingston and Doughty), and firms engaged in the manufacture of tools and equipment.

The textile machinery sector in contrast continued to maintain a leading role within the industry. Although its share of engineering employment declined somewhat from 23 per cent in 1948 to 19.5 per cent in 1971, the total number employed continued to grow until 1971, the peak year (6,235 workers), only to fall away dramatically by 1974. The industry locally was in the hands of a small group of large firms, several of them old established family firms that in some cases were part of larger conglomerate groups. Thus Stibbe was an old family firm, as were some of the firms in the Bentley Engineering Group such as Bentley Engineering and Wildt, Mellor Bromley. Bentley Engineering (like the British Shoe Corporation) became for a time one of the stars in the Sears firmament. The 1970s, however, saw the rapid growth of a relatively new firm, Camber International. Moreover, smaller firms survived in textile machinery components, usually on a subcontract basis, or in making very specialized machinery or building and reconditioning old machines.

Even in the light engineering trades there was considerable variation in the experiences of different sectors. The manufacture of typewriters was a case in point. This constituted a significant sector of the engineering industry but was almost entirely one firm, based on Imperial Typewriters, which at its peak directly employed about 1,400 workers and through subcontracting had a more extensive

A worker at Imperial Typewriters, late 1960s

impact locally. Despite being one of the original and largest typewriter firms in the UK, it failed to respond quickly enough to technical and product changes, and was overtaken by relatively new firms such as Olivetti. Taken over by an American conglomerate in the 1970s, Imperial Typewriters was closed down in Leicester in 1974 as a consequence of rationalization with continental interests.

By contrast, the machine tool sector in Leicester continued to enjoy considerable success, although this industry has been the graveyard of many famous names nationally. Employment in this sector was 12 per cent of employment in engineering in 1948, rising to 17 per cent at its highest level of employment in 1970 (5,553 workers). Here again a number of pre-Second World War firms were the subject of outside takeovers and mergers. Among the larger firms were Jones and Shipman, Adcock and Shipley (now Bridgeport Machines, part of an American company) and Frederick Pollard. There were a number of other firms, such as the medium sized Moss Engineering and J.W. Bamkin, making specialist machines and a group of firms making major tooling components or units (e.g. broaches and measuring tools). This industry owed much of its relative success in Leicester to concentrating on higher volume standard machines, particularly drilling and milling machines, rather than depending on highly sophisticated specialist equipment.

Finally, in this discussion of the engineering industry in Leicester, account has to be taken of three more broad groups with a diverse range of products and processes.

These were, firstly, the firms making assembled machinery or sub units, such as printing equipment, metal can manufacture (Metal Box), hand and press tools and so on. Secondly, process firms engaged in metalwork processes, metal processing and the making of components such as springs, valves, castors, fasteners and screws (mainly as subcontractors). Thirdly, and the largest sector, a range of firms generally referred to as 'general' or 'precision' engineers – a statistically residual group, but one that in Leicester constitutes a very substantial section of the industry. Again most of these firms originated as subcontractors making components, or part components, usually involving metal cutting and grinding with possibly minor sub-assembly: they did not produce a product of their own.

In this subsidiary branch of the industry larger firms were exceptional, yet over 4,000 workers were employed in 1974, most of them in small (or very small) firms. Many of the latter were relatively young firms, established largely in response to a combination of skilled labour shortages and government restrictions on major investment, which provided market conditions and opportunities for individuals to set up their own small businesses. A ready supply of second-hand equipment and relatively simple factory space requirements facilitated this. Given such circumstances and the high rate of dependency on subcontract work there was a high birth/death rate in this sector. Nevertheless, older firms that developed particular skill levels or engaged in more specialist precision processes have proved to be highly successful and durable. Many of them developed markets outside the mainstream of Leicester engineering dealing with firms in the motor, aero, defence and high technology industries, including firms, such as Rolls Royce, where there was a degree of mutual interdependence. The forging of such links has in fact led to the emergence of a group of firms working exclusively for the air and motor industries. In 1948 firms involved in these two sectors already employed 2,044 workers, which by 1962 had risen, albeit briefly and erratically, to 5,353 workers (subject to the vagaries of the employment statistics). They still employed 3,400 workers in 1971.

Another sector with strong local origins and a similar pattern of employment was that of instrument engineering, in which the leading firm (Rank Taylor) was associated with the manufacture of lens and camera equipment, and metrology equipment. Reid and Sigrist, another firm in this sector, was subject to mergers and take-overs to become part of Racal. By 1971 this sector employed 2,287 workers.

Electrical and Electronic Engineering

The growth and development of the electrical and electronic engineering industry must be regarded as one of the key developments in the industrial structure of the Leicester area during the post-war period until the mid-1970s and even to the present time. The industry evolved from its pre-war and wartime roots to replace the footwear industry in employment terms as the third largest manufacturing industry by the late 1960s/early '70s with 10,183 workers and a 9.3 per cent share of local manufacturing employment in 1974. It was also highly innovative in terms of

Employees of the engineering firm Frederick Parker are told of the company's latest success, 1969

the development of products and markets. The industry was one of the most dynamic sectors in this period, not only through the expansion and development of the major firms but also through the formation of new and small to medium-sized firms producing a range of products for a variety of markets.

The three locally founded firms dating from pre-war times were Gents (alarm and clock devices), Davenset (at one time making electric floats) and Parmeko (various types of switches and solenoids). All three developed new products and markets and were taken over by companies from outside the area (Exide, Westinghouse and Sears respectively).

The wartime firms included BTH, although following mergers its factory in Leicester became the base for Thorn Lighting, engaged as the name suggests in the manufacture of electric lamps. Two vacated wartime sites provided locations for the development of the largest firms in the Leicester industry – AEI at New Parks and English Electric at Whetstone. The latter's arrival marked an important move into electrical power generation (including nuclear power) and the site subsequently became the base for major research and development activity. Once again, however, merger and take-over activity in the 1960s – this time on the part of Lord Weinstock – led to the merger nationally of English Electric and AEI along with GEC and Marconi, among others, to form the GEC group. The subsequent rationalization was to Leicester's advantage with development and expansion at New Parks and Whetstone, including a move away from the earlier electro-mechanical bias into electronics, and with it the development of new markets.

Other Manufacturing Industry

Among the other manufacturing industries contributing to the diversity of Leicester's industrial structure, the food industry should not be overlooked. It had grown nearly 80 per cent by 1967 when it had 5,541 workers, although this still represented a relatively small share of local manufacturing employment. The growth in numbers employed came about mostly from the expansion of locally based firms as they developed national markets. As a consequence of this growth, the local industries became vulnerable to take-over and subsequent rationalization and closure. This is what happened to Frears and Black, for example, with the Frears Biscuit Co. taken over by the multi-national Nabisco company in the 1960s. The local firm of Walkers, the pork butchers, provided another example. Here growth was dependent on the making of potato crisps, which began in a modest way in the late 1950s/early '60s, and then rapidly expanded. The business was divided, with the crisp business subsequently taken over by an American food group, General Foods. The pork butcher side was also absorbed by a larger concern after expanding into a major supplier of the retail multiples. Similarly, the rationalization of the food and sweet industry that began in the 1960s led to another successful local firm, Fox's glacier mints, succumbing to a take-over by the Rowntree Mackintosh group, but retaining its factory in Leicester.

Printing and cardboard box making are other industries which were essentially local firms in origin, dependent on the local requirements of the textile and footwear

The arrival of light industry in Leicester brought firms such as Walkers Crisps to prominence

trades, but which subsequently expanded and diversified into wider national markets. Indeed, Leicester during the post-war period became a significant provincial printing centre.

It also became a centre for the rubber and plastics industries, the former dependent entirely on the firm of Dunlop. This firm moved into the making of polymer engineering products after the formation of Dunlop Metalastik. The plastics industry provided another illustration of a business which developed in part from the changing needs and technologies of the local traditional industries only to find the same technology had wider applications in other industries. From being chiefly the suppliers of components to local industry, existing and new firms diversified into a wider range of product areas and markets such as toys, teaching aids and plastic dispenser units and so on. The firm of English Glass showed the way in this transition by developing from its pre-war concern with making reflective glass beads for use in pedal cycles (as suppliers to Dunlop) to making various ranges of both glass and plastic products. It then specialized in glass and plastic lenses and reflectors, and the making of specialized plastic dispensers for the food and chemical trades. Another firm which turned to the production of plastic containers (blown as opposed to moulded plastics) was the old toy-making firm of Cascelloid (as transformed into BXL). Taken together, employment in the rubber and plastic industries grew nearly threefold to a peak in 1965, when it had 6,678 workers and a share of 5.8 per cent of local manufacturing employment, but this had fallen to 4.2 per cent by 1974.

Service Industries

The overall increase in employment in the post-war service sector in Leicester, as shown earlier, was dependent on major growth (at least in percentage terms) in most sectors. From 1955 to 1974 employment in three sectors grew a little over half as much again – gas, water and electricity (51 per cent) transport and communication (52 per cent), and distributive trades (51 per cent). One sector (miscellaneous services) grew by 85 per cent and three sectors more than doubled. The latter included insurance, banking and finance (183 per cent), professional and scientific services (123 per cent) and public administration (128 per cent). Nevertheless, despite these high percentages, it can be argued that all these sectors were essentially responding to the increase in demand for services arising from normal urban growth plus changes in the range and complexity of services. The growth of employment in service industries did not mean that Leicester was shifting in any marked degree towards a service-based economy in this period. Moreover, with a few exceptions, Leicester did not acquire major service firms and institutions with regional or national markets. Nor did it benefit from the growth of regional government offices in the 1960s. The only organizations to establish major offices were the East Midlands Gas Board, the insurance group, Hogg Robinson, and the Leicester Building Society, which established its headquarters at Oadby.

Detailed trends in employment are readily explicable by changes affecting the city. Thus a short term growth in employment in public administration was a consequence of developments in local authority services in the late 1960s and early '70s. The sustained increase of employment in professional services was the product of a growth in educational services, particularly the expansion in higher education. Employment growth in distribution was largely a product of the way Leicester emerged as a major wholesale distribution centre for the footwear retail industry and increasingly in other sectors, as a consequence of its position in relation to the new motorway network constructed in this period.

The Economy in Recession, 1974–5

As already noticed, the period from 1948 until 1974 was one of negligible unemployment levels, with only some 1 per cent of the labour force being unemployed in the second half of the 1960s and the rate never rising above 3 per cent until January 1975. However, between June 1974 and January 1976 there was a fourfold increase in unemployment. In Leicester, as in the country at large, this marked the beginning of a recession which brought the long post-war boom to an end. But what was worse in the case of Leicester was that from about mid-1974 the relationship between the local and national pattern of employment began to diverge. During the period before 1974 unemployment levels tended to move in sympathy with national levels, the downturns locally tending to be sharper but the recoveries more rapid. In the months after 1974 the growth of unemployment began to diverge from the national pattern, and at the peak of unemployment in mid-1976 was briefly worse than the national rate.

The impact of such a change on the wider public consciousness was cumulative as the realization grew that the economy was not what it had always seemed. Nevertheless, as with previous peaks in unemployment there was still a feeling that bad though this was, things would get back to normal. It was the closure of a number of long-standing firms in traditional industries that really began to make Leicester people realize that things were about to change. Two notable pillars of the local economy closed within weeks of each other in 1975. Stibbe, the textile machinery manufacturer, collapsed soon after moving into a new purpose-built factory at New Parks. This was partly related to the move and a failure to dispose of its factory in Great Central Street (still empty in 1992), but more especially to the decline in the market for textile equipment. Second, there was the decision of Litton Industries to close the Leicester operations of Imperial Typewriters. Later came the closure of the Frog Island factory of Nabisco Frears, another well-known firm, to be followed by the closure of Wildt, Mellor Bromley, the textile machinery manufacturer, a prelude to the dismemberment of the entire Bentley Engineering Group. Despite the workforce occupation of the Wildt, Mellor Bromley factory on Aylestone Road in March 1977 the factory was eventually shut, many workers lost their jobs and the city lost a major hosiery machine manufacturer.

Another factor of immediate concern at the time to officers and some elected members of the City Council was the growing stock of vacant offices in Leicester. It was estimated in 1974 that nearly 5.5 million square feet of vacant office space was available in the city centre, amounting to about 21 per cent of total office space. The expansion of office space had been based on the belief of both planners and developers in the late 1960s and early 1970s that Leicester, along with many other cities, would benefit from the growth of office-based services nationally, but more specifically through migration from high rental London. Office developments were seen as an opportunity to widen the base of the local economy and provide new areas of employment. Despite having one of the lowest levels of office rentals in the UK, the city failed to attract sufficient firms to fill them. For Leicester, the hope that an expansion of office employment might offset any decline in manufacturing employment was never realized and it was not until the mid- to late 1980s that the level of office vacancies was finally reduced. There are still questions remaining about the role of office expansion in job creation and its contribution to broadening the city's economic base.

Moreover, according to the *Leicester Economic Study*, all the features of the onset of recession – unemployment rates, firm closures and empty offices – were in reality symptoms rather than causes of the city's economic problems. The fundamental problem, the study claimed, was the structural weakness of the economy because of the continued role and importance of the traditional industries. Discounting footwear, the two industries of textiles and engineering accounted for over 57 per cent of manufacturing employment and 27 per cent of total employment in 1974. A wider and possibly more realistic interpretation of the figures can be made by including clothing with textiles and adding into the engineering category related metal foundry working, instrument and vehicle engineering. Then the two 'industries' together accounted for 65 per cent of manufacturing employment and almost a third of total employment in that year.

By comparing local and national employment data it can be shown that a relatively small group of manufacturing industries – textiles, mechanical engineering, clothing and, despite its decline, footwear – were over represented in Leicester's economy. Other manufacturing industries including the growth industries, such as electrical engineering, were on a par with the national pattern, but several industries – including food and drink – were under represented in terms of employment, which was also the case for some of the service industries. If we look at product/process groups rather than industries then it can be shown that five such groups had a progressively higher representation in the local economy well into the recession. This is indicative of an increasing concentration of the local economy on a relatively small group of products – a conclusion that is very much at odds with the idea of Leicester as a diversified economy.

Employment and Economic Structure, 1976–89

The period from 1976 to 1981, when the first new type of census of employment became available, covers the most critical years of the recession in the local economy. The unemployment figures show that after the peaks of 1975–6, there was a pattern of short term fluctuations: levels of unemployment oscillated around 12,000 or in percentage terms between 4.6 per cent and 6.6 per cent of the workforce, marginally below national levels but nevertheless devastating for a community used to extremely low levels over a number of decades. Unemployment levels climbed to 14,000 in 1981, only to rise further and higher to a post-war peak in March 1985, when there were over 18,000 adults in Leicester claiming benefit. The next four years saw a steady fall in this number, but from November 1989 unemployment levels started to rise again, indicative of both national and local recession.

Underlying these basic figures were significant and arguably disturbing trends in the pattern and nature of unemployment, notably the longer duration of unemployment and the incidence of unemployment within and between particular groups, such as young and older people, and in particular ethnic groups.

Table One: Percentage Changes in Employment 1981–9

	Leicester per cent	G.B per cent
Manufacturing	-14.3	-14.3
Construction	-21.5	-0.7
Services	+21.3	+17.9
Total	+ 3.1	+ 5.5

One of the most important changes has been the continuing shift in the balance of employment between the main sectors in the economy. Thus the percentage decline in manufacturing employment in Leicester – matching the national figure – and amounting to a loss of nearly 14,000 jobs, has been offset by a larger than national increase in employment in the service sector, amounting to over 24,000 jobs. The overall balance shows a relatively static picture, with a small percentage growth amounting to just over 7,000 jobs, somewhat below the national figure. As in the previous decade the service sector gained a greater share in local employment, while the share of manufacturing declined. In 1989 only 35.4 per cent of the city's employed population was engaged in manufacturing compared with 59.3 per cent in the service sector. But the shift towards a more service-based economy should not be exaggerated. In Great Britain as a whole the share of manufacturing employment in 1989 (at 23.1 per cent) was less than in Leicester and the share of employment in the service sector (at 68.7 per cent) correspondingly more. In fact, there was very little change in the degree of concentration of service employment in Leicester over the 1980s.

Looking more closely at the fortunes of Leicester manufacturing industry through the employment figures, the first thing to be said is that there has only been a slight decline in the relative share of local manufacturing employment on the part of the two traditional industries of mechanical and general engineering and knitted textiles during the 1980s, although both sectors have suffered a considerable decline in absolute numbers of workers. Percentage changes in employment for these and

Hosiery workers protest against the effects of foreign competition during the TUC's day of action in 1980

other main industrial groups are set out in Table Two below for the period 1981–9.

In the case of textiles and clothing much of the decline was concentrated in the later part of the decade. Up to 1987 the textile industry seems to have held its own in employment terms, with the level in that year not much different to 1976. But over 6,000 workers were lost between 1987 and 1989, about a quarter of the workforce. The only section to remain really buoyant in an otherwise difficult period was the making up section (the employment figures for which come under the broad product category of leather, footwear and clothing) and there is also evidence of considerable growth of firms engaged in the wider field of clothing manufacture. But for the core textile industry – still an important employer – continuing pressures are already leading or are potentially likely to lead to even more drastic changes than have occurred so far.

Most of the pressures already noticed intensified in the later 1980s. The particular demands and changing fortunes of the large retailers continued to affect local suppliers. The rise and subsequent eclipse of Next, whose headquarters are at Enderby, is an illustration, albeit a rather flamboyant one, of the problems that this brought. The level of imported textiles was still a serious problem in the early 1990s, when there was much local concern about the impending run-down of the Multi Fibre Agreement, which gave some degree of protection. Nevertheless older firms remained in production, notably the firm of Corah, albeit diminished in size and importance and controlled by an Australian investment company. Furthermore the basic structure and character of the textile industry in Leicester had remained intact, although there is considerable contemporary argument over whether this structure is best suited to future need and change.

Table Two: Employment in Manufacturing Industry 1981–9

	Employment per cent	Share of total per cent
Textiles	-23	24
Leather, footwear and clothing	+24	18
Mechanical /General Engineering	-15	23
Vehicle and Aero Engineering	-47	-
Instrument Engineering	+12	-
Machine Tool	-25	3.6
Textile Machinery	-30	1.1
General/Precision Engineering	-	6.0
Electrical Engineering	-45	6.8
Rubber and Plastics	-29	4.0
Food and Drink	- 8	6.5
Printing and Packaging	+12	6.9

Taking into account all the different branches, engineering still had a share of 60 per cent of local manufacturing employment in 1989. But the fortunes of different branches have been very diverse over the 1980s. Thus employment in vehicle and aero engineering fell drastically but instrument engineering enjoyed modest growth. Both machine tool and textile machinery, previously major product sectors within the engineering industry, suffered marked decline. However, the machine tool industry managed to survive to retain a significant presence in Leicester, and employment was still only about 13 per cent below that of 1976 before the onset of the deep recession of 1978–81. By the early 1990s most of the major firms as well as smaller specialist firms were still in production, although they were probably smaller and had been variously subjected to rationalization and reorganization. By contrast the textile machinery industry had become a mere shadow of its former position, with employment by 1989 below 1,000 workers – a far cry from its post-war peak of over 6,000 workers in 1967. But general and precision engineering – still a significant sector – showed considerable resilience, with no change in employment and a marginal increase in share of employment.

The performance of the remaining Leicester industries over the 1980s had also varied considerably. The electrical engineering industry, for example, which enjoyed growth throughout the 1960s and early '70s suffered considerable losses in employment since then. By 1989 employment was less than half the peak level of 1974, while share of manufacturing employment fell from 10.6 per cent in 1981 to 6.8 per cent in 1989. The rubber and plastics industry has also seen a contraction in employment. One contributory factor was the structural and corporate changes within Dunlop Metalastik arising from merger and take-over activity within the Dunlop Group. Other firms, especially in the plastics sector and engaged in subcontract work, were affected by the fortunes of customer firms.

By contrast the food and drink industry had become a significant industry in Leicester by 1989. The closure of a major bakery, and previously the closure of Nabisco-Frear's main factory, was offset by the expansion of both Walker and Son, the pork butchers, and Walker's Crisps, and more recently that of another meat and food product firm, R.F. Brookes, a major supplier to Marks and Spencer and other large retailers. But the only manufacturing industry besides instrument engineering to register growth during the period was that of printing and packaging.

Finally, there are the service industries for which the available data is set out in Table Three to show that the largest of these industries enjoyed considerable growth over the period from 1981 to 1989, and at the latter date provided an important share of total employment in the city.

Table Three: Employment in the Service Industries 1981–9

	Employment change per cent	Share of total employment 1989 per cent
Wholesale distribution	35.7	5.5
Retail distribution	5.5	9.3
Insurance banking etc.	48.0	8.6
Public administration	9.4	14.7
Medical services	29.8	6.2

Expansion of employment in wholesale distribution was facilitated by the development of industrial estates with good road communications. Leicester, along with other parts of the county, became a substantial centre for distribution within the region and the UK. Such a development has been welcomed as helping to compensate for job losses in basic manufacturing, although it should be noted that modern distribution tends to be land rather than labour hungry. Growth in retailing is in keeping with national trends and particularly reflects the establishment of large retail outlets as well as changes in retail operations with longer opening hours. As with wholesale distribution the real employment effects are modest, given the high degree of part-time and casual working. Despite the remarkable growth of employment in the banking, insurance and related sectors, there is no real evidence of Leicester having become a financial centre.

The considerable growth in medical services over the period might be partly a consequence of hospital building during the 1980s to overcome considerable deficiencies in such provision in the Leicester area. The more modest growth in public administration, only amounting to about three thousand jobs, might seem to be at odds with Central Government policies and actions to curtail the role of local government.

The Size of Firms

So far, this review of Leicester's economic and industrial structure has been confined to structural change as manifest mainly in employment patterns. But there are other aspects of the economy which have contributed to the particular character of the city in recent years, and these need to be touched on even if briefly. One of these aspects is the role of small firms – frequently seen as an important feature of the city contributing both flexibility and flair to its economic life. But how far was Leicester in the later twentieth century still a city of small firms?

An industrial survey prepared by the Leicester City Planning Department in 1964 was inclined to think it was. This gave details of firm size by manufacturing establishment within the then Leicester County Borough. Just over 85 per cent of establishments had under 100 workers (and 40 per cent employed fewer than nine) as against under 1 per cent employing over 1,000 workers. However, the total share of employment of the smallest establishments (2.6 per cent) was very small. A more extensive survey undertaken for the *Leicester Economic Study Report* in 1974 relating to manufacturing industry showed that in the Leicester Employment Exchange Area over 80 per cent of manufacturing firms employed under sixty workers, 69 per cent under thirty workers, and 54 per cent under fifteen workers. At the other end of the scale only fifteen firms employed over 1,000 but there were marked disparities within these. The conclusion of this report, however, was that the popular view of the role of the small firm in Leicester should be modified. It seems that the proportion of small firms is no greater in Leicester than nationally or regionally. The more important feature of the Leicester economy, this report argued, was the relative insignificance of larger firms rather than the relative significance of small ones.

More recent but limited data for Leicester City from the 1987 Census of Employment shows that 75.5 per cent of firms employed under twenty-five workers and accounted for 18.7 per cent of workers. By contrast, firms employing over 1,000 workers accounted for only 0.1 per cent of firms but employed 19.7 per cent of workers. Although these figures are not strictly comparable with the earlier surveys there is evidence to suggest a growth in the small firm sector during recession. One way this happened was when redundant or disillusioned managers and others decided to set up in business on their own rather than becoming unemployed, although there was inevitably a high death rate amongst such firms. At the same time there is evidence to suggest that the most significant feature of the

Leicester economy during the 1980s was the decline of the larger firms either through closure, reduced size or break-up through rationalization. Thus while the conclusion of the *Leicester Economic Study Report* noted above still applies, there has possibly been a proportional increase in the number of small firms and a decline in larger firms over the 1980s.

There also seems to have been a revival in the importance of family networks in establishing new enterprises, especially among the new Asian business community. But there were relatively few of the old indigenous family firms left in the city by the end of the 1980s, and among the white business population the old concept of family dynasties in business seems to have almost disappeared. According to research being carried out at the University of Leicester on wealth accumulation, the heads of small firms do not generally expect their children to come into the business. Nor do they expect to accumulate large fortunes. Most of the small entrepreneurs had acquired relatively modest levels of wealth, and with one or two exceptions the small number of people in the city and county with considerable fortunes had accumulated that wealth elsewhere.

Concentration of Ownership

It has frequently been claimed, as already noted, that one of the keys to Leicester's economic success was the continuing division of ownership characteristic of the city's business structure. The city was never dominated by a few giant companies, as in the case of some of the older industrial cities of the north. However, in an earlier section we gave examples of the way that larger concentrations of capital became involved in the local economy during the expansive period of post-war growth and especially in the 1960s. It is worth attempting to make some assessment therefore of the extent and influence of the large corporate groups with a stake in the Leicester economy.

The influence of concentrations of corporate capital was manifested in the economy through acquisition, merger and the establishment of subsidiaries. This concentration of ownership enabled a large firm to control different stages in the production process or to acquire competitors working in the same stage of production. In addition the large firm was able to exert a powerful influence on the local economy in more indirect ways through its management policies for instance, such as its purchasing or other market processes, and as a major employer it could influence labour supply and wage levels in the city more generally. The ability of a large corporate owner to exert dominance was clearly more apparent in smaller one-industry sectors, but undoubtedly the largest firms in Leicester have influenced the structure and performance of the local economy, despite its diversity and scale.

There is evidence on the role of the large corporate groups in Leicester in the *Leicester Economic Study*, using data for 1974. The report sought to identify for manufacturing industry which firms were part of these groups, and which firms were themselves the parent companies of groups. Within manufacturing industry as a whole the fifteen largest groups together accounted for over 32 per cent of employment. The two largest groups employed nearly 11 per cent of manufacturing employment and both had service industry interests in Leicester. In one notable case the subsidiary firm was at the time the largest employer in the private service sector in Leicester. The fifteen groups together owned forty-seven individual firms in Leicester. Only five of the groups were Leicester based and with one exception these tended to be among the smaller of the groups. Three further groups were American owned, the rest primarily British based. In terms of industrial products, five groups were primarily engaged in the textile/clothing industries (in one case this also included textile machinery and packaging), five were basically in mechanical engineering and four others respectively in electro-mechanical engineering, electrical/electronics, rubber/plastics and food. Although the degree of concentration of ownership within the textile/clothing industry was not as high as in engineering, the largest fifteen groups within this industry still employed 40 per cent of textile/clothing workers.

In more recent years, however, there have been indications of profound changes in the role of such groups within Leicester's economy. The available evidence suggests that the impact of recession has led to a decline in the scale of operation of the large groups, particularly in those industries especially vulnerable to the vicissitudes of economic change. In some cases, as we have seen, there were major closures of constituent firms, in other cases the pruning out of smaller subsidiaries, while a major rationalization of operations was frequently followed by the decision to get out of the less profitable manufacturing sectors while retaining interests in the more profitable fields, almost invariably in the service sector. Thus many of the older established firms which had major interests in Leicester have either disappeared or are mere shadows of their former selves. In some cases the larger groups have themselves been subject to take-over and merger, with consequential rationalization of operations.

Reference has already been made to major changes within one of the largest groups, Sears Holdings, most of whose manufacturing operations had either disappeared or had a very minor presence by the early 1990s, while its largest remaining interest, the British Shoe Corporation (now Sears) has suffered from cuts in the wake of the recession on the High Street. The GEC/AEI group, while still an important force within the city itself, has nevertheless rationalized its operation at Whetstone, including the development of part of its site into small industrial units. Reference has previously been made to other well-known firms such as Corah, now under Australian control, and the British United Shoe Machinery Corporation, part of its factory turned into a retail complex and no longer part of AUSM. The impact of the decline of such firms has not only been in terms of employment but through the loss of subcontract and other work for many local businesses.

While it has been the absolute decline and loss of employment in particular key product sectors which has been the most important factor impinging on Leicester's economy in the 1980s and early 1990s, changes in ownership and related firm size have possibly affected the economic and social character of the city in more subtle ways.

Female Employment

An account of Leicester's employment structure must include some discussion of the role of female employment, if only because much of Leicester's prosperity has been historically attributed to employment opportunities for women workers and their apparently 'high' earnings as well as to the adaptability and dexterity of a female pool of labour experienced in factory work, which was attractive to firms considering establishing in the area.

An extensive analysis of the 1973 figures in the *Leicester Economic Study* revealed that females constituted 41 per cent of total employment. As the national figure for the same year was 39.2 per cent this means that there was a greater proportion of female workers in Leicester, but not of the order previously assumed. Nationally there has been a marginal shift in female employment since the early 1960s, but in Leicester the proportion had remained fairly constant (40.1 per cent in 1965). Data from the 1987 Census of Employment for Leicester City shows that female employment constituted just over 48 per cent of total employment. Within the manufacturing and services sectors it was 38.2 per cent and 55.4 per cent respectively.

Generally the role of female employment has been considered to be more significant within the context of manufacturing rather than in the service sector where high female levels are regarded as the norm. Of particular importance are the levels of female employment at industry level. Certain predominantly female employing industries stand out, notably textiles and clothing (including footwear). However, in sub-sectors of a number of other industries there remain a

Women at work in the hosiery trade, early 1960s

predominance of female workers – cardboard box manufacture and electrical engineering for example.

However, to properly assess the importance of women workers in Leicester, it is necessary to measure the number of people available for employment in terms of activity rates. For Leicester female activity rates have tended to be markedly in excess of most Standard Regions. Further, the activity rates for married women have been greater than those for all females, giving credence to the reputedly strong tradition of 'working wives' in the city. It was the contribution of married female workers to household income that was the significant factor in the purported prosperity of Leicester. This income contribution seems to have become an even more vital factor during the bottom of the recession in 1979–81 when lay-offs and redundancies hit male employing firms, particularly in engineering and construction, and there were reports available indicating that in many households the wife became the main bread winner.

Ethnic Groups

The most outstanding post-war change in the social and demographic structure and character of Leicester has been the influx into the area and in particular into the city itself of large groups of people from the Commonwealth, mainly Asian groups – initially from the Indian sub-continent but subsequently from East Africa. This 'great migration' as it became known had been preceded by a smaller influx of Afro-Caribbean groups. Leicester became essentially a multi-racial city with more than a quarter of its population of largely Asian extraction. Different ethnic groups have well-established roots in the area, given that a number are now third generation immigrants. They have had a significant impact upon the local economy.

In terms of employment, the initial influx of people mainly from the West Indies and the Indian sub-continent was prompted by the shortages of labour in many industries and services (transport, hospitals, etc.) during the boom period of the late 1950s and through most of the early '60s. The entry of the Ugandan Asians in 1968 was prompted primarily by political events but they were attracted to Leicester for mainly economic reasons.

A survey by MORI in 1990 for Leicester City Council showed that the Asian workforce was concentrated in manual and less skilled occupations with only small participation in the managerial and professional occupations. This lack of representation in higher level occupations may account for the popularity among ethnic groups of entrepreneurial activity, although Ugandan Asians brought to the city a considerable background of experience in business and commerce. Thus from the early 1970s members of ethnic groups, most notably the Asian groups, began to make an important contribution to the Leicester economy as entrepreneurs, helping to create a distinct ethnic business sector.

There has been little substantial empirical research into this development, but it is quite evident that in keeping with tradition and origins, the initial and still major concentration of ethnic business has been within general retailing and wholesale distribution (particularly clothing and textiles but also food). This kind of economic activity came to be strongly concentrated in the main Asian areas of the city where it was geared to meeting the particular needs of such markets, which in retailing has involved a diversification from food retailing into wider product sectors such as jewellery, travel services and so on. However, there has also been the entry of Asian retailing into markets largely serving the white as well as the Asian population, particularly in lower order goods such as general food stores and newsagencies. At the same time the growth of the ethnic minority population has given rise to opportunities for the establishment of a wider range of services, including car repair and wholesaling, but also more professionally based services such as estate agencies, property investment and development, financial and legal services. Some of the established Asian entrepreneurs are allegedly among the wealthiest in the city.

By the 1980s the extent and scope of these ethnic business sectors were clearly identifiable within the local economic environment. Less obvious but nevertheless significant has been the emergence of ethnic businesses within the manufacturing sector. This was concentrated particularly in the clothing and textile trades but with ethnic representation also in general engineering and more recently in food processing. As with the service sector many such firms started by supplying the ethnic market, but have subsequently expanded into the wider market. Many of the new manufacturing and distribution concerns were located within the main ethnic residential areas such as Evington Valley Road/St Saviours Road and Belgrave Road/Melton Road. These areas provided an ethnic labour supply, especially female, and also had a substantial stock of industrial premises vacated as a consequence of recession and the decline of older traditional firms. Such developments have led to the emergence of a small but very dynamic business and professional entrepreneurial class within the Asian community.

Suburbanization and Decentralization of Industry

Industrial and economic change in Leicester has in turn influenced and moulded the spatial pattern of industry and, more recently, office based services. Fundamentally this has involved two related developments: first, decentralization – that is, the absolute decline and/or movement of firms from the central and inner areas of the urban area; and, secondly, the process of suburbanization – which refers to the growth of industry in the urban/rural fringe through inward migration of firms from outside the area, the outward movement of firms from the inner city and the establishment of new firms seeking green field sites. All these processes have been a familiar aspect of modern urban and industrial change.

In Leicester, the economic crisis of 1974–6 prompted concern about the level of decentralization of industry, primarily at this time as a consequence of decline and closure rather than relocation, and the consequences this had for unemployment levels in the inner city. Subsequently the inner areas tended to suffer from net losses in employment as a consequence of inward and outward relocation of firms. When vacant industrial premises in the inner area were eventually reoccupied, as they generally were, the density of employment was almost invariably lower in employment terms. On the other hand, the outer areas continued to be attractive to relocated established firms as well as new firms, indigenous firms as well as new entrants.

The processes of decentralization and suburbanization have continued through the 1980s. Within the city the last remaining major area for industrial development was Hamilton New Town to the north-east. The main development immediately outside the city was the Meridian Business Park next to Junction 21 on the M1/M69, but also in the same sector out of the city in villages such as Blaby, Whetstone and Enderby. There have been similar if more modest developments in other mainly industrial villages such as Syston and Barrow as well as the smaller county towns such as Hinckley which has attracted considerable investment because of its location with regard to the road network. Perhaps the best known of the local large-scale developments has been Magna Park near Lutterworth, which attracted firms such as Volvo and Asda.

Despite these developments, and the impact of recession on the older city based industries, the inner area has still managed to retain some industrial activity and has not suffered from the scale of decline seen in many other older industrial cities. At the same time there is undoubtedly a two-way pull both with regard to industrial development and also office premises.

Since the late 1980s there has been a trend toward the suburbanization of office based business – a somewhat novel development for cities such as Leicester, which has important implications for the future of the city centre given its traditional and paramount role as the centre for office based business services. The problem of the vacant office stock in Leicester was largely resolved by about 1988 with only unlettable offices remaining. Since 1989 there have been suggestions within the property sector of a growth in the demand for office space in Leicester and calls for a relaxation of restrictions on new office development on the part of planning authorities. This argument has been accepted and in consequence a development of new office building has taken place, as well as the conversion and refurbishment of existing offices. While most of this has been in the city centre, such as the developments in St Margaret's and in Conduit Street (near the railway station), a substantial amount of office development is being undertaken in the Meridian Business Park. In addition there have been other developments elsewhere in the urban/rural fringe, including the construction of a new headquarters by the Alliance and Leicester Building Society on the former Carlton Hayes hospital site at Enderby. However, there is no evidence to suggest a general trend towards the decentralization of existing office based businesses, since most of the new developments have involved firms relatively new to the area.

Intervention in the Local Economy

In the mid-1970s initial recognition that all was not well in the local economy was confined mainly to a small group of officers and elected representatives within the

City Council, along with local academics engaged in economic and industrial research. Following the *Leicester Economic Study* – undertaken for the City Council – there was a growing recognition that the local economy was undergoing considerable structural change, and a determined attempt was made to develop a range of new economic initiatives and policies. This marked a major change in the way that local authorities viewed their role in regard to the local economy, which was also politically significant given the attitude of central government from 1979 onwards. Before the mid-1970s the only real interface between local authorities and the industrial and economic structure was through the allocation of land for industrial and commercial use and general planning controls. After this period the local authority adopted a much more interventionist stance.

The first of the new economic initiatives in Leicester were mainly reactive to the particular economic events of the mid-1970s – the initiation of research into the economy, as already described, and the formation within the Estates Department of the Leicester Promotion Campaign, which was very much prompted by concern over the levels of vacant office stock. Internally there was eventually the establishment of an economic development unit under the Chief Executive, with major responsibility for economic initiatives and to co-ordinate all those activities and powers of the council that might impinge upon local economic performance. There were parallel developments at county council level.

Central to this more vigorous approach on the part of the council was the availability of funding through the Inner Area Programme. While the money that could be raised by the local authority was severely limited by legal constraints on their financial powers, there was enough funding available to finance a range of new projects aimed especially at specific groups as, for example, ethnic minorities. In some cases new projects were funded through inner area initiatives of the county; others – particularly improvements in the socio-economic and physical environment – through the designation of Industrial Improvement Areas and also through separate policy initiatives with regard to housing. Obviously most of the effort went into inner area projects, but these had a ripple effect on the wider city.

Other initiatives have included the establishment of a range of advisory services: the Business Advice Centre, advisory services for ethnic business, co-operative development agency, and support and help for a range of voluntary organizations. Within the city council's own organization there has been intensive scrutiny of its operations in terms of the help or otherwise given to particular economic activities, as, for example, practices within the Estates and Planning Departments and the council's own employment and training policies, including a long standing initiative to develop school–industry links. There has also been both internal as well as external research into specific issues.

During the heyday of these policy initiatives a number of more radical ideas were proposed, but these have tended to wither from lack of funding and more especially because of central government pressure through cuts and curbs in public spending (including capping). Towards the later 1980s certain programmes were cut back and central government shifted the emphasis to its own schemes, for example the introduction of Task Force and more recently the City Challenge projects.

Economic initiatives on the part of both the city and county have tended therefore to revert to those activities which were traditional and within the normal workings of the local authorities, and thus acceptable to central government. These included the allocation of industrial and commercial land, planning permission, advisory and promotion services – all essentially of an enabling rather than pro-active nature.

How far such initiatives will help to overcome Leicester's economic problems in the twenty-first century is still unknown, given the arguments that have been advanced in this survey about the fundamental nature of the challenges to the economic future of the city. All the evidence that is available suggests that notwithstanding the many changes that have taken place in recent decades, Leicester's economic and industrial structure is still based on manufacturing and characterized by dependence on a relatively small range of manufacturing industries, a number of which have been highly vulnerable to external economic processes of change and still remain so. Although the growth in the number of service industries is a major development, this has largely involved, it would seem, a degree of catching up and a response to the changing demands and needs for services, particularly in a large and growing urban area, rather than the establishment of Leicester as a major commercial centre.

Further Reading

The main sources for the inter-war period are the Trade Directories, the *Daily Mail Trade Reviews* and publications of the Leicester Chamber of Commerce. The references to inter-war probates comes from research undertaken by Dr David Reeder at the Centre for Urban History, University of Leicester.

For the post-Second World War period the basic source is employment data – the employment series arising from the implementation of National Insurance from 1944 and the new type census of employment from 1981. The chapter provides a summary of a more detailed analysis carried out by Dr Clive Harrison and available from him at the Leicester Business School, De Montfort University. The fullest source of information on the Leicester economy is the *Leicester Economic Study* referred to in the text and consisting of the Stage 1 Report (1976), the Stage 2 Report (1977) and six more detailed reports plus a summary report (all 1982). Other surveys include the privately commissioned survey by the Financial Analysis Group: *A Business Survey of Leicester and its Companies* (1972) and the *Leicester Economic Trends Survey* prepared by Leicester University Department of Economics, Vol. 1 Nos 1–3 (1986–8). This statistical data can be supplemented with information about local companies from numerous published local business histories. The *Leicester Mercury* frequently provided brief portraits of leading city firms and businessmen. Information about attitudes towards and strategies of wealthholding in contemporary Leicester is currently being gathered by Dr Kate Mulholland of the Department of Sociology, Leicester University.

Chapter Three

POLITICS

Leicester's political life in the twentieth century can be understood at two levels: local politics, in the sense of the politics of the council and the relationship of active politicians to the changing currents in the life of the city; and national politics, in the sense of the place of the city in the nation. This chapter will outline developments at these two levels.

Local politics in Leicester in this century has been characterized by a general decline in the participation of the social leaders of the city in the affairs of the council. Prominent social leaders – leading manufacturers in particular – have steadily ceased to seek public office or pursue a political life. Instead they seem to have opted for alternatives, particularly philanthropy. In place of these social leaders, new men and women dependent on party have taken their place, and many of the decisions and policies that have shaped the life of the city have been taken as a consequence of the interaction between those party men and women with the officers of the corporation. Thus party and technocracy has replaced social-political leadership.

National politics, too, has been reshaped. At the beginning of the century Leicester was a Liberal city. Nonconformist manufacturers had worked the machine of the Victorian two-member borough system to maintain an almost unbroken Liberal hegemony throughout the nineteenth century. Admittedly, by the beginning of the twentieth century this dominance was being moderated by the rise of organized Labour. But Britain was still not a democracy when war broke out in 1914, and so the political life of the city perceived in national terms and observed through parliamentary elections often concealed class divisions. However, after the First World War a more democratic arrangement was established between 1918 and 1928. This development restructured the politics of the nation and was witnessed by a reshaping of the politics of the progressive left, especially in manufacturing centres like Leicester. Its other effect was to permit a period of Conservative dominance at national level from 1918 until 1945. During those years the Conservatives had some presence in every government except two – the Labour minority government of 1924 and the second Labour government of 1929 to 1931. Thus in a twenty-seven year period the Conservatives dominated in twenty-four of those years.

In Leicester, where Liberalism and a Lib-Lab pact had held sway before 1914, the inter-war years were a period of flux. The constituency of Leicester South in fact became solidly Conservative throughout the period 1918 to 1945. The remaining two seats, Leicester West and Leicester East, showed frequent changes but one feature became clear – the traditional Liberals only won a straight victory in Leicester West on one occasion, in 1931. Admittedly, a National Liberal, supported by the national coalition coupon, was returned to Leicester East in 1918. But for the remainder of the period Labour fought to assert itself in the east and west of the city. It was successful, only really losing out in 1924 and 1931; but in effect Leicester became a Labour city in the politics of the nation. Labour fought against various forms of anti-socialist fronts – tacit electoral agreements between the Liberals and the Conservatives as well as open campaigns.

Similar developments occurred in local municipal politics. Political realignment was the common experience of many manufacturing centres – Wolverhampton, Coventry, Nottingham, Sheffield, Crewe, Bristol, St Helens and Salford. In this sense, then, the experience of Leicester was mirrored elsewhere. Liberalism markedly weakened, losing seats in national parliamentary elections and often being unable to find candidates or funds to contest municipal elections. In seventy of the largest municipal boroughs in England, of which Leicester was one, Liberal candidates declined from 19 per cent of the total number of candidates contesting seats in 1921 to 15 per cent of the total in 1925. The increase in Labour's ability to contest seats was more or less increasing in inverse proportion to that Liberal decline. At the same time, the politics of the Right was also being reshaped and confused by an increase in the number of independents, and again Leicester was not left untouched by this phenomenon. But Leicester did not see the formation of a solid Independent grouping on the council as was the case in Sheffield, for example. Nor was the decline of Liberalism in Leicester's municipal politics as dramatic as it was in Birmingham or Manchester where the Liberals completely gave up contesting some working-class wards. There is no doubt, though, that Leicester Liberalism, from having been so dominant, was assiduously undermined in the inter-war years.

After the Second World War Leicester has been predominantly a Labour city in the politics of the nation. In municipal politics the city council had, for the first time, a Labour majority in 1945. This was lost within three years and the post-war pattern of swings between Labour and Conservatives was set in place. The dynamics of local politics were transformed in the 1960s and the 1970s due to two main structural features – the decline of many traditional industries and overseas immigration. These two developments transformed the politics of the Left. Factories like Stibbe's and Imperial Typewriters closed, and when the Wildt, Mellor Bromley factory closed in 1977 it was occupied by its workforce for fifteen days. Immigration, particularly Asian immigration in the 1970s, also redefined the Labour Party, overturning the leadership that had dominated since the 1950s. By the last decade of the century it would be impossible to explain the politics of the city without reference to the impact of race. Leicester East was to be represented by an MP of Asian origin and the deputy leader of the city's Labour Party was also Asian.

Labour was the dominant party in the council after local government reorganization in 1974, and in 1983 it won forty out of fifty-six seats. Nine of those forty Labour councillors were Asian.

These broad contours show how the shape of Leicester's politics, municipally and nationally, had changed over the century. Obviously more detailed examination will reveal many complex issues, but perhaps above all an appreciation of the political transformation of the town rests on an understanding of its changing social and economic structure. At the beginning of the century the political demarcation lines were drawn by class and religion. By the end of the century they were drawn by class and race. Labour had become the focal point of political loyalty for the most socially cohesive group in the city – the Ugandan Asian population. Thus equal opportunity had come to define so much of Labour's politics. Of course there were many other factors at work, and a closer examination of both municipal politics and parliamentary elections will reveal the rich patterns of the city's political life.

Municipal Politics up to 1945

The modern municipal politics of Leicester really begin in 1891. It was in that year that the town boundary was extended to include what were then seen as outlying places – Belgrave, Aylestone, Knighton, North Evington and Newfoundpool. The extension was in effect the political and administrative recognition of the town's growth in the nineteenth century. From the revolution in local government in 1835 Leicester had been a Liberal town. Hosiery manufacturers and merchants, later boot and shoe men, dominated the council. In 1881 about 60 per cent of the town council was made up of businessmen, but by 1901 businessmen only made up half of the council; and by 1931 they made up a third. This presence held fairly solid until just after the Second World War, when business interest on the council rose to almost a half but thereafter fell away again to about a fifth in the mid-1960s.

These broad contours raise some basic questions. Who were the men and women who have sought public office during the twentieth century? What were their social origins? What motivated them to seek office? What were their political affiliations? What issues divided them? In the middle years of the nineteenth century there had been a considerable overlap between the social élite and the political élite. Leading citizens had sought public office as a legitimate way of expressing their social status within the public domain. Between 1871 and 1891 about a third of the town's aldermen had left more than £50,000 in their wills and some left considerably more than that. For example, Sir Israel Hart left £193,000 in his will in 1911; Arthur Wakerley left £128,000 in 1931; and Edward Wood left £172,000 in 1917. For the upper sections of the business classes public office was a duty and those who took up a public life were held in high regard. Thus the *Wyvern* newspaper praised Hart for putting himself forward for the mayoralty on no fewer than four occasions. There was apparently a kind of consensus at the beginning of the century – success in business deserved to be rewarded with public office. Thus Sir Edward Wood

Thomas Rowland Hill was President of the Leicester ILP 1917–18, and a prominent member of the City Council after the First World War

when interviewed by the *Leicester Guardian* in 1904 claimed that 'the present basis of business is a personal one. . . . Today the populace gives honour to him whom they regard as a successful wealth getter.' Both Hart and Wood, two old style 'city fathers', were men who contributed to charity and participated in the political life of the town, shaping its municipal policy and provision. They were motivated by a desire to donate their business expertise to the public domain. Importing private entrepreneurial skills into the public sphere was regarded as a positive advantage. However, when Arthur Wakerley, a prominent builder, was challenged in the 1897 municipal elections about whether his knowledge of council business had enabled him to make personal profit, he denied the claim, saying it was a 'black and cruel falsehood'. Thus there was a fine balance to be struck: it was acceptable to contribute private expertise to public affairs, but public position could not lead to private advantage.

If at the beginning of the century the notion of public service was an ideal of the town's leading businessmen it was probably already beginning to have less attraction. The wealthiest businessmen were already less evident on the council even before the First World War. After the war wealthy businessmen only made up about a tenth of the council's membership; and by 1931 their representation had fallen to about 5 per cent. Admittedly some of the wealthiest businessmen continued to be prominent as aldermen throughout the 1920s, and Jonathan North held the mayoralty throughout the First World War, continuing to be a member of the council until 1935. These developments should not lead us to the conclusion that

William Billings was an engineer businessman who was Lord Mayor from 1934 to 1935 and another example of the 'city father' politician

Leicester's businessmen withdrew into county society. Some leading families did move into the county – the Corah and Faire families are two notable examples. There does not seem to have been any significant intermarriage between Leicester business families and the county gentry. Nor do Leicester's businessmen seem to have sought a political life on the county council until the 1930s. Instead, they seem to have sought other ways of maintaining their élite status. Philanthropic work was the most favoured activity. Thus Samuel Faire, having been prominent in the Liberal split in 1886, becoming president of the Liberal Unionist Association and therefore following the Chamberlainite wing of the party, seems to have spent his latter years in charitable work. He was president of the Private Fire Brigades Mission and president of the Leicester Ragged School Mission as well as a trustee of the Leicester Royal Infirmary. His brother John was chairman of the Provident Dispensary and chairman of the Leicester Temperance Society. Sir Edward Wood, who had been mayor in 1888, chose to give support to hospitals and Baptist churches and provide university scholarships for students at the Wyggeston schools.

There had in fact been a kind of consensus between the classes in the nineteenth century and elements of that consensus persisted into the twentieth century. This is perhaps revealed by the agreement struck in parliamentary politics between the Liberals and the emergent Labour Party. In 1903 James Ramsay Macdonald of the Labour Representation Committee and Herbert Gladstone, Liberal Chief Whip,

The Unemployed March to London in June 1905 was the climax of a campaign that had begun the previous year. Unemployment remained a crucial issue in the November municipal elections, with Labour campaigning on the 'right to work'

concluded their now famous electoral pact. It was of great importance nationally and of particular significance for Leicester. The pact secured MacDonald's return as one of two MPs for Leicester in 1906. In 1910 MacDonald wrote: 'I am sensible of the very great efforts made by the leaders of the Liberal Party in Leicester to secure a united vote for me.' MacDonald had represented class co-operation *par excellence*. But that co-operation was probably very fragile and it was certainly broken up by the war. MacDonald's stance on the war was unacceptable to the patriotic sections of the Labour Party and unintelligible to the electorate, and he lost his seat in the 1918 Coupon Election. In municipal politics it is the same story. Before the war there was a certain stability and between 1909 and 1915 slightly less than one fifth of the members of the council were new members or had been elected within those years. Indeed in 1911 only 19.6 per cent of the wards were contested in the local elections. Between 1918 and 1926 over 60 per cent of the seats were contested. The politics of the war had had a polarizing effect and Jonathan North was drawn to say that it was necessary to 'counteract the poisonous doctrines put forward by the pacifists'. This was a direct attack on MacDonald. The Labour Party was to begin making great incursions into local politics in these years. It was partly a consequence of the extension of the franchise in 1918 but there was also a realignment between the Conservatives and the Liberals. In the 1920 municipal election Labour faced six straight fights with Liberals and five with Conservatives as the two traditional parties tactically withdrew candidates to avoid split votes. The agreement was still operating in 1925 and Labour specifically began to address the problem, arguing that the manoeuvre was bound to fail as it was dishonest. Labour was now able to proclaim itself the party of 'straight dealing'. According to the pro-Labour newspaper, the *Leicester Pioneer*, there was a 'Grand Holy Alliance' to thwart Labour. What was happening was probably a re-alignment of the lower middle class around the Conservatives. As the larger businessmen withdrew from the political arena of city politics so the Liberal party weakened. MacDonald had already reflected in 1918, saying: 'There was a time when Leicester Liberalism was a strong robust faith expounded by strong men of independent minds and massive ideas. . . . I could not dissociate these giants from Leicester Liberalism. Their spirit brooded over the town.' By the late 1920s the giants had all but gone. Only George Hilton, the son of Stephen Hilton and chairman of Hilton shoes; Jonathan North, the chairman of Stead and Simpson; and John Mantle Hubbard, a hosiery manufacturer, remained as old style businessmen on the aldermanic bench.

The middle-class allegiance to Liberalism that had been so strong in Leicester, bound together by nonconformity, philanthropy, temperance and moderate programmes of municipal improvement, was now being dissolved. It was not

Charles Bennion was the Chairman of the British United Shoe Machinery Company. He first entered the council in 1891 as a Conservative. The Liberals regarded him as a progressive who gave freely of his time performing public duties in the 'city father' tradition

immediate but it was nonetheless quite rapid in the 1920s. Signs of this breakdown of support were seen in the suburbs where middle-class houseowners began to see their interests as ratepayers as distinct and separate from those who might possibly benefit from municipal services. The most notable new middle-class interest group to emerge in the 1920s was probably the ratepayers' association. It was particularly attractive to shopkeepers and small tradesmen who feared increases in rates, which would have been detrimental to their businesses. Thus Frank Gadsby, a picture framer, stood as a Ratepayers' Association candidate in 1932 for St Martin's ward before standing as a Liberal in St Margaret's the following year. He was unsuccessful on both occasions. Ratepayers' associations were also attractive in the suburbs. One such association was formed in Humberstone in 1924 and it was affiliated to the Leicester Federation of Owner Occupiers. By 1938 the Humberstone Association was nominating candidates for the Humberstone Parish Council. Ratepayer groups generally allied themselves to the Conservative Party. The interests of the house-owning middle classes enabled Conservative politicians to argue that Labour politicians were hopelessly idealistic. Thus in 1919 in Aylestone Ward the Conservative candidate claimed that he would lead the 'moderates' against the 'mad hatters'. Such a stand received the support of the President of the Aylestone Liberal Association who said that he was against the 'theoretical, visionary and quixotic methods of the Labour Party'.

Labour's growing strength in this period was due to its organization and there was a strong tradition of working-class organization in the city. The Leicester branch of the Independent Labour Party was formed in 1894 but the lasting impression it made on Leicester politics is demonstrated by the fact that it was the largest in Britain at the end of the First World War. A number of factors were responsible for making Leicester's working-class politics so vibrant at the start of the twentieth century. Leicester's reputation as a radical city had been well deserved for most of the previous century. In part this was a consequence of Leicester's trade structure that had continued to employ a mix of skilled and semi-skilled labour in large numbers considerably later than other factory-based towns. While this avoided the mass politics of some northern towns the low wage levels endemic in a system of outwork in the hosiery and shoe trades created problems of its own; and it encouraged an approach to politics which was to an extent sectionalized. This sectionalized approach to politics was starting to break up at the beginning of the century as the threat of unemployment, even among skilled men, began to grow. Consequently the 'radicalized sectionalism', as Bill Lancaster has called it, gave way to 'social reformism' which was personified by James Ramsay MacDonald.

The persistence of artisan culture was reflected in Leicester's success at building a stable secular society and by the enduring popularity of gradualist improvement forms of Liberalism. Both of these were generally recognized as forms of radicalism that attracted skilled workmen. As the nineteenth century came to a close the skilled status enjoyed by so many for so long was increasingly undermined by changes in working practices, the impact of machinery and also of foreign competition. At the

Leicester's Labour politics moved sharply to the left in 1917–18 and a Labour Party conference on militarism was held at the Temperance Hall in February 1918. Will Crooks is addressing the conference. MacDonald advocated open diplomacy in line with the Labour Party's War Aims Memorandum. MacDonald's criticism of the government's war policy contributed to his crushing defeat in the 1918 Coupon Election

same time some sections of the Leicester working class had been able to actively promote the culture of socialism. Alongside a lively and active City Labour Club the Labour Church movement was successful in Leicester long after the phenomenon had declined nationally. Most important of all, the Labour movement in Leicester had its own highly successful newspaper, the *Pioneer*. Edited initially by Tom Barclay, a veteran of Secularist and socialist agitations, it quickly established itself as the foremost radical paper in Leicester. Retaining a deliberately popular format, the paper contained sports reports as well as a wide range of news and comment.

After 1918 Labour was able to form a strong constituency organization. It also had the backing of the Trades Council, which actively campaigned in the immediate post-war period and sponsored many candidates. Labour's determination extended into every area of public policy and it was able to fight local elections on the burning issues – unemployment, health and housing. Admittedly some of Labour's campaigning was couched in utopian terms, as was revealed by the Labour candidate in Latimer Ward in 1927, who said he stood for the abolition of unemployment; higher wages and better

Leicester Labour Councillors and members of the Board of Guardians, c. 1915. The administration of the Poor Law became a vital issue for Labour in the 1920s

conditions; good houses at reasonable rents; improved education and a municipal savings bank. Unemployment in particular was a strong issue for Labour. Although it was often claimed that Leicester was a prosperous town it had not completely avoided difficulties. Unemployment and poverty were ever present. In fact unemployment had risen to 14,000 in January 1921, and the resources of the Poor Law Guardians were completely exhausted. A protest march to the Guardians' offices in Rupert Street in September 1921 resulted in a full scale riot. Subsequently Amos Sheriff initiated the 'Leicester Work Scheme'. While it did not completely solve the problems it was a practical solution and a clear indication that Labour could influence policy. Thus a seat on the Board of Guardians was a legitimate aim for Labour men and women who sought to humanize the administration of the Poor Law. But here the older parties were still in a strong majority – thirty-one to seventeen in 1923.

Throughout the 1920s Labour continued to make inroads into the council so much so that the alliance between the Liberals and the Conservatives was consolidated in 1926 and the two parties produced a joint broadsheet warning the city's electorate of the impending doom: 'Political power may soon pass to a party sworn to a policy of plunder.' Alderman Swain claimed: 'Leicester is at the cross roads. Two more socialists and the dark lane is entered, the lane is ill-lit, ill-paved, with ditches on either side and no fences. . . .' The election of 1928 was vigorously fought as the Conservatives and the Liberals realized that Labour only needed two more victories to assume greater influence on the council and its sub-committees. There was in fact an open anti-socialist pact and the two older parties expressed their opposition through the united broadsheet, *Leicester Calling*. The anti-socialist

William Hincks was Secretary of the Charity Organization Society and an advocate of temperance reform. He became Lord Mayor in 1936

candidates – a mixture of Liberals, Conservatives and Independents – got the backing of the town's leading businessmen and the town's two leading newspapers, the *Leicester Mercury* and the *Leicester Mail*. The array of businessmen who were drawn into the fray was impressive. They all warned that Labour's schemes were extravagant and dangerous and would lead to high rates. Thomas Fielding Johnson opined that Leicester's prosperity was due to individualism; and Harry Percy Gee argued that socialist theories were 'unsound and fallacious'. Labour pressed on campaigning on its now almost traditional issues – housing, health and abolition of the existing rating system. Tactically it answered the charge of extravagance by hitting out at what it called the excessive salaries of Corporation officials at the expense of decent wages for workers.

Perhaps the most divisive issue of the inter-war years in municipal politics revolved around disputes over the administration of public assistance. The reforms of local government in 1927 meant that the corporation took over responsibilities that were formerly dealt with by the Board of Guardians. Labour sought to use their stronger presence on the council – they had never gained much influence on the Guardians – to bring about a more constructive approach to the problem of unemployment. In 1930 Amos Sheriff was blocked in an attempt to introduce a public works scheme. In October 1931 he proposed that the Public Assistance Committee should not work the 'means test'. This was supported, with one exception, by the other Labour members of the committee, but was voted down by a combination of Liberals and Conservatives. Emily Fortey claimed that Labour was seeking to operate the test 'humanely'. The question of the means test was to be a constant source of conflict between Labour and the older parties for the rest of the decade but in 1932 Labour successfully implemented a scheme of works of 'public utility', although implicit in Labour's proposal was the charge that unemployment had been aggravated by the means test. This was too much for the Conservatives who moved an amendment to remove all reference to the means test. The amendment was carried but Labour voted against, mustering twenty votes. It had truly arrived and it was able to influence the policy of the council.

Despite these clear political antipathies there was still a certain agreement about the nature of public service that persisted throughout the 1920s and 1930s and even to beyond the Second World War. There was even some agreement about the wide-ranging responsibilities of municipal government. Thus, although Alderman Swain could warn of the dangers of socialism in 1926 he was quite happy ten years later at his own mayor-making ceremony to boast that there was scarcely a phase in the life of any citizen from 'pre-natal existence to burial that was not touched by the activities of the governing body'. He went on to extol the virtues of public service

Public ritual remained an important means for the city's political élite to confirm their status. This civic procession was in 1934, when William Billings was Lord Mayor

that would have been subscribed to by the late nineteenth-century city fathers – Sir Israel Hart, Arthur Wakerley and Edward Wood. 'Those who devote their time,' he said, 'their leisure time and their abilities to public service, can hope to do no more than serve their day and generation without thought of recognition or reward.' The degree of co-operation within the council had been revealed as early as August 1931, when the Corporation had given its support for savings in expenditure, and the council agreed, without dissent, to defer all schemes of capital expenditure. Plans to extend the education service were halted and not resumed until 1936.

Leicester's Municipal Politics, 1945–74

In the post-war period the political fortunes of the parties often reflected events at Westminster. So, in terms of electoral performance in the municipal polls, there were marked fluctuations in support for the parties and these often ran contrary to the levels enjoyed in parliamentary general elections. Thus Labour success at Westminster was often associated with Conservative success at local level. The Liberals were very much in decline throughout the 1950s and 1960s and their ward associations in the city were in a lamentable state by the 1960s. Admittedly the Liberals had won five seats on the city council in 1962 but in 1964 the local agent

Charles Keene was probably the last of the 'city fathers'. He became Lord Mayor in 1953. His work on post-war reconstruction and education were his greatest achievements

for the party, John Holmes, was owed £200 in back salary. Holmes in fact resigned in March 1965 and the Liberal Annual General Meeting heard that there were still many unpaid bills.

In the years immediately after the war the city was dominated by Labour and the party was fortunate in the talents of two men – Charles Keene and Mark Henig. Both were businessmen and in many respects they conformed to the old style 'city father' municipal leader. Keene had already amassed considerable experience in pre-war politics. Born in 1889 he had first entered the council in 1926. He had been particularly interested in education becoming the city's representative on the University College Council in 1928. He also became a governor of the College of Art and Technology. During the war he became chairman of the Air Raid Precautions Committee where he showed, according to Mark Henig, 'characteristic clear thinking and sound exposition'. It was this ability that established his central position in the affairs of the city council after 1945. In that year he became chairman of the Reconstruction Committee, which in 1953 instigated an ambitious programme of slum clearance and the redevelopment of St Matthew's. He continued with his involvement in education, particularly with the College of Technology and the Gateway School. When he received the freedom of the city in 1962 his political colleagues recognized him as a man with 'breadth of vision, foresight and a stimulating influence on the post-war planning of the city'. Charles Keene was imbued with the ideals of public service. He was not a socialist but he saw Labour as a device for getting things done. In that respect he was an old style Liberal 'improver'. Like Charles Keene, Mark Henig was also able to devote

Mark Henig was treasurer of the City
Labour Party after the Second World War

considerable time to a political life. Henig was the son of a Jewish immigrant who had settled in Leicester in 1908 and established his own wholesale hosiery enterprise. Henig was a great organizer and was a member of numerous council committees including Finance, Education, Water, Publicity and Rating. He was treasurer of the city Labour Party. On the Conservative side the most prominent figure to emerge was Ken Bowder. He represented Westcotes Ward and was one of the council's most able debaters. He became vice chairman of the Housing Committee and was also a member of Town Planning, Health and the Rating and Valuation Committees.

Party conflict in the post-1945 era centred around the extent and scope of municipal provision. Labour was essentially the party of 'improvement' just as the Liberals had been in the nineteenth century. The Conservatives on the other hand were the party of 'economy'. Thus in 1952 when Ken Bowder fought the Westcotes Ward he argued: 'Just as the household . . . has to be wisely and properly organized so must the town hall against waste and extravagance.' The Conservatives had already attempted, while they had a majority, to eliminate 'waste and extravagance' in 1949 by bringing in a firm of private consultants to examine the corporation's efficiency with a view to reforming its administrative organization. But conflicts about public expenditure were most acutely revealed on the question of housing. For example, in the 1953 municipal elections the Conservatives fought Abbey Ward arguing that keeping the rates down was a priority and therefore council house provision needed to be kept under control, although there was a priority to house the old. The issue of housing also illustrates the interaction of national politics with local issues. The Conservative government's controversial Rent Act of 1957 was vigorously attacked by the Leicester Labour Party in the 1958 municipal elections. The Rent Act had removed rent controls and Labour argued, with some effect, that it was a 'landlords' charter'. At the same time Labour maintained that the government's high interest rates handicapped Leicester Council in achieving its house building targets. Nevertheless 1,400 dwellings had been built in 1956–7 and shops had been provided on New Parks estate and Eyres Monsell. Work was also underway to provide shops and community centres on Thurnby Lodge, Stocking Farm and Mowmacre. Nevertheless, the assumed position of Labour produced vitriolic attacks from the Conservatives. Labour had by now adopted the role of 'defender of the faith' on matters of public provision, especially on housing and education. The Conservatives on the other hand perpetually argued for restraint of public expenditure, dubbing Labour as the party of extravagance and high rates. Thus in 1957 Florence Coltman, a Conservative candidate standing in Newton Ward, adopted an almost Disraelian stance on matters of social welfare for the elderly but railed on Labour, saying: 'High rates [were] a burden to everyone.' Some Conservatives went further, anticipating the Thatcherite antipathy to the whole philosophy of public provision, arguing that it eliminated the virtues of hard work and independence. Thus Dorothy Russell contesting Castle Ward in 1957 forthrightly asserted that the 'socialist municipalization of houses, would be the means of strangling private property . . . [and] . . . the destruction of thrift. . . .' By contrast Labour was able to portray the Conservative Party as a menace to all forms of public provision. In 1958 Labour campaign literature focused on a rather vague Conservative proposal to introduce a means test for would-be council house tenants. It was, Labour claimed, a 'spiteful and unfair attack'. Labour was able to refer to its successes in house building in St Matthew's and clearing the slums in Wharf Street.

What were the social characteristics of the two main parties in this period? Labour, apart from businessmen like Keene and Henig, recruited many of its would-be councillors from the ranks of trade union officials who were active in their local ward organizations. At the end of the Second World War trade union officials made up about a fifth of the city council's members. By the middle of the 1950s councillors with obvious working-class occupations or who were trade union activists had come to make up 34 per cent of the council's membership, and although this figure fluctuated with electoral fortunes the trade union element remained a strong presence within the Labour group on the council right through to the 1960s. Thus in 1964–5 36 per cent of the council was made up of trade union officials and working-class men and women. Railwaymen were particularly prominent in the 1950s, putting forward Arthur Marriott, George Antill and Percy Watts. The Amalgamated Society of Engineers was the route by which Sam Barston came to the forefront of the local Labour Party in the 1960s. Barston became chairman of the Youth Employment Committee and was a most effective politician. Arthur Gratrix was also a member of the Amalgamated Society of Engineers. He led the Thurnby Lodge Tenants Association in a campaign against the rent rebate scheme in 1965 and had stood for the council as a communist in 1967. He later became a Labour Councillor and became chairman of the Parks Committee. One of Labour's most energetic councillors was, undoubtedly, Lily Marriott. She represented Abbey Ward, became a member of the Rents Tribunal and one of Labour's most experienced committee politicians. By all accounts she was a woman of considerable ability, showing an exceptional grasp of detail on matters of finance as well as on education and welfare.

The Conservative Party relied heavily on businessmen, shopkeepers and women. In 1949–50 almost half the council was made up of businessmen including hosiery manufacturers, boot and shoe men and builders. Conservative 'housewives' formed an important element of the Conservative Party at local level. In the 1956 municipal elections the Conservatives put forward twice as many women candidates as Labour. All the Conservative women candidates defined themselves as 'housewives' in their campaign literature and the party agent asserted that women candidates were popular and the *Leicester Mercury* in 1955 claimed that the election campaigners were giving 'considerable prominence' to 'the housewife and her budgetary problems'. A Conservative councillor such as Monica Trotter gave unstintingly of her time, performing her work in the old style manner of duty just as the old style city fathers had done fifty years earlier. The most formidable

Conservative 'housewife' politician was undoubtedly Irene Pollard who eventually became party leader on the council. The greatest asset for those who sought to be active in municipal politics was time. It was often difficult to obtain time off work, and so trade unionists whose unions had negotiated concessions from employers, businessmen who could leave their firms (Mark Henig left his company in the hands of his brother), and 'housewives' were often well placed to pursue a career in local politics.

The Transformation of Council Politics, 1974–90

The 1970s mark a watershed in Leicester's political scene. A marked transformation was brought about as the consequence of two major issues – education, particularly the comprehensive schooling debate, and immigration in the wake of the Ugandan crisis. These two matters rocked the local Labour Party to its foundations and the ensuing transformation of the party was highlighted by the emergence of a new generation of Labour politicians who challenged the old leadership, which seemed increasingly unable to come to grips with the new political agenda. These overtly political questions were debated against a backdrop of indifferent economic performance and the decline of Leicester's staple industries. Greville Janner voiced his concern in the House of Commons in 1972, pointing out that the rate of unemployment had doubled since 1970, adding that 'tremendous hardship' had arisen in what was a 'previously prosperous city'.

In 1972 the Labour Party had gained a majority on the city council with the Conservatives decisively defeated. According to John Manders in his study *Leicester Schools 1944–1974*, 'the imminence of local government re-organization . . . released some of the constraints which had traditionally moderated the politics of local government in Leicester'. Fear of the Leicestershire Plan for comprehensive education was eventually to cast the city's Labour leadership in a reactionary light. The ageing Labour leadership (the deputy leader Syd Bridges was in his seventies), was imbued with civic pride and was convinced of the great progress that had been made in the city's education service since 1944. Now, local government re-organization as a consequence of the Redcliffe–Maude proposals made the possibility of the imposition of the county plan on the city an immediate reality. The issues were immensely complex as were the social and political reactions of the various interest groups – the city and county officers, teachers in city secondary schools, parents and councillors. The Labour leadership in the city was unable to stomach the imposition of the county plan and so appeared to be opponents of comprehensive education. This was to be the source of the first ideological fracture within the Labour group. The second issue stemmed from Amin's coup in Uganda and the consequent expulsion of the country's Asian population. On 6 September 1972 the city council took the remarkable step of placing an advertisement in the *Ugandan Argus* advising intending migrants not to come to Leicester. Edward Marston, the Labour leader, believed that he was responding to local concern that an influx of immigrants would damage the city's already vulnerable prosperity. Accusations of xenophobia and racism followed and the local press had a really substantial issue to report. However, nine Labour councillors rebelled against the party line, which the *Leicester Mercury* interpreted as a 'socialist challenge' against the old guard as represented by Bridges and Marston. Whether it was a 'socialist challenge' is debatable, but among the nine rebels it might be said that they represented that element who had benefited from higher education, and included Jim Marshall, Dorothy Davis and the Revd Mr Billings. Marshall was in fact to become the new Labour leader in 1973.

The aftermath of the immigration issue saw an increasing polarization of politics around the question of race. In the 1976 municipal elections the National Front came within sixty-one votes of victory in Abbey Ward. The Front fought a skilful campaign avoiding violence, which had often been its trademark elsewhere. Its leader, the solicitor Anthony Read Herbert, sought to appear reasonable and moderate. In 1973 the Front had put forward twenty-six candidates and gained over 17,000 votes. It had not succeeded in winning any seats but its importance was revealed by the fact that Labour lost sixteen seats to the Conservatives. The National Front was also able to capitalize on the decline of Leicester's once prosperous economy. The Mansfield Hosiery strike and in particular the Imperial Typewriter dispute, which lasted for fourteen weeks and largely involved newly

In May 1974 a strike started at the city's Imperial Typewriter factory. It lasted fourteen weeks and the initial dispute over bonus payments was subsumed by issues of racial discrimination. Press coverage depicted striking Asian workers as violent militants. The National Front capitalized on the dispute as part of its unsuccessful push to gain seats on the city council between 1974 and 1976

recruited Asian workers, proved to be one of the most explosive disputes in the history of the city's industrial relations – akin, for the passions it stirred, to the Grunwick dispute. What began as a dispute over bonus payments quickly mushroomed into a series of demands concerning the election of shop stewards, opportunities for promotion, and better pay and conditions for women workers. In 1974 the number of manual workers at Imperial was 1,650, of whom 550 were white. However, the seventeen-strong shop stewards' committee was predominantly white. Many Asian workers had been unable to stand for election as shop stewards as the rules of the Transport and General Workers' Union required a two-year membership as an essential qualification before being allowed to stand for an elected office. To begin with forty workers went on strike at the Copdale Road works, but by June 420 workers had been sacked. The media coverage of the strike, which tended to depict the striking Asian workers as militants, inevitably aggravated existing racial tensions. This undoubtedly contributed to the National Front's success in the local elections of that year and by 1976 the Front was gaining 18 per cent of the votes in the local municipal elections. Subsequently support for the Front fell away and Valerie Marret in her comprehensive study of this episode believes that much of this was due to the campaign of the Inter Racial Solidarity Campaign. It might be thought that this organization was a prime example of a 'new urban left' type caucus. It certainly influenced the new city Labour Party that was emerging behind the leadership of Jim Marshall. The 1976 municipal elections had seen a swing to the Conservatives and former Labour group leader, Edward Marston, lost his seat.

After 1974, when Leicester was relegated to the status of a district council as a consequence of the Local Government Act, there was a steady transformation of the Labour group. Most notable was the emergence of the school teacher contingent. In 1975 Peter Soulsby and Derek Fryett entered the council. By 1985 the list of school teacher councillors was substantial – Soulsby, Fryett, Trobe, Newitt and Bett. Many had graduated from NUT activism and some had tested their political ideas in the campus conflicts of the 1960s. It was students from Leicester University who staged a sit-in at the Admiral Nelson public house in 1964 in protest against a colour bar being operated by the landlord. Labour was now more overtly ideological although it was not without pragmatism. At the same time Labour became increasingly dependent for its electoral support on members of the Afro-Caribbean and Asian communities. The Indian Workers' Association was most adept at getting its voters out. By 1983 there were nine Asian councillors on the council and they were all in the Labour group. They represented the inner city wards of Abbey, Belgrave, Spinney Hills, Latimer and Rusheymead. The Labour Party's leadership now became markedly middle class and professional in character with a much stronger attachment to socialist principles than had been the case in the 1940s and 1950s. In the 1983 elections Labour had forty out of the fifty-six seats on the council; a quarter of those were Asian, and they probably acted as power brokers between the Asian community and the Labour Party. The Asian councillors had not yet grasped

In the later twentieth century Leicester's politics was transformed by the issue of race, as this demonstration in the 1960s shows

the leadership of the party although the dispute over the Kensington Street improvement scheme showed the significance of the Asian community. The decision of the Housing Committee to press ahead with a scheme to demolish fifty-three properties in Kensington Street and Westbourne Street produced a powerful lobby against the chairman of the housing committee and the proposal was withdrawn. It was a rare event for the recommendation of a committee chairman to be overthrown but it demonstrated the importance of the Asian community in Belgrave. (In 1982 46 per cent of the households in Belgrave were headed by a member from the New Commonwealth.) The dramatic change that immigration had had on the inner city was clearly impinging on the city's municipal politics. Leicester experienced some rioting in the early 1980s but it was not as violent or pervasive as the unrest in other parts of the country – Brixton in south London, Handsworth in Birmingham, the St Paul's district in Bristol – where there were large immigrant populations. Nevertheless a House of Commons Select Committee on Race Relations and Immigration visited the city in March 1981. It heard considerable evidence from city community leaders, members of the professions and local politicians. The City Council's own *Survey of Leicester 1983* showed that 45.5 per cent of young Afro-Caribbeans and 38.5 per cent of young Asians were unemployed. Subsequently programmes of inner urban aid were dispersed via the

Department of the Environment and the City Council to revitalize inner city areas that had been designated priority zones. The politics of the inner area became crucial to immigrant groups who were now able to penetrate many of the indigenous political structures of the city. Arguably the Asian community has been much more successful in this area than the Afro-Caribbean community. These developments were gradually revealing new community structures, new patterns of social-spatial segregation, which in turn were undoubtedly changing the patterns of power distribution within the local political arena.

Parliamentary Politics, 1900–18

During the nineteenth century Leicester was a stronghold of the Liberal Party. This was also true of the first part of the twentieth century, but the Liberals were soon to be replaced by Labour. The conflict between the Liberals and Labour in the inter-war years allowed a period of some success for the Conservatives, but since 1945 the city's left-of-centre tradition has been reasserted by the Labour Party, whose grip has only rarely been shaken but never broken. The outcome of elections in Leicester has also been shaped by the evolution of the franchise and by periodic changes in constituency boundaries. The electoral system in operation in Britain between 1900 and 1918 had been established by the Third Reform Act of 1884 and the associated redistribution of seats in the following year. Leicester remained a two-member borough like Derby, Blackburn, Halifax, Oldham, Newcastle, Preston, Portsmouth and Sunderland. The city as a whole therefore formed a single constituency and an elector could cast two votes. This had suited the Liberals, who ran two candidates in tandem. The party tactic was to present two candidates who were acceptable to the different social and religious groupings within the electorate. Thus in 1894, at a by-election caused by the retirement of both the sitting Liberal MPs the Liberals put up two candidates – Walter Hazell, a philanthropic businessman and Henry Broadhurst, the general secretary of the TUC. This dual ticket arrangement – a mainstream Liberal acceptable to the local manufacturers and a Lib-Lab acceptable to the 'respectable' working-class voters – was a highly effective means by which the Liberals could maintain their support in the two-member boroughs, and Leicester is an example *par excellence* of this phenomenon. However, Broadhurst's election did not please the Leicester ILP who had put up their own candidate, Joseph Burgess, in 1894. In 1900 the ILP made another challenge, this time putting up James Ramsay MacDonald who held the ILP vote at 4,164, only a few hundred fewer than Joseph Burgess had mustered in 1894. The disruptive effect of the ILP challenge to the Liberal and Lib-Lab balanced ticket resulted in the defeat of Walter Hazell, letting in the Conservative candidate, Sir John Rolleston.

This was a salutary lesson for both the Liberals and the forces of organized Labour, and within three years the Liberals and the LRC of which MacDonald was secretary, concluded a secret electoral pact whereby the Liberals gave the LRC a free run in over thirty constituencies. It was negotiated by MacDonald and Herbert Gladstone, the Liberal Party chief whip, and signed on 6 September 1903 at the Leicester Isolation Hospital, where MacDonald had been admitted after an illness. One of the first products of the pact was the regularization of the position in Leicester, where, after some pressure from Gladstone, the local Liberal Association agreed to accept Broadhurst as the mainstream candidate for the Liberals with MacDonald as an LRC candidate who could challenge Rolleston. The pact was triumphant in 1906 and the Conservatives, in disarray over the policy of tariff reform, were routed. In Leicester Broadhurst secured 14,745 votes and MacDonald gained 14,685, almost double that secured by Rolleston. Thus the old Liberal sponsorship of Lib-Labism had now been turned to Labour's advantage in Leicester.

The period from 1906 to 1911 saw the heyday locally and nationally of the Lib-Lab 'progressive' alliance, and in the two general elections in January and December, fought over the 'people's budget' and the reform of the House of Lords, MacDonald and his Liberal partner Crawshay-Williams held off their Conservative challengers by comfortable margins. However, after 1911 the pact came under increasing strain and in June 1913 when Crawshay-Williams resigned his seat the Leicester Labour Party nominated its own candidate, Alderman George Banton, who had been, along with Thomas Frederick Richards, one the pioneers of the ILP in Leicester. Banton's candidature was in contravention of the pact, and Labour's National Executive Committee refused to endorse his candidature. MacDonald

George Banton was Leicester's leading ILP politician. He first entered the council in 1896. He became President of the local branch of the LRC in 1904 but he always remained firmly on the left, being an advocate of a 'people's peace' in 1918

A demonstration of the Leicester Branch of the Women's Social and Political Union, c. 1913

subsequently ran on a joint ticket with a Liberal, Gordon Hewart. MacDonald was seemingly vindicated but the pact had sapped the vitality of the Leicester Liberal Association, and the position of Liberalism in the city was already showing signs of vulnerability apparent to the local Labour leadership, even before the First World War overwhelmed and divided the Liberal Party nationally.

The war proved a great test for the country's political institutions. The long battle over conscription in 1916 meant that the granting of universal male suffrage was inevitable when the war was over. In 1914 two in five adult males still did not have the vote. The extension of the franchise meant that the Leicester electorate grew from a little under 27,000 – the number qualified to vote in the 1913 by-election – to a total of 114,230 in the 1918 general election. (The franchise was to admit all women in 1928, and so in Leicester the number of qualified voters in the 1929 election increased to 160,572.) At the same time the legislation of 1918 abolished the old two-member boroughs that had been so beneficial to the Liberals. Leicester was to have three separate seats. Leicester East consisted of the wards of Belgrave, Latimer, Spinney Hill and West Humberstone; Leicester South comprised Aylestone, Castle, Charnwood, De Montfort, Knighton, St Martin's and Wycliffe wards; Leicester West was made up from Abbey, Newton, St Margaret's, Westcotes and Wyggeston wards.

These new arrangements quickened the decline of the Liberals in Leicester and facilitated the rise of Labour. However, it was not a straightforward matter not least because of the problems created by Ramsay MacDonald's criticism of the diplomacy of the British government. MacDonald was not a pacifist and nor was he pro-German, but his opposition to the government's alliance with Russia split the Labour Party at national level and MacDonald resigned his chairmanship of the party. He was replaced by Arthur Henderson as leader of the so-called patriotic-Labour section of Labour MPs in the Commons. In Leicester MacDonald's stand had far-reaching repercussions. MacDonald's position in Leicester had owed much to Liberal patronage since the inception of the pact of 1903. Moreover, MacDonald's criticisms of what he had called profiteering in the hosiery industry had met with hostility from the town's hosiery manufacturers. Further, because of his hostility to the war he opposed conscription when it was introduced in 1916. This was too much for the Leicester business classes, and at the Chamber of Commerce annual general meeting there was a call from the new president that MacDonald's name be removed from the list of patrons of the Chamber on the grounds that MacDonald's lack of patriotism had brought shame upon the town. Anti-MacDonald sentiment continued into peace-time. In 1918, when Germany's defeat was in sight, Alderman Sawday, a leading Liberal, publicly disassociated himself from MacDonald. Sawday's attitude also found support from some sections of the working class in Leicester, principally the local branch of the British Workers' League. At a mass meeting organized by the League in April 1918, there was a call to 'disinfect' Leicester after the recent 'pacifist gatherings'. This was a direct reference to MacDonald's call for a 'people's peace'. Patriotism also influenced the

The Liberals had been the dominant force in nineteenth century Leicester. Their 1918 campaign was unable to resist the Coalition's coupon candidates who made a clean sweep in the city's new constituencies

Ramsay MacDonald had been rejected in 1918 but was given the freedom of the city in 1929. MacDonald became prime minister for the second time in 1929

ILP, where Jabez Chaplin was the leading critic of MacDonald's position. It was hardly surprising then that in the 1918 election MacDonald was trounced by the patriotic candidates. MacDonald stood in Leicester West against a coalition candidate, J.F. Green, supported by the Lloyd George coalition coupon. At national level the election was a test of the prime minister's wartime record but in Leicester it became, according to David Marquand, 'a referendum on the character and patriotism of MacDonald'. MacDonald's defeat was crushing and the Coalition made a clean sweep in Leicester's three new seats. Thus, from having been the city where the Liberal accommodation of Labour between 1903 and 1906 had borne such rich fruit and where Labour organizations were quite strong, Labour was wiped off the electoral map in 1918. MacDonald's stance had been peculiarly damaging.

Parliamentary Politics, 1918–45

After 1918 the electoral history of the three Leicester seats diverged. In 1922 J.F. Green defended his seat, still as a coalition Liberal loyal to Lloyd George. The seat fell to the Labour candidate, Frederick Pethick-Lawrence, who undoubtedly benefited from the disunity among the Liberals whose two candidates in fact gained more votes than Pethick-Lawrence. However, Lawrence was able to hold the seat until 1931 when he was defeated by E.H. Pickering, a Liberal who was given a clear run without a Conservative standing. In 1935 the seat was won by Harold Nicolson, the diplomat, who had fought under the banner of 'National Labour'. He was part of a small group of Labour MPs who continued to support MacDonald and the National Government after the financial crisis of August–September 1931. After 1937 Nicolson was part of a group of MPs who supported Churchill and Eden against the government's appeasement policy. Thus after Pethick-Lawrence had lost the seat it was clear that Labour had no real hold on Leicester West and it was not until 1945 that Labour was able to recover its position, when Barnett Janner gained the seat, polling over 20,000 votes to Nicolson's 13,000 votes. (Nicolson had merely stood as a 'National' candidate and a supporter of Churchill.)

The Conservative Party was the main beneficiary of the conflict between the Liberals and Labour in the inter-war period. The benefits it derived from the division of the anti-Conservative vote were clear in the history of the other two Leicester seats. In March 1922 Gordon Hewart, the sitting National Liberal member, resigned upon his promotion to Lord Chief Justice of England. Labour successfully put up the old war-horse, George Banton. However, there was a general election in November 1922 when the Conservatives withdrew their support for the Lloyd George coalition after the famous Carlton Club meeting. Banton lost the seat in a straight fight against a National Liberal, Henry Evans. Evans had the tacit support of the local Conservatives and in the following short parliament he accepted the Conservative whip. In the subsequent general election of December 1923, which Baldwin had mysteriously called to fight on the issue of tariff reform, Evans stood as a Conservative. This time Banton won in a three-way contest by a margin of 4,915 votes. Thus he formed part of the Labour contingent that secured the first, minority, Labour government. Labour's position was precarious and MacDonald was eventually forced to go to the country again in the autumn of 1924, and Banton lost the seat to the Conservative John de Vere Loder. The seat remained Conservative until 1929 when it was retaken by Labour; but again in the crisis of 1931 it reverted to the Conservatives who held it until 1945. These changes were a consequence of the struggle between the Liberals and Labour but there was probably also a gradual re-alignment of support between the Liberals and the Conservatives, with the latter gradually picking up votes from the middle classes, who were abandoning the Liberal creed that they had supported before the First World War.

The relationship between middle-class voting preference and the Conservative Party was most clearly demonstrated in Leicester South. Here the Conservatives held the seat throughout the whole period 1918 to 1945 with the single exception of 1923, when it was taken by a Liberal. In 1945 Labour made a clean sweep of the three Leicester seats with Terence Donovan, Herbert Bowden and Barnett Janner. This result was formative – Leicester became a Labour city in the heart of a Conservative county; and Labour also had a majority on the city council.

Parliamentary Politics, 1945 to the Present

The predominance of Labour within the city of Leicester since 1945 has been partly a function of electoral boundaries. Middle-class suburbs that might be natural areas for support for the Conservatives have been part of the constituencies of

Harborough, Bosworth and Blaby. Conservative success within the city has been intermittent and unusual. In 1949 there was a nationwide redistribution of constituency boundaries and in Leicester's case the city was divided into four constituencies. The first of these, Leicester North-West, consisted of Abbey, Newton, St Margaret's and Westcotes wards, and was the safest of the three seats that were normally Labour territory. Since 1945 this division and its successor, Leicester West, have been represented by two members of the Janner family, both lawyers and prominent figures in the world of British Jewry. The seat was won by Barnett Janner in 1945, and he retained it with comfortable margins until his retirement in 1970. Janner had originally been a member of the Liberal Party and had represented the East London constituency of Whitechapel. His place was taken by his son Greville Janner and this inevitably led to some accusations of nepotism. Greville Janner then moved across to the new seat of Leicester West in 1974, for which he has sat ever since.

The second safe Labour seat was Leicester North-East, which comprised Belgrave, Charnwood, Humberstone and Latimer wards. Throughout the period 1950 to 1974 it has been represented by Labour – Terence Donovan, Ungoed-Thomas and after 1962 Tom Bradley, who had been a prominent figure in Northamptonshire local government. Labour's hold on the North-East division was becoming increasingly tenuous in the later 1960s and this was in part due to the effects of immigration. It is difficult to chart exactly the effect of immigration on voting behaviour but it is probable that in the first instance it broke up the traditional working-class support for Labour candidates in the older inner wards of the city. Bradley faced a challenge from an Anti-Immigration Society candidate who

Greville Janner succeeded his father as Labour MP for Leicester North-West in 1970 and continued to represent Leicester West after 1974

captured 1,616 votes in 1970. Bradley's overall majority in that election was only 891. As the number of immigrants grew so middle-class residents moved out, and gradually areas became clear ethnic minority enclaves. Many of the areas of Belgrave and Highfields contain an Asian population of between 45 and 65 per cent of the total. For example the area of Crown Hills to the east of Highfields and of Rusheymead to the north of Belgrave have become attractive to more middle-class Asians who have sought to move up the housing market. Afro-Caribbean people can be found living in all parts of the city but still fully a third of that population has continued to live in Highfields. These kinds of concentrations have proved vital to Labour's political strength within the city during the last two decades of the century.

Leicester South-East initially comprised Evington, Knighton, Spinney Hill and Wycliffe wards, and thus included the leafy suburbs. In the redistribution of 1955, which did not affect any of the Leicester constituencies, the Conservative majority in the South-East became virtually impregnable when the Oadby Urban District, outside the boundary for local government purposes, was added to the parliamentary seat. Charles Waterhouse, who had represented the old Leicester South constituency between 1924 and 1945 took the new South-East division in 1950 and held it until 1957. The seat remained in Conservative hands until the 1970s when further boundary adjustments reduced the number of constituencies to three. All three seats became marginals and the effects of immigration were now much more clearly felt.

It was Asian immigration rather than Afro-Caribbean immigration that has had the greatest impact on Leicester's parliamentary politics. The Asian population had begun to grow from the early 1960s, but it was given a rapid and dramatic boost by the expulsions from Uganda in 1972. Asian populations living in other parts of East Africa have followed their Ugandan counterparts as the various African nationalisms have made the lives of Asians in Africa more difficult. Thus Ugandan Asians have been followed by Asian peoples from Kenya, Malawi and Tanzania. These peoples have found the task of assimilating to life in an industrial western city not without difficulty, but in many respects they have been successful. By 1981 people of Asian origin made up 22.1 per cent of the total population in the city. The social and spatial arrangements of a modern city have naturally produced concentrations of Asian people in particular districts of the city. A national ranking of parliamentary seats by percentage of non-white population according to the 1981 census found Leicester East to have the thirteenth highest proportion with 26.3 per cent and Leicester South the fourteenth highest with 25.3 per cent. In political terms this has sustained Labour's hold: the Asian community has a strong tradition of registering to vote, turning out on polling day, and maintaining a strong loyalty to the Labour Party. In the shorter term Asian immigration has also produced neo-fascist campaigns. The activity of the Anti-Immigration Society in the 1970 general election has already been noted, but it was followed by more serious challenges from the National Front who fought all three Leicester seats in the 1974 and 1979 elections. In February 1974 the Front gained 3,662 votes in Leicester East (7.4 per cent) and in Leicester West it obtained 2,967 (6.4 per cent). Evidence that its

Anti-racist demonstrations became a dramatic means of mobilizing opposition to the National Front in the 1970s

appeal was more to the feelings of fear and resentment among the poorer sections of the inner-city white working class was borne out by the poorer showing of the Front in the more suburban middle-class constituency of Leicester South. Here the Front polled 1,639 votes in February 1974, only 3 per cent of the poll. In the national context, of the fifty-four candidates run by the Front in February 1974 its performance in Leicester was its best performance and that in Leicester South was its sixth highest. This performance was at the peak of the political furore about immigration, against the background of the Imperial Typewriter dispute which had begun in May 1974; and a mass demonstration in Highfields by 6,000 people when the police had refused to ban a National Front march in support of white workers at Imperial Typewriters. Although the Front continued to be a threat in local politics its significance in parliamentary politics quickly declined: support for Front candidates in the 1979 election fell by 50 per cent, with a best showing of 469 votes in Leicester West, only 1 per cent of the poll. The effect of race was still present, however, and in Leicester South Jim Marshall actually increased his majority over the Conservative candidate from 1,133 to 1,998. Labour in fact held all three Leicester seats, which meant that it bucked the national trend in favour of Margaret Thatcher, the largest swing in a general election since 1945. Labour did well in other areas outside London where there were sizeable immigrant communities. It is difficult to tell how immigrant communities viewed the Conservatives at this time, but in Leicester South during the last few days of the electoral campaign a leaflet printed in Gujerati identified the National Front with the Conservative Party. The leaflet apparently contained the local Labour Party agent's name. The Labour Party agent and Jim Marshall both issued apologies. It was an unfortunate incident, and precisely what effect it had on voting behaviour will probably never be discovered; but it demonstrates the powerful effect that race was having on the city's politics.

Since 1974 the most significant party battle has been between Labour and the Conservatives. In Leicester West Greville Janner's majority was 8,652 in February 1974, but since that time it has gradually dwindled, to only 1,201 in 1987. In Leicester South the seat was held by the Conservative, Tom Boardman; but he was ousted in the October 1974 election by Labour's Jim Marshall. No doubt this owed much to Marshall's stand against the Labour old guard who had wanted to discourage Asian immigration following the Ugandan crisis. Marshall enjoyed the support of the Indian Workers' Association and in 1979 Marshall increased his majority slightly, despite a national swing against Labour. The seat was still highly marginal and in 1983 the seat reverted to the Conservatives whose Derek Spencer defeated Marshall by a mere seven votes. Marshall bounced back and recovered the seat in 1987, squeezing out the Liberal vote which had damaged him in the previous election, and gaining a majority of 1,877.

Leicester East was less of a cliffhanger, but its history from 1974 to 1979 was more reflective of national developments. Tom Bradley, who had held Leicester North-East from 1962 to 1974, held Leicester East from 1974 until 1979. However, he followed Roy Jenkins into the Social Democrats and so in 1983 had to defend the seat against a Labour candidate, Patricia Hewitt. As is often the case in these three-cornered contests, Bradley's support syphoned off potential support for Labour, and so the seat was taken by the publicity conscious Conservative Peter Bruinvels, who gained a majority of 933. His crass outspokenness made him a natural target for Labour even during the zenith of Thatcherism. Labour put forward Keith Vaz, an articulate lawyer of Asian background who had worked in community law centres in the city's immigrant districts. Fears that an Asian candidate might produce a white backlash proved groundless. Vaz polled 24,074 to 22,150 for Bruinvels. Thus Keith Vaz became Britain's first Asian MP since the Communist Saklatvala in 1923.

Since 1979 Leicester's geographical position in the middle of the nation has been paralleled by its politics. At first in 1983 the city appeared to be at one with the pattern in the west Midlands and the south. Then in 1987 it seemed to revert to being a Labour stronghold along northern lines, akin to Liverpool, Leeds or Newcastle, and provided a significant contribution to Labour's few seats in England. As the twentieth century entered its final decade Leicester was once more, as it had been in 1906, solidly in the hands of the main left-of-centre party in British political life.

Further Reading

Armitage, F., *Leicester and the First World War* (c.1930)

Bennett, J.D., *Who Was Who in Leicestershire* (1975)

Cook, C., *The Age of Alignment in Electoral Politics in England 1922–1929* (1975)

Hartopp, H., *Roll of the Mayors of Leicester* (1935)

Jones, P., 'The Recruitment of Office Holders in Leicester 1861–1931' *Transactions of the Leicester Archaeological and Historical Society*, LVIII (1981–2) pp. 64–77

Lancaster, Bill, *Radicalism, Co-operation and Socialism: Leicester Working Class Politics 1860–1906* (1987)

Marquand, D., *Ramsay MacDonald* (1977)

McKinley, R., (ed.), *The Victoria County History of Leicester and Leicestershire*, vol. IV (1958)

Nash, D.S., *Secularism, Art and Freedom* (1992)

Newitt, N., *The General Strike in Leicester* (1976)

Newman, A., 'Sir Israel Hart of Leicester', *Transactions of the Leicester Archaeological and Historical Society*, XLIX (1975) pp. 43–51

Simmons, J., *Leicester: Past and Present*, Vol. II (1974)

Walker, M., *The National Front* (1977)

From the Leicester Reference Library Local History collection

Anrurar, M., *Votes and Policies: ethnic minorities and the General Election of 1979* (1980)

Fenn, G.W., *Candidates in a Municipal Election, Leicester May 1956* (n.d.)

House of Commons Home Affairs Committee Race Relations and Immigration Sub-Committee Session 1980–81: minutes of evidence, 13 March 1981 (1981)

Leicester Inner Area Programme Annual Report 1985–86 (1986)

Leicester Corporation: Conferment of Freedom of the City upon Harry Percy Gee and Alderman Ernest Wilford (1950)

Street Disturbance 11–13 July 1981, Leicester City Council (1981)

Survey of Leicester 1983, Leicester City Council (1984)

South Leicester Conservative Association Knighton Ward Branch: *Knighton Local Government Guide 1977* (1979–81)

Leicestershire Record Office

Recordings of speeches made at the award ceremony of the granting of the freedom of the city to Alderman Keene

Records of the Leicester Liberal Association 1882–1923

Minute Books of the South Leicester Liberal Association 1940–71

Humberstone and District Ratepayers and Property Owners Association, 1939

Labour Party Circular explaining the party's propaganda and press policy, 1936

City of Leicester Labour Party

Box of miscellaneous photographs and election campaign literature. Valuable evidence was supplied by John Phipps (former town clerk)

Chapter Four

MUNICIPAL PROVISION: EDUCATION, HEALTH AND HOUSING

Afeature of twentieth-century urban history has been the gradual decline in the importance of civic culture from its heyday in the later nineteenth century. But in Leicester the erosion in the significance of municipal office and in the extent of municipal powers was not marked until the 1970s. Moreover, during the inter-war years the activities of the Borough Council began to affect the life of the city in new ways as local government was given further administrative responsibilities. This chapter focuses on three of these. It describes the development of health and welfare services in the city, and the making and implementation of key aspects of municipal policy with regard to education and housing. It begins with the period before the Second World War, when guides and handbooks deliberately set out to represent the Borough Council as a pioneering and progressive municipal authority.

Pre-Second World War

During this period the Labour group built support in the Council, as already described, by closely relating to the new responsibilities for education, health and housing plus the relief of unemployment, seeking to project an image of Labour as the party of progress and civic idealism. But councillors in other parties also subscribed to this credo. There were differences of approach, of course, and the Tory councillors were more inclined to see themselves as a ratepayers' party. Yet despite acute party controversy over particular issues, the continuity of council membership fostered the formation of a broad consensus about the importance of council services. Until as late as the 1970s a long-serving group of established councillors from all parties influenced the tone and style of council business. During this period it was customary for the mayor and chairmen of committees to alternate between the main parties, whichever group was in power.

The relative prosperity of Leicester in the years between the two World Wars was a factor in helping the Council establish an early reputation as a progressive authority. Despite the support given to cuts in local government expenditure in

Leicester City Council in session, c. 1928

1931, the general level of spending was maintained throughout these years. The rate in the pound also steadily increased from 7*s* 9*d* to 14*s* 10*d* over the period 1918/19–40/41, notwithstanding the rate reductions of 1932. The forward looking reputation which the Council acquired owed much to the ideas put forward by the Council's new administrative officers and the support these received from a group of strong-minded councillors.

Among those influential in shaping policies in health (including mental health) and education, the first two women councillors rate special mention. Mrs Ellen Swainston, a leading member of the Conservative and Unionist Association, was the first woman to be elected to the Council: she was elected for the Belgrave Ward in 1922 as a 'parents' candidate' in opposition to recent measures taken by the Education Committee. Mrs Swainston was a long-serving chairman of the Mental Deficiency Committee. Emily Comber Fortey, returned unopposed for Labour in a by-election in St Margaret's Ward in 1923, was exceptional for the times in holding a degree in science. She was also a member of a Catholic order. However, until the election of Miss Frisby, these two women ploughed a rather lonely furrow on the Council: in the words of Emily Fortey, 'we must regretfully admit that the political and economic equality of the sexes is still a claim rather than an achievement'. What Emily Fortey particularly regretted was that there was only one woman on the Housing Committee.

The Reorganization of Schooling

In 1956 an official handbook claimed that the Education Committee had always pursued a policy of vigorous development which 'has earned Leicester an enviable reputation among education authorities'. This claim seems to derive mainly from developments in the inter-war years. As John Mander, Head of Schools Division in the post-1944 period pointed out in 1980: 'By 1939 the LEA had enjoyed for some fifteen years the reputation of being a forward looking Authority and a good Authority to work for. In part this reputation rested on material provision in the schools; in part it was cultivated; and in part it rested on an early "Hadow" reorganization and early establishment of nursery classes.' To this could be added the early establishment of the school medical service and appointment of a school psychologist as well as pioneering developments in special education. These efforts to be in the vanguard of educational movements, however, created problems when ideas changed.

The driving force in seeking to improve the school system was F.P. Armitage, former head of the modern side at St Paul's school, London and Director of Education in Leicester from 1919–45. He was supported by an education committee which had remarkable continuity of personnel. These included such leading figures as Councillors North, Keene, Oram, Fortey and others, many of whose names were to be commemorated in the titles of schools and colleges. The redoubtable Emily Fortey was of particular importance in bringing the Labour Group in support of the school reorganization plan, and for the interest she had in backward and handicapped children. Although an advocate of greater equality for women she was nevertheless in support of the principle embodied in the reorganization plan of setting up single sex schools.

School reorganization or regrouping was an attempt to extend the provision of top classes in elementary schools. The idea was to get rid of the all-age schools inherited from the previous century by splitting them into infant/junior and senior schools with classes organized into ability groupings – i.e. streaming in the modern parlance. This was seen as necessary for modernizing the senior age curriculum. It also enabled junior schools to be large enough to accommodate two streams, with the A stream as a forcing house for secondary selection. But these advantages were not apparent to many parents and the introduction of regrouping in the northern district ran into considerable opposition: parents withdrew children from school and, as already noticed, put up a candidate at the local elections.

However, regrouping was supported by Labour councillors because of the director's ideas for improving access to secondary education. These involved the introduction in 1923 of a basic subjects eleven-plus examination organized by the teachers. The results in the first year provided ammunition for expanding places in secondary education, which was done by creating two new municipal grammar schools and designating some of the senior schools as intermediate schools. The latter were a unique feature of Leicester's educational provision. Thus it could be claimed that Leicester came nearer than most other LEAs in achieving the aims of the Consultative Committee's Hadow Report in 1926 of 'selection by differentiation'. The director had anticipated the thinking of the report, and the Leicester scheme was cited in it.

Until the local expenditure cuts of 1931 the city education authority had made full use of the free place regulations with 50 per cent – the maximum allowed – of entrants to secondary schools awarded free places, and resisted attempts to introduce special places rather than free places or to raise fees. They also made an effort to overcome the pressures for early leaving that were particularly acute in Leicester because of the availability of employment. But in 1931 cuts in educational spending and changes in governmental policy affected educational opportunity locally. Plans to raise the school leaving age were scrapped, while a Board of Education circular raised the minimum fees for secondary schooling and declared that free place children should now be means tested. Despite local protest meetings by teachers and political groups, and a proposal by the secondary education subcommittee, on the instigation of Charles Keene and Emily Fortey, to adhere to existing fees, the Education Committee agreed to chairman Sir Jonathan North's motion that the government proposals be accepted.

Besides reducing educational opportunity, the new fees accentuated the differences between the secondary grammar schools. The Wyggeston Boys, Wyggeston Girls and the Collegiate School were considered Leicester's most socially desirable schools. As a result they charged higher fees and limited the number of means-tested special places available to pupils from elementary schools (to 25 per cent in the case of the Wyggeston schools and to only 15 per cent by the Collegiate). Newarke Girls School, City Boys, Alderman Newton Boys and Girls and Gateway Boys all charged the minimum allowable fee of 9 gns and took the balance of special places to achieve the overall figure of 50 per cent. This helped to create a two-tier system amongst the secondary grammar schools in Leicester.

The cuts also affected educational expenditure, and some plans, as for instance the building of the Gateway Girls school, were abandoned. Yet although the early 1930s were years of financial stringency, the record of the authority over the inter-war years as a whole stood up well comparatively. There was no great pressure of population increase to contend with, but the redistribution of population and the regrouping proposals entailed new school building and a modernization programme. Nursery schools were provided and thirty-five new council schools. In the latter classes were made progressively smaller, specialist teaching introduced, new science rooms and art classes created. The Education Committee made particular efforts to promote practical instruction in schools and to extend night school provision for the fourteen to eighteen group introducing preparatory courses to the College of Arts and Technology for which it also had a responsibility. The

Local nursery school provision in Leicester

quite exceptional interest shown in technical education was reflected in the founding of the Gateway School in 1928, a project of Charles Keene. Another strong concern in this health conscious city was the provision of games facilities and gymnasia.

The annual reports of the committee reflect the interest they had in improving the standing as well as efficiency of the schools. This was not always successful judging from the steady flow of truancies reported, and the way that some schools achieved reputations as difficult schools. Nevertheless the reports tell of efforts to provide outings, encourage social activities and promote *esprit de corps*. Particular attention was paid to the intermediate schools, which in drawing pupils from different parts of the city were recognized as lacking the traditions of the grammar school. By the 1930s according to some old pupils they were in no way inferior – 'they had a uniform, they did homework, and they played rugby'.

But it was in the growth of facilities for the education of handicapped, backward and what became known as maladjusted children that Leicester gained a nationally recognized ascendancy. This was because of relatively early moves in trying to identify and cater for different kinds of problem children with separate institutional provision. The Committee had anticipated national legislation in founding special schools for blind and handicapped children, and did so again in provision for mentally defective children – initially in an existing school (Willow Street) and then in a new school (the Haddenham Road Experimental) linked into the authority's developing psychological service.

The founding of the school psychological service reflected a growing national interest in child guidance and teaching programmes, but in Leicester it was also a logical consequence of reorganization and the director's belief in the possibility of selection and classification so as to better allocate children to appropriate educational niches. A keen advocate of intelligence tests, he influenced the decision to develop this service with a psychologist in charge (rather than a child guidance clinic with a psychiatrist in charge as in some other authorities). R.B. Cattell, the best known of the early appointments (1933), succeeded in developing the service on a broader basis and with more diagnostic and therapeutic work involving the use of psychotherapy to treat children with behavioural problems – an aim supported by the director, who wanted a consultative service for teachers and parents. Cattell's successor, Dr Katherine Bridges, went further in promoting the role of the psychiatrist and did much to publicize the theory and practice of special education as it was then understood. Haddenham School was changed to Manor House School in the post-war era and recognized as a special school for maladjusted children in 1949.

But in Leicester as elsewhere, inter-war ideas about special provision for handicapped children and the nature of special education eventually went out of fashion. In particular, the maladjusted school movement in which Leicester continued to have a prominent part, did not develop in the way its pioneers had expected. Similarly the strength of the conviction of the inter-war authority in the possibilities of classifying children and in the benefits of streaming were to be strongly challenged in the years after 1944.

Towards a Healthier City

Leicester's progressive tag was also connected with the work of the health and housing committees. The growth in the range of activities of the health department and the involvement of the council in building and letting houses were both developments that raised the profile of the council in the city and in certain respects nationally.

On his retirement in 1935 Dr Killick Millard, the medical officer of health since 1901, drew attention to the expansion in the staff of the health department with the addition of assistant medical officers, sanitary inspectors and health visitors. Millard had not welcomed every new accretion of responsibility, but his period of office was informed by a coherent philosophy of health that in common with other leading medical figures at the time, such as C.J. Bond, consultant at the Royal Infirmary and President of the Leicester Medical Society, was underpinned by eugenic ideas about the importance of maintaining the calibre of the racial stock. Millard was in some respects a controversial figure, because of his advocacy in a semi-private capacity of euthanasia and sterilization; and some of the proposals he brought before the health committee were advanced for the time, creating problems in his relationships with councillors. But there can be little doubt that his outlook was a key factor in the crucial early stages of the development of health policy in Leicester.

Dr C. Killick Millard (Leicester's medical officer of health) with his staff, in the 1920s

The high incidence of infant and child death at the beginning of the twentieth century was a key factor in extending the concept of public health to include welfare. While overall mortality rates had fallen gradually from 27.3 per 1,000 in 1875 to 17.8 in 1900, 174 in every 1,000 babies born in the latter year still died before the age of one. Deaths of children under five accounted for 44 per cent of all deaths in the town in 1900, many of them due to epidemic diseases such as diphtheria, measles, scarlet fever and infant diarrhoea. Although other factors were never overlooked, ignorance on the part of mothers, and working-class mothers in particular, was seen as playing a major role in the high incidence of illness and death of town children. Alongside continuing efforts to improve its physical environment, the early years of the twentieth century were thus marked, A.J. Waddington commented in 1930, by 'an active crusade . . . to dispel the ignorance of young mothers as to the proper care of their children, and to assist them in every way to rear healthy children'.

New initiatives were taken before the outbreak of war gave a new impetus to infant welfare work. The appointment of female sanitary inspectors in 1895 and 1906 – or health visitors as such officers came to be known – was the first indication of a new departure in public health policy. Initially appointed to carry out inspections of workshops and other premises employing females, the work of the

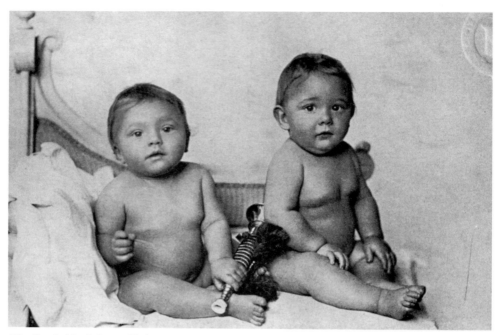

The first babies fed on milk from the Leicester Municipal Milk Depot, 1906

visitors expanded within a short time to include home visits to mothers of new-born infants and sufferers from tuberculosis and their families. The purpose of these was to advise on infant feeding and the prevention of infection. In 1906 the council also opened a Municipal Milk Depot on Belgrave Road. At this time, however, the Council's Sanitary Committee placed much reliance on the activities of the Leicester Health Society, founded in 1906 to organize voluntary effort into the work of improving the health of the town. By 1915 the society employed two full-time health visitors and could also call on the services of twenty volunteer workers, each assigned to specific districts where they visited the homes of new-born infants. Between 1909 and 1915, with some financial aid from the Sanitary Committee in the form of rented premises, the Health Society had opened nine 'Schools for Mothers' offering instruction in childcare and infant welfare clinics. Another quite separate voluntary initiative was the Newton Ward Infant Consultation Centre which, apart from some medical supplies, was also self supporting. Leading by example, middle-class volunteers were often able to tread where public health officials were greeted with suspicion.

In 1917 Dr Millard paid tribute to the co-operative effort of the voluntary sector and the local authority in helping the city's mothers. But at the same time he showed an acute awareness of the factors which limited its effectiveness: of the inequalities of wealth, of access to adequate diet, decent housing, medical care and more besides. As he said: 'Poverty has always been a great enemy of infant life.' The understanding that many married women in Leicester worked from necessity rather than choice led the medical officer to support the continuation of wartime day nursery provision into peacetime, albeit reluctantly, since 'it was an open question whether it might not be better if the money which it costs to subsidize day nurseries were spent in subsidizing mothers to stay at home'. Nevertheless, in 1920, the Council did take over responsibility for two of the three day nurseries that had been provided during the war by the Leicester Day Nursing Society with government financial aid. In the meantime, the Maternity and Child Welfare Act of 1918, eased the financial burden by way of grants covering up to 50 per cent of 'approved' expenditure. Alongside additional health visitors, the Council now appointed Dr Ada Macmillan, former resident medical officer at Groby Road Isolation Hospital, as an assistant medical officer with specific responsibility for maternity and child welfare.

The growth of statutory involvement in this field did not mean the voluntary sector was supplanted. Unpaid volunteers still helped to run the Council's infant welfare centres – the former 'Schools for Mothers' – while a certain number were co-opted to its Maternity and Child Welfare Committee, one of the requirements of the 1918 Act. Among them was Miss E. Windley, daughter of Alderman Thomas Windley JP, chairman of the Sanitary Committee and its successor, the Health Committee, for a total of forty-six years.

Immediately after the First World War efforts were made to improve the quality of ante-natal care and provide additional lying-in accommodation: the number of ante-natal clinics was increased and in 1919 the Council purchased and converted Westcotes Grange for use as a municipal maternity home. This was intended to alleviate a situation where a surge in the birth rate coupled with a severe shortage of housing meant that many pregnant women were found to be living in lodgings or with friends, in conditions unsuited to a home birth.

In the inter-war years, inadequate diet, repeated child bearing or the economic necessity of working late were all factors that increased the risk of complications in pregnancy and childbirth, but very often women most in need of institutional care were least able to afford it. At 2 gns a week for an average stay of two weeks, fees for the Westcotes maternity home were beyond the reach of many working-class families, although they could be reduced in 'necessitous' cases. The rules of the Royal Infirmary excluded maternity cases except in cases of severe complications, and for those unable to afford a private nursing home the only alternatives were the maternity hospital, opened in 1905 by the Provident Dispensary, or the North Evington Infirmary on Gwendolen Road. The former only provided twenty beds and the latter was an institution of the poor law to which there was still much popular resistance, despite commanding buildings that earned it the popular title of 'the palace on the hill'. When the Infirmary passed to the control of the Council, following the local government reorganization Act of 1929, to become the City General, it developed its own maternity service and over 500 babies were born there in 1938. There was now 'no hesitation on the part of all classes of patients, necessitous or otherwise, in seeking admission'.

However, a large proportion of babies continued to be delivered at home, and women unable to afford the fees for a doctor or midwife still relied on the services of a local 'handywoman', whose other speciality was laying out the dead. In the course of implementing the Midwives Act of 1936 health officials identified around seventy such women in the borough, and soon afterwards the Council obtained an order from the Ministry prohibiting the employment of any but qualified women to attend a woman in childbirth 'for gain'. Under the provisions of the same Act a Municipal Midwifery Scheme was introduced in 1937.

The concentration on working-class mothers in the inter-war years was a reflection of the higher incidence of infant mortality rates in the inner working-class municipal wards such as Newton, St Margaret's and Wyggeston. In Leicester a pattern of mortality, highest in the inner areas and declining towards the outer, applied to all deaths in all age groups and remained largely unchanged for many years despite the fall in actual rates of death. Already by 1920 the overall death rate had fallen to 12.1 from 17.8 in 1900, while over the same period the infant mortality rate was virtually halved to 89 per 1,000 live births. Even in Newton Ward the rate fell to 111 per 1,000 between 1918 and 1922, and continued to decline thereafter. But the fact remains that differential rates of infant mortality persisted in Leicester throughout the pre-Second World War period, as Table One shows.

Table One: Contrasts in Infant Mortality in Leicester 1901–36
Ward infant mortality: deaths per 1,000 births

	1912–16	1921	1924	1927	1931	1934	1936
Newton	173	102	124	141	163	49	52
Wyggeston	193	112	139	123	98	69	44
St Margaret's	169	154	122	103	125	36	114
Wycliffe	92	30	73	85	25	113	129
Westcotes	82	59	54	59	42	28	44
Aylestone	91	95	70	92	70	79	47
Knighton	59	53	60	51	21	10	27
City Average	115	86	79	75	64	53	58

Council activity in health and welfare was carried forward into new areas by the founding of clinics. Behind this movement, and the associated practice of home visiting, lay the need as perceived by health officials to identify and change the behaviour of families most vulnerable to ill health. But the attentions of school nurses at the regular headlice inspections, and of home visitors attached to school clinics, were sometimes resented by families who saw themselves picked on rather than helped. This was particularly the case in the early days of the School Medical Service, which had been introduced voluntarily in Leicester three years before national legislation. Initially the service was confined to the medical inspection of school children, and was 'said to be largely ineffective and useless, because, after defects were discovered no provision was made for remedying them'.

The most common problems detected were defects of sight and hearing, skin conditions, and tooth decay – the latter, it was said in 1921, so common 'that people are apt to accept it as a natural and necessary evil'. Private remedies for such problems cost money that many working-class families could ill afford, and so over a period of time the School Medical Service developed an alternative network of central clinics providing treatment. By 1940, in addition to the usual dental, opthalmic, ENT and skin clinics, these included an orthopaedic clinic, and an artificial sunlight clinic for children suffering from anaemia or debility; and if the long-suffering ratepayers had to subsidize these along with much else, then in the view of Dr Warner, the school medical officer, it was 'money well spent. . . . Wise expenditure . . . in improving the health of the rising generation is true economy.'

In so far as illness and premature death, particularly of the family breadwinner, were in themselves major causes of poverty, then prevention could be argued for in more general terms as 'good economy', and in the absence of any certain medical cures for many epidemic diseases, the only practicable course. When it came to dealing with epidemics the range of options was limited. In regard to smallpox, for example, the exceptionally strong feeling against compulsory vaccination that developed in Leicester in the later nineteenth century ensured that only a small minority of infants born in the town were ever vaccinated. In the event Leicester does not seem to have suffered any more severely during smallpox epidemics than other towns with high levels of vaccination, and much of the credit for this was given to the alternative 'Leicester Method', which a former MOH had devised. This involved strict isolation of sufferers, the thorough cleansing of homes and the quarantine of contacts.

In fact, serious as it could be, fewer people died from smallpox than from other epidemic diseases. Although quite exceptional, the influenza epidemic of 1918 claimed over 1,000 lives and around 500 more deaths occurred in the following spring. In 1924 429 cases of diphtheria were recorded, 34 of them fatal; in 1938, 701 cases with 33 fatalities. As late as 1945–6 an outbreak of diarrhoea was still capable of raising the infant mortality rate. Beyond isolating victims to prevent further infection, medicine could do little either to prevent or cure such diseases. Much depended on the general health of the sufferer, which was influenced in turn by such factors as income, diet and housing.

However, successive medical officers argued that the public should do more to help itself with regard to avoidable illness. What Millard called the excessive consumption of alcohol was a case in point, a matter on which he had a particular interest as a member of the Leicester Temperance Society and advocate of the legal prohibition adopted in the United States after the First World War. In the absence of such a measure in Britain, Millard and his successors had to rely largely on efforts to educate and persuade.

This was not the only moral issue: in 1930 the two contentious subjects of birth control and the prevention of venereal diseases were introduced into the annual reports. On the provision of birth control advice Millard believed that moral sensibilities were impeding a service that in his view held the real key to improvements in the quality of infant life. The 'conspiracy of silence' as he put it on the part of the middle class about birth control had to be overcome. His advocacy resulted in the setting up of a birth control clinic in the city, although the MOH was dissatisfied with the way the Ministry restricted the giving of advice to married women who had attended the maternity and ante-natal clinics.

There were moral dilemmas too over what role the health department should play in combating VD, given the prevalent belief that in a great majority of cases this was transmitted 'through the promiscuous or illicit relationship of the sexes'. But Millard's belief that the provision of medical information should take precedence over moral concerns led to a programme of public and workshop lectures on venereal disease, although every lecture 'should include the true statement that the ideal preventative against venereal disease is complete loyalty between husband and wife'. However, as Dr C. Hamilton Wilkie, the doctor appointed to take charge of this work noted, the success of any scheme of VD education would ultimately depend on a guarantee of treatment that was not only effective but confidential, a service provided in Leicester by arrangement with the Royal Infirmary.

The importance of 'prompt recognition' had also been accepted at an early date in relation to other diseases such as cancer. Thus in the 1920s representatives of the Council, Poor Law Board, Royal Infirmary and medical practitioners joined forces to form the Leicester Cancer Committee. Primarily an advisory body it also opened a Cancer Control Clinic to aid the early diagnosis of cancers of the breast and uterus, the most common forms of the disease among women. One of the first such clinics in the country, it was run in co-operation with the Infirmary, and offered free examinations.

The proportion of deaths caused by cancer in the earlier twentieth century was, however, relatively low by comparison with those due to tuberculosis: 158 per 100,000 population in 1910 for example for all forms of TB, and 124 for pulmonary TB alone. Many more suffered for years from the physical suffering and economic hardship which this disease brought. Pulmonary TB was especially common in Leicester among male shoemakers and female hosiery workers. Particular groups of shoeworkers suffered higher rates of infection than others: finishers, for example, who commonly inhaled dust produced by buffing and scouring processes; and clickers, who often suffered from 'bootmakers' chest, a deformity of the rib cage caused by long hours bent over a cutting board, and compounded by a 'thorough hatred of open windows'. Clicking presses went some way to prevent the former, while in the view of the MOH as early as 1907, the whole town would benefit from more active 'ventilation sentiment'. Indeed the Sanitary Committee issued a poster urging the people of the city to 'refuse to work in a close, stuffy or polluted atmosphere'.

The National Insurance Act of 1911 went some way to ease the financial burden on TB sufferers and the Council also provided medical treatment with the aid of a government grant. This included a Dispensary, opened in 1911, with institutional care for TB sufferers provided mainly at the Isolation Hospital in Groby Road, although only those thought to have a reasonable chance of recovery were normally admitted. The Education Committee provided an open air school at Western Park and in 1929 the Health Committee took over a convalescent sanatorium, which had been financed from public subscriptions. But until the development of effective drugs after the Second World War, full recovery depended mainly upon the patient's own determination, and ability to live, for some years at least, a greatly restricted life. Nevertheless both the incidence of infection and mortality did decline over the years: by 1935 the death rate from all forms of the disease had fallen to 98 per 100,000 population and to 91 in the case of pulmonary TB. Social and environmental factors were at least as important as medicine in this decline. According to the Tuberculosis Medical Officer in 1936 : 'Good homes in healthy areas, where there is ample fresh air and sunlight' was 'the most important step yet taken in preventing the spread of disease' – a view supported by the average TB death rate in that year of 7.8 per cent on the municipal estates, and a recovery rate of 29 per cent, against figures of 12.7 per cent and 15.6 per cent respectively for the city as a whole.

Nevertheless medical and institutional provision by the Council was an increasingly important aspect of its contribution to the health of the city, including the mental health of its inhabitants. In the latter respect the main responsibility was the borough asylum, extended in 1901, and again in the 1930s, and renamed the City Mental Hospital, subsequently The Towers. In the early 1930s it catered for around a thousand patients, roughly a third of them residents of Derby admitted under a special arrangement. After 1930 new legislation made it possible for patients to be admitted on a voluntary or temporary basis 'thus evading the "stigma" of certification', and contributing to the liberalizing of the regime. The Council also had responsibility from 1914 for the care of the 'mentally deficient', which it discharged initially by taking over a small charitable home founded by Annie Clephan and acquiring new premises for a girls' home. This was followed in the early 1920s by a major development at Leicester Frith. The Committee's work however went well beyond institutional provision. Many of those with mental handicaps were able to live in their own homes with the aid of financial grants, while in 1929 an Occupation Centre was opened to train some twenty to thirty adults in 'good habits as well as the simpler forms of manual work', thereby 'obviating the necessity of adopting the costly course of institutional care'.

The main responsibility in hospital provision centred on the City General, the ex-poor law infirmary taken over in 1930. This had been built in 1905 at a cost of almost £80,000 and in the nine months from the April in the year of transfer it treated a total of 1,772 in-patients. Although the stigma of the poor law was lost, some of the old restrictions survived. The elderly can well remember the high spiked railings surrounding the hospital grounds, guarded at each end of a long drive by locked gates, where local people waited for a ticket to visit followed by an unseemly dash up the drive, so as to preserve as much of the short visiting period as possible.

Other institutions acquired after local government reorganization in 1929 included the workhouse – which never did lose its stigma but functioned eventually as a geriatric hospital (Hillcrest) – and the cottage homes for poor children at Countesthorpe consisting of schools, infirmary and workshops as well as living accommodation. The latter was supplemented eventually by the provision of 'scattered homes' in various parts of the city as ideas changed about the value of isolating poor children.

But hospital provision, as with other aspects of health and welfare work remained heavily dependent on charitable and voluntary bodies in this period. The Leicester Royal Infirmary was one such example, entirely supported by donations and subscriptions, the former mainly from local companies and societies, with subscriptions raised through the Hospital Saturday Society founded in 1903. All those who contributed in this way were eligible for admission: except for emergencies patients were only admitted on the ticket of a subscriber. The Hospital Saturday Society was a chief source of regular income, which rose to £80,000 in 1939. Much of this was used to finance convalescent homes in Leicestershire and beyond. On a smaller scale, hospital facilities were also provided by the John Faire Hospital, opened by the Leicester Provident Dispensary in the early twentieth century. The Dispensary itself was managed after 1911 by a panel of local doctors.

The queue for polio vaccination

Operating as the Leicester Public Medical Service, with doctors paid on a per capita basis, and fifty lay employees, it was a unique venture that attracted national attention.

Public charity and private philanthropy were always a major source of support in other areas of health and welfare too. The Charity Organization Society continued to support what they regarded as deserving families, supplemented by the activities of the Children's Aid Society. But there were also organizations that made provision for people with various handicaps, notably the Wycliffe Society for the Blind, the Leicester Guild of the Crippled and the Leicester and County Mission to the Deaf and Dumb. On the other hand, as this section has shown, there had undoubtedly been a marked growth in local council provision for health care. By 1939 this included provision of maternal and child welfare services, school medical services; school meals and milk; dentistry; TB programmes; services for infectious diseases, VD and ENT conditions; birth control advice; cancer schemes; and municipal hospitals, clinics and occupational centres. With the exception of the School Medical Service, all these were the responsibility of the public health department and added considerably to the work of a department that had been mainly concerned with sanitation and food adulteration. From the point of view of the local authority the inter-war years might be described as the golden age of public health.

Municipal Housing and the Attack on the Slums

One of the environmental concerns of the Health Committee was the condition of the older working-class streets of houses close to the centre of town, most of them erected before the introduction of building bylaws in 1859. In these poor districts where courtyards of houses co-existed with slaughter-houses, factories and warehouses, health problems were particularly acute. In one such area, a district now occupied by St Margaret's bus station, surveyed by the medical officer in 1929, the committee was told of the lack of washing and toilet facilities, with outside toilets usually shared between several families. There were no storage facilities for food and a lack of dustbins, which meant that meagre yards were often scattered with rubbish. In these damp, insanitary and dilapidated houses population density was ten times the average for the city. The incidence of TB, smallpox and scarlet fever was higher, while the infant mortality rate, a sensitive indicator of environmental conditions, was nearly double the city average.

During the 1920s the Health Committee was critical of the Housing Committee for concentrating on the building of council houses for better-off families. They made repeated recommendations on this subject making reference to health visitors' reports and the incidence of tubercular cases among the poor. But in the immediate post-war period the priority of national and local government was to deal with the housing shortage that had arisen rather than the condition of existing property.

The Council made a vigorous start on a housebuilding programme by erecting 1,384 houses with the help of the subsidies provided under the Housing Acts of

1919 and 1923. A further 103 houses were built under the houses for sale scheme. Yet there were still over 3,000 applicants outstanding. The housing emergency lay behind the decision of the Council to develop a more ambitious programme of council housing under the terms of the Wheatley Act of 1924, which gave the local authority greater autonomy over design and finance. This was when the decision was made to concentrate development on green field sites at Saffron Lane and Braunstone as these were likely to be more economical and give better control than *ad hoc* developments within the city where space was limited. It was also intended to bring the 1,200 acres of land purchased from Major Winstanley into the city's town planning scheme by the construction of a ring road through the site. Councillors were inspired by the idea of making this purchase in order to form a working-class estate on garden suburb lines. The development at South Braunstone was to be locally designed as a showpiece estate with tenants carefully selected for the houses. These were provided with up-to-date amenities and large gardens, and provision was made for playing fields and other recreational areas.

The Council also sought to meet local cultural aspirations for parlour-type houses but financial necessity dictated the building of some non-parlour-type houses, and because of the shortage of building materials the Council experimented with building 1,000 concrete houses on the Boot pier and panel system. They resisted, nevertheless, the urging of the Ministry of Health and their own Health Committee to build smaller and cheaper houses. The view of the Housing Committee seems to have been that the provision of council housing for the better off would eventually benefit the poor through a process of filtering up into vacant accommodation. But the impact of the council house building programme was blunted by the increase in the number of households in the city during the 1920s.

In 1932 Dr Millard was forced to conclude that Leicester was little better off regarding the rate of houses to families than at the end of the war. Two years earlier he had urged the full use of the Greenwood Housing Act of 1930 for the relief of overcrowding. This Act reflected a developing concern at national and local level about the slum problem, a concern that was as much affected by moral as health considerations. In Leicester concern was not only articulated by members of the health committee and the professionals. The formation in November 1929 of the Leicester Voluntary Housing Association on the initiative of Canon Linwood Wright brought a valuable housing pressure group into being. Canon Wright's parish of St Marks included some of the worst housing conditions, and it was his opinion that since the state and local authorities seemed incapable of clearing the slums, then help should be sought from the voluntary sector. However, by the early 1930s there was a consensus of opinion among those prominent in civic life that the Council should deal with the slums, although there were differences of approach on how best to do it.

One source of dissension was the divergence of views as between the Health Committee and its chief medical officer. Dr Millard believed strongly that 'housing needs rather than ability to pay' ought to be the chief criterion in deciding who

Sir Jonathan North opening the Martin Street playing fields, 1927

should be allocated municipal houses; but he was not in favour of large-scale slum clearance. One reason for this was his belief that Leicester did not really have any 'plague spots' similar to those in other industrial cities. He also believed it was better to keep the old in the environment to which they were accustomed if it could be improved by repairs. The priority for rehousing in his view should be families with children: 'Let our slogan be "Save the children from the slums!" to which we may add, "Keep the old houses for the old people".' The Health Committee did not accept his arguments for improvement areas, and relations deteriorated when the chief sanitary officer was invited to submit clearance proposals.

In fact the Health Committee had already been active in seeking to restart a slum clearance programme under the Leicester Corporation Act of 1928. While this scheme had to be shelved because of inadequate powers and the opposition it created, the Committee was in a position to push through a proposal for clearance under the provisions of the Housing Act of 1930. The Green Street–Sandacre Street scheme gained Ministerial approval in 1932. By anticipating new legislation Leicester had managed to start work on slum clearance before most other authorities. However, the proposals for ambitious five-year programmes of clearances under the powers of the Housing Acts of 1930 and 1933 ran into more difficulties and created much opposition. The proposals of 1933 were rejected by the Council and the political deadlock that ensued was broken only by the acceptance of a compromise solution, which reduced the extent of clearance in favour of improvement areas. A move by Councillor Harrison to recoup investment on the Braunstone estate by selling out to private builders was defeated, but the compromise solution caused dissension in the ranks of the Labour group, and area clearance became a major issue in the local elections.

Another reason for the slowing down in the rate of progress was the failure of the council to appoint extra sanitary inspectors to cope with the new work. Account has also to be taken of the obstructive manoeuvres of the Leicester Property Owners and Ratepayers Association over the terms of compensation in particular areas. In addition, the County Court played a part in frustrating slum clearance by dealing sympathetically with appeals against demolition orders.

Although property owners were partially successful in getting all the local Tory and some of the Liberal councillors to curb the extent of the council's slum clearance programme in the early 1930s, from 1934 the pace of clearance and rehousing began to gather a fresh momentum. By this time lower building costs and a fall in the rate of interest made the financing of rehousing schemes much easier. Moreover, the Council was forced to redesignate improvement areas as clearance areas after the Housing Act of 1935. This Act also enabled the Council to pool rents charged under the different Housing Acts. In 1930 a differential rent scheme had been adopted, which scaled rents according to the level of income and number of persons in a household. Under the 1935 Act it was possible to use surplus income from existing tenants to subsidize the lower rents of the re-housing schemes. By the end of 1939 a total of 110 clearance areas had been designated, affecting 12,477 people. In Leicester 3,159 houses had been demolished, which was close to the Health Committee's preferred target. The total of houses erected by the Housing Committee in the period 1921–39 at 9,107 was over 50 per cent of the output of the private sector in the same period (16,642).

The impact of municipal housing on the quality of life of working-class people in the inter-war years has been much discussed by historians. It seems clear from the Leicester experience that there were losses as well as gains. On the plus side, as we have already noted, the medical officer was able to argue in the later 1930s that they had contributed to improvements in the health of the city, particularly the incidence of TB. There can be no doubt too that many families enjoyed the better amenities of the council houses. In a booklet on the inter-war council estates recently published by the Leicester Corporation, oral testimonies are provided from present-day older inhabitants of the excitement and anticipation that they experienced in moving out to what must have seemed a 'new Jerusalem'.

On the other hand even the best of the new estates lacked shopping and social facilities and although tenants' associations were formed it was not until 1938 that a first mention is made of the building of premises for community centres. Apart from these drawbacks, the cessation of general needs housebuilding after 1930 and the imposition of economies on local authorities meant that the council houses under

*Barnett Janner MP inspects slum housing
conditions*

the 1930 Act were of a lower standard of construction and amenity, which was to create problems later as they aged. The policy of moving slum cleared tenants *en bloc* to designated estates had the advantage of replicating many community ties, but the concentration of these tenants in particular estates created social problems and exacerbated social divisions within the working-class community in Leicester. The obvious example of this was the social as well as the physical separation of South and North Braunstone. The latter never seems to have overcome the stigma of being developed for slum-cleared tenants in the 1930s and this district came to be designated by social workers and teachers in the post-1945 years as a 'difficult estate'.

The Post-1945 Years

In the immediate post-war years there were many continuities with the pre-war period in respect of personnel. Until the mid-1960s Council business was generally conducted in an atmosphere of political moderation. Thereafter the old consensus arrangements began to break down and the Council became more politicized. One reason for this was that issues such as housing policy and educational reorganization themselves became more politically controversial at a national level. Then there were the challenges and distinctive problems of the immigration issue. The escalating scale of capital expenditure was also a factor, particularly in the 1960s when total expenditure ran at an all-time high and rates had increased to 27*s* in the pound before the new valuations in 1963. At the same time the scope for local autonomy began to be eroded as central government increasingly sought to impose financial restraints on local authorities.

The post-war years also saw the scale and complexity of municipal administration increase, and witnessed a growth in the number of officials required to operate services. This brought up questions about the cost and efficiency of local government. It also raised questions about the relationships between professional workers – rent officers and welfare workers, for example – and the public. The more extensive involvement of the council in the planning process from the 1960s raised other questions about the extent to which local communities were participating in decisions that drastically affected them. In the second half of the twentieth century it was not only the expenditure but the organization of local government services which came to be seen as problematic leading to local powers being circumscribed. In Leicester a sudden change was made by the reorganization of city and county government in 1974 following the recommendations of the Maude Commission. In some respects this year marked the end of an era as some of the city's responsibilities for major services, such as education, were taken over by a reconstituted county authority. Nevertheless, the reorganization still left Leicester as the largest non-metropolitan authority in the country.

The Move to Comprehensive Education

Perhaps one of the most contentious of all the issues with which the Council had to deal was the move to comprehensive education. To describe how this was achieved provides a case study of the pressures and constraints affecting municipal policy in the post-war period. It also illustrates how the old set-up inhibited change and put Leicester behind other cities with regard to the timing of secondary reorganization. The contrast with the experience of the Conservative-controlled County of Leicestershire, where the Director of Education had initiated an experiment in comprehensive education as early as 1956, was quite striking.

One reason for the reluctance of the Council to drastically change the organization of secondary education was that the Education Committee in the 1950s was composed of long-serving members of both parties, who regarded themselves as architects of a flexible system that gave plenty of opportunities for young people to better themselves. The moderates who led the Labour group were closely identified with this system, which had evolved from the school reorganization of the 1920s. To some extent they also had faith in the selection process that had been placed in the hands of the teachers with the formation of a General Examination Council and was further modified in the 1960s, culminating in the abolition of the selection examination altogether. The leading Labour spokesman for education, Councillor Charles Keene, chairman of the Education Committee from 1953, opted for developing greater flexibility in the system as regards transfer rather than outright change.

As in other cities the development of new council housing estates provided an opportunity for a limited experiment in comprehensive education, but proposals in the early 1960s to set up a comprehensive school on the New Parks campus site was defeated by local opposition and another proposal to turn the new Beaumont Leys school into a ten form entry comprehensive was turned down by the minister as unrealistic. Otherwise the changes made in this period to 1965 and beyond were mainly aimed at strengthening the secondary modern schools. The Director of Education Dr Elfred Thomas, writing in the *Municipal Journal* just before these developments, admitted that at the secondary stage there was no doubt that the appropriate organization of education posed a problem that had yet to be satisfactorily solved. Leicester, he pointed out, 'was not wedded to any single solution'. Dr Thomas was convinced that Leicester parents had no great enthusiasm for comprehensive schools, and that the best way ahead was through the expansion of O-level teaching in the secondary modern schools. To facilitate this development the intermediate schools lost their status as selective schools and resources were put into building and amalgamating secondary modern schools to create four form entry schools throughout the city.

The beginnings of the move to comprehensive education dates from the early 1960s when the political mood began to change, with the Labour Party in Leicester following the national lead and announcing their intention of pressing for a full comprehensive system. This seems to have reflected grass roots pressure. In addition, the apparent success of the experiment in comprehensive education in the county was affecting the perceptions of Leicester parents. The supporters of comprehensive schooling pointed to the considerable out-migration of city residents attracted by the county school system. This aspect of the matter came to a head in relation to the projected extension of the city boundary when coachloads of parents with children in county schools turned up at a public meeting at the De Montfort Hall to protest. In 1969 the boundary issue flared up again when Hamilton School in the county area was moved back to the City and de-comprehensivized. This was the immediate background to the formation in 1970 of the Leicester Group for Comprehensive Education, a small group of mainly Liberal activists affiliated to the Campaign for Comprehensive Education, who set out to persuade the city to become comprehensive by adopting the county system.

Such pressures were bound to affect the attitudes of the old guard of Labour councillors. The private papers of Sir Charles Keene show how this long-standing chairman of the education committee was pushed into a half-hearted conversion to abolishing the selective system. In 1964 the Education Committee anticipated circular 10/65 requesting all local authorities to submit schemes by inviting the director to report on how the abolition of eleven-plus selection could best be achieved. The report merely reviewed the advantages and drawbacks of various options. Hence the setting up of a working party chaired by Professor Tibble of the Leicester University School of Education to include councillors and teacher representatives to work out a scheme best suited to city needs and resources. It was this working party that recommended a two tier system differing in major respects from the county model and involving the idea of common schools to the age of sixteen, but with separate routes thereafter, making use of Further Education Colleges with new sixth form colleges for the more academic group.

The working party on comprehensive reorganization was in being for eight years, made two revisions to the original scheme and produced thirty-five reports. In other cities besides Leicester plans for secondary reorganization were a cause of much local controversy and this was especially acute when councils attempted to push schemes through without much consultation. That charge cannot be levied at Leicester, where the director went to great lengths in the early years of the plan to hold meetings with governors and parents. On the other hand there can be no doubt that the city had a strong preservationist tradition that was sustained by a small group of prestigious figures, led by Sir Mark Hennig, many of them ex-grammar school pupils who had a natural resistance to tampering with the educational system. Leicester had very little private schooling and no direct grant grammar schools, so its élite were dependent on the municipal grammar schools, and particularly the Wyggeston schools, which were seen as important in the city's history. This helps to explain the strength of feeling in the city and why the idea of turning the leading schools into sixth form colleges (rather than a uniform scheme of all through comprehensives) was eventually thought to be the only answer.

There were several reasons why comprehensive reorganization took so long to achieve in Leicester. One was the changing political complexion of the council in the late 1960s with the return of the Conservative party to local control. Leading conservatives supported groups defending the grammar schools and criticized the neighbourhood basis of the proposed reorganization in a city with a large number of council housing estates. Under pressure from the national Labour administration the Conservative dominated council reluctantly agreed to a reorganization scheme in 1969, but back-pedalled as soon as the Conservatives came back into power at the national level. It was the prospect of the council's educational powers passing to the county with the impending reorganization scheme that precipitated the bringing forward of new schemes only to have them frustrated by central government. Both a Conservative-backed scheme for an area by area reorganization in 1971 and a Labour-backed scheme for what the *Leicester Mercury* described as 'instant comprehensives' in 1973 failed to secure the approval of the Conservative Secretary of State.

Leicester was unique in the way that the comprehensive issue came to be caught up in city–county tensions. This was because the reorganization of local government left the way open for county spokesmen on the new Education Committee, and the new Director of Education, to take the initiative of putting the county scheme on to the city agenda. The procedure adopted by the Director, Andrew Fairburn, involved the appointment of a chief officers management team to review all the options suggested over the years including alternative six (the original city two tier scheme as amended subsequently) and a new alternative seven (the county two tier scheme). In effect the choice came down to the last two alternatives, and it was around these that council and local opinion polarized. Alternative seven was strongly opposed by a reconstituted Labour Group, critical of what they called county thinking, as well as by representatives of city teachers antagonistic towards the county system.

Against a background of hostile teacher activity and emergency council meetings in 1974 a reconstituted *ad hoc* committee was formed to cost and report on both alternatives six and seven in an attempt to resolve what was being increasingly perceived as an intolerable saga. Although the committee was divided its main report seemed to favour the city scheme, notwithstanding a note of dissent from the Director; and with local opinion hardening, the Council adopted a revised version of alternative six on 3 November 1975. Much was made of the importance of ending the uncertainty about Leicester schooling and recovering the morale of its teachers. The scheme as implemented was based on eleven to sixteen comprehensive schools plus three sixth form colleges and two mixed eleven to eighteen schools, with a promise of a third at Beaumont Leys. But while the city scheme had won the day, the new school system was to incorporate ideas of community education which had been pioneered in the county. Indeed, once the issue of comprehensivization had been settled the process of reorganization went through remarkably quickly and smoothly, enabling the school system to cope with the new educational challenges of the later 1970s and the problems associated with the need to absorb increasing numbers of immigrant children.

Parents protest against cuts in education spending in 1980

New Problems and Challenges in Health and Welfare Provision

In 1938, with the death rate at its lowest on record and the infant mortality rate at a level 'unbelievable twenty years ago', the MOH insisted that 'an industrial town need not, and should not, be a death trap', provided there was no relaxing of efforts by the council. Over the inter-war years, as we have seen, the concept of public health had been considerably extended with the growth of health care services based on clinics, which complemented the medical responsibilities acquired through the school medical service and municipal hospitals. This was accompanied by a shift in thinking about preventative care among public health practitioners towards increased emphasis on the education and surveillance of individuals and families, with a view to changing individual lifestyles and improving personal hygiene: 'teaching the people the way of health', as the long serving Medical Officer, Dr E.J. MacDonald, put it in appointing a Health Education Officer in 1945.

In the post-war years, however, the role of prevention and the standing and influence of the local authority health department became more problematical. By the 1950s preventive medicine was being eclipsed by hospital-based curative medicine. Health care policies, incorporated into the social policies of an expanding welfare state, were determined at national rather than local level. How then did the city's health and welfare services respond to changes in national policy and the emergence of new needs?

The National Health Service Act of 1946 created a tripartite structure of health care in Britain. The immediate impact of this on the local authority was the transfer of the municipal hospitals – the City General, the Isolation Hospital and Westcotes – to the Sheffield Regional Health Board. The NHS was not, as many pre-war MOHs had confidently expected, established around local government services, and the separation between prevention and cure left the public health departments with a fragmented collection of services. Nevertheless Dr MacDonald, a quietly determined officer, was optimistic for the future and sought to develop a coherent remit for preventive health activities under the auspices of Section 28 of the 1946 Act, which referred to the possibility of developing welfare services around the prevention of illness, support for those suffering from illness and after care services. In the event no policy for integrated services of this kind was developed nationally and in the absence of a long term strategy the services grew piecemeal. There were also problems of co-ordination with the hospital and general practitioner services.

Another aspect of MacDonald's vision in 1947 was the importance of continuing to provide scope for partnership and co-operation with the voluntary sector. The voluntary worker he saw as providing a 'a friendly, humane and personal touch that would otherwise be lacking'. But the overall trend after 1946 was for health and welfare services to become increasingly taken over by professionals as responsibilities and workloads increased.

Before the Act the health department's role in the prevention and detection of disease had been enhanced by the introduction of immunization for diphtheria in

1942 and the start of the mass radiography service in 1945. But the emphasis of post-war expansion was once more on better provision of clinics and other services for mothers and young children. Proposals were advanced for an increase in the number of ante-natal clinics, some in the city centre, others in outlying areas, a scheme for eight post-natal clinics, additional infant welfare centres, and day nurseries, and an expansion in the number of domiciliary midwives. Joint or branch clinics had been opened just before the war and these were to be extended and eventually transformed into health centres. Other developments in health care included the home help service, started in 1946 and to be mainly employed at first in cases of confinement. Health visiting continued although there were always staffing shortages and health visitors acquired additional responsibilities, for example the giving of talks on mothercraft to senior schoolgirls. Pre-war responsibilities for district nursing were continued by the District Nursing Association as the Council's agent, and an expansion of the Council's ambulance service was envisaged with provision for a new ambulance station at a site on the Welford Road. Health propaganda became a formal responsibility with the cartoon figure of Dr Fosse as its 'symbol and mouthpiece'.

In 1948 the Council also acquired entirely new welfare responsibilities, notably the domiciliary mental health service, a new service under the National Health

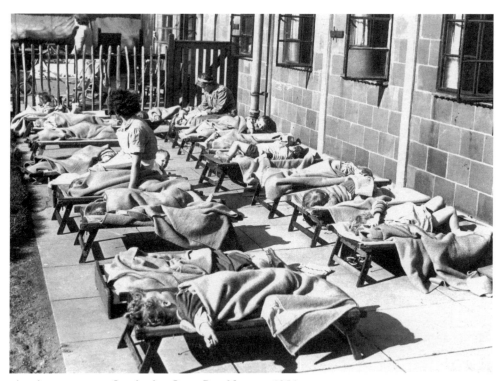

An afternoon nap at Sparkenhoe Street Day Nursery, 1951

Service Act, and responsibility under the Children Act of 1948 for the care of children 'deprived of a normal home life'. This last responsibility entailed the formation of a new Children Department and appointment of a children officer. The department not only took over responsibilities previously shared between the Public Assistance Committee and Health and Education departments, but also acquired new responsibilities for delinquency and its aftercare.

During the post-war years the school medical service continued to function as a Council responsibility and here there was not merely growth but increasing specialization of services. In Leicester provision was made for a new partial hearing unit, a new ESN school (High Leas) and a range of new clinics: an Eneuresis clinic (Richmond House), a Minor Ailment clinic, Audiology clinic, and overweight (nutrition) clinic to mention some of them. By the early 1960s, however, pressures were developing on the routine work of the service. The speech therapy department was under pressure, for example, from the closure of clinics, and experiments were made in selective medical examinations in order to release resources for giving more priority to handicapped children.

In contrast to the growth of medical intervention in children's lives, Leicester was a pioneer of home and community based treatment of disease with innovations during the 1950s in the treatment of diabetes. By taking patients out of the hospital context, this initiative to some degree 'demedicalized' diabetes, making it a condition manageable within the everyday lives of patients. Diabetes clinics started in Leicester in the inter-war years, but this work was much further developed by Joan Walker, a consultant physician at the Leicester Royal Infirmary who conducted major surveys of the incidence of the disease and developed methods of home treatment, including in 1952, the first diabetic health visitor service.

By this time the pattern of disease generally in the city was beginning to change as the reports of the MOH in the 1960s emphasized. In 1965 the senior medical officer, B.J.L. Moss, remarked on how improvements in environmental conditions and advances in medical treatment, particularly the use of antibiotics, had reduced the incidence of infectious diseases. Some of these were being replaced by the 'new diseases of an affluent society'– road traffic accidents, heart disease and cancer of the lung. But what most concerned him was the increasing preponderance of the elderly in the population, which was putting pressures on hospital accommodation and creating new problems for the local authority. He made a special plea for better heating and a rapid expansion of the meals on wheels service currently provided by the WVS.

The health report of 1971 was especially informative on the health problems of the city and the problems confronting the local authority. Over the period from 1963 both the overall death rate and the infant mortality rate were persistently higher than in England and Wales generally. The report speculated on the effects of immigration on this and the concentration of immigrant practices in areas in which general conditions of housing were poor, attracting large numbers of patients at risk. Fluctuations in the levels of infant mortality were also associated with the absorption

Leicester's meals on wheels service was staffed by 200 members of the Women's Voluntary Service

of new immigrants. This anticipated the way that in more recent years the infantile mortality rates among the Asian population attracted attention as research revealed raised perinatal mortality and a poorer quality of obstetric advice in this population. Subsequent research also identified an excess of coronary heart disease among male migrants from the Indian subcontinent.

The 1971 report showed also a new concern about environmental issues – the hazards being created on new estates, for example and asked: 'are present-day developments the slums of the future?' It stressed the importance of combating pollution and the role of public health inspectors in the smoke control areas programme. Attention was paid to health education and how teaching and advice was directed to school children, expectant mothers and those who attended the new cytology clinics. Wider campaigns on such issues as smoking and the misuse of drugs were also underway. But the major theme was the need for 'urgent and radical rethinking' because of growing pressure on the community health services.

The rethinking taking place, however, involved the setting up in 1972 of a new Department of Social Services in order to bring together the existing services of the Children and Welfare Departments and the social service elements of the Health Department. The aim was to better use the specialist skills of social work staff trained as child-care officers, welfare and rental welfare officers, while 'endeavouring to use resources generically as a comprehensive field force'. The new directors' strategy, however, had to take account both of the findings of an internal management review and the demands of new legislation for children, the disabled and the elderly that was imposing extra responsibilities and straining resources. The theme of this strategy, as applied to the elderly for example, was to move away from the 'emergency help' represented by residential care 'to encourage self help, family support and neighbourhood and community help'. To this end the director proposed a community plan with Age Concern Leicester as a key element. The emphasis on family and community support was also evident in the argument for community care for the mentally handicapped rather than segregation in separate establishments and, in the field of delinquency, the idea of making Desford Boys Home part of a community homes plan. It was also thought necessary to penetrate into the community more by means of Family Advice Centres, and schemes involving parents and teachers in neighbourhood plans.

The Health Department itself – to be absorbed in 1974 into the new Area Health Authority – was also affected by new thinking as the concept of community health emerged to redefine the role of public health specialists, and an attempt was made to integrate public health into the NHS through a community physician. It was not until the later 1980s that a new stress on prevention and health at the national level led to a renewed emphasis on the public health responsibilities of the Health Authority and the appointment of a Director of Public Health.

Housing Policy, Social Deprivation and the Housing Crisis

In the post-war period the subject that more than any other dominated the routine business of the Council as well as raising difficult policy issues was municipal housing provision and projects of slum clearance. It seems ironic, therefore, that despite all the effort put into the housing programme over the years, commentators in the 1980s were talking again of a housing crisis. This seems less an indication of lack of energy on the part of the Council, which vigorously pursued its housing policies, as of financial restraints and the distinctive problems of the city.

The history of municipal housing provision in the post-war years is of recurrent drives to catch up with housing demand and reduce waiting lists. One such drive was instituted immediately after the end of the Second World War. Imbued with a new spirit of optimism and reconstruction, the Council accepted the estimate of its Housing Committee that 10,000 houses would be needed straight away, and that 56,000 houses would be needed over the next thirty to forty years if the aim of demolishing all pre-1904 houses by 1976 was carried through. As in the period after the First World War, however, meeting the housing shortage took priority and it was not until 1953 that slum clearance was renewed in earnest. From then on tensions existed between the provision of new housing, the rehousing of slum cleared tenants, and the improvement of older housing areas.

The major post-war development was the New Parks estate intended to be completed within three years. The Housing Committee was also worried about the geographical distribution of the working-class population around the city, since the bulk of municipal housing at that time lay to the west and south, while there were large and expanding industrial areas to the north and east. Hence the move to acquire and develop land on the Stocking Farm Estate and Scraptoft Valley. Post-war progress was hindered by shortages of labour and materials, and delays in the acquisition and preparation of sites. In consequence only 3,918 houses had been erected by 1951, short of the target, and these included 600 factory assembly (Easiform) houses and 500 steel-framed houses. By that date the waiting list stood at 14,012 people who wanted to move into council houses.

The building programme accelerated in the 1950s and by 1955 it was possible to claim that more dwellings had been erected since 1945 than in the twenty years from 1920–40. The main demand was for three-bedroomed family houses, but the Housing Committee became increasingly concerned about the unbalanced nature of the estates, and began to provide flats (the first group of these at Aikman Avenue) and bungalows for older tenants. They were more conscious than in pre-war years of the need to provide facilities, and approval was given for the construction of shopping parades and precincts, churches, public houses, schools and community centres. They also employed a team of welfare officers.

With the reinstatement of slum clearance, the tempo of rehousing accelerated, with provision for 1,400 families whose houses had been demolished as unfit. By the late 1950s the number of houses let by the Council had increased fivefold on the 1946–51 figure at an expenditure of over £10 million. In 1957 the financial implications of this programme were such that the Council decided, on the recommendation of the Housing Committee, to end building for general needs and limit the future building programme to 600 houses per annum for slum clearance reinstatement purposes. Once again the housing programme had run up against the barrier of financial restraint.

There was also a shift in priorities with the beginnings of the reconstruction of inner-city areas rather than wholesale relocation to suburban neighbourhoods. The new phase had been anticipated as early as 1957 when the Housing Committee drew attention to the extensive demolitions then going on in the city. The rebuilding of the St Matthew's area had now started. This commitment to demolition and reconstruction was to bring rapidly new social problems in these inner-city districts, which were rarely anticipated at the time.

The clearance programme focused on physical structures with the number of demolitions reaching a peak in 1972–3: this was followed by a peak in public sector building in 1976. Thereafter the rate of demolition slowed down as Leicester came to be affected by the 1974 Housing Act and its influential Renewal Strategies circular. An approach was advocated based on the principle of gradual renewal, which involved a greater attempt at renovation combined with a lower rate of demolition.

These changes came against the background of a new agitation, in Leicester as elsewhere, for measures to tackle what was perceived as the poor housing and social

St Matthew's Estate under construction, c. 1960

St Matthew's community centre in the 1970s

conditions of the inner city – the so-called urban problem that was dramatically highlighted in the social literature of these years. The Leicester Shelter Group was to the fore locally in drawing attention through its research reports to the seriousness of the situation. In a survey of housing conditions based on the analysis of census data 1961–71, they concluded that the city's overall housing shortage had not been eliminated and by some important indicators housing conditions had worsened. The improvement in average figures over this decade, they argued, 'concealed appalling and often worsening conditions in Highfields and Spinney Hill and the North Braunstone council estate'.

As has been described already in an earlier chapter, Leicester initiated a vigorous renewal strategy on the basis of a well-considered and flexible plan of housing action areas and general improvement areas. Yet, if anything, local concern about the city's housing situation intensified in the 1980s. By this time many organizations were reporting on the shortage of housing in Leicester and the problems of its inner districts. Agitation culminated in a local enquiry into housing in the city and county, undertaken at the request of the Leicester Housing Associations Liaison Group and chaired by the Bishop of Leicester in 1986.

There were several reasons why housing problems seemed to intensify over the 1970s and '80s. One was simply the ageing of the housing stock. In 1976 the council's renewal strategy team estimated that over a half of the older terraced housing required substantial improvement. Despite recent progress in housing rehabilitation the average age of stock was increasing. In 1985 the Council report *Leicester Faces a Housing Crisis* estimated that 4,950 houses in the city could be classified as unfit, 7,433 houses were without basic items, and that just under a third of the city's stock of housing, 33,482 homes, was in need of very substantial repair. According to a document about the Council's housing investment programme of 1986–7, the problem of disrepair and lack of amenities was particularly severe in pre-1945 council housing – approximately 28 per cent of council dwellings. As a priority, it was thought necessary to initiate a major rebuilding programme to replace the concrete system-built houses, now found to be defective. The Housing Department at this time estimated that 1,167 pre-1919 houses, 3,682 inter-war houses and 10,000 post-war and early 1950s houses required immediate and substantial improvement due to rapid deterioration that could not be inhibited.

The city was also faced with a considerably increased demand for housing. This was partly due to the extraordinary growth rate of the population, which in the 1950s and 1960s had been four times that of England as a whole, as well as the subsequent pressure from the flow of immigration in the 1970s. There were also social as well as demographic factors at work that increased the rate of household formation. Among these were the growing number of young people aspiring to form their own households, the increase in the number of the elderly in the city, and the incidence of divorce and separation – all factors that had an impact on the number of household formations and hence the demand for housing.

The supply of housing on the other hand was affected by restrictions on public

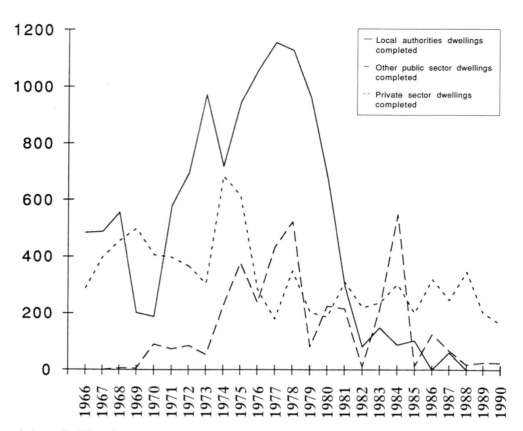

Leicester Building Completions

expenditure and changing policies towards council house provision. There was a dramatic decrease in the contribution of the local authority to new housing starts over the ten-year period from 1975. (see graphs) Whereas the local authority was contributing 66 per cent of new housing starts in 1975–7, as against 22 per cent from housing associations and 12 per cent private sector, in 1985 the local authority contribution had fallen to 3 per cent as against 26 per cent by housing associations (which represented a decline from 48 per cent in 1981–2) and 71 per cent private sector. Waiting lists for council property remained high at over 10,000 during the 1980s, and there were especially acute problems of the under supply of accommodation for single people, the elderly and large families. Single people formed over half of the waiting list.

The housing associations had developed initially to provide housing for special groups such as the elderly, single people and ethnic groups as well as care and support for people suffering from mental and physical handicaps, ex-offenders, battered wives and young unsupported mothers. Despite financial aid from the

Sheltered housing for the elderly in New Humberstone, 1983

government-aided housing corporation they were unable to meet the growing demands put upon them. Hence the importance of hostel provision in the city on the part of the Council and voluntary agencies for different groups of homeless people. An action plan initiated in the mid-1980s by the Council's hostel working party involving all agencies and interests represented a significant attempt to achieve a comprehensive approach and was especially commended in the report of the housing inquiry.

From the point of view of the social workers and representatives of the environmental professions, the most intractable problems were presented by the concentration of the most deteriorated housing and the worst living conditions in the inner city districts. The census of 1981 revealed that although there had been improvements overall in housing amenity, there were striking contrasts between inner and outer districts. The severity of Leicester's problems in this regard was brought home by OPCS (the Office of Population and Census Statistics) in 1982 on the basis of a study of adverse conditions in British cities based on the use of eleven measures of deprivation taken from the Census. Of the cities with more than 30 per cent of their population living in adverse conditions, Leicester was the fourth highest with a figure of 37 per cent. As the Leicester Housing Association subsequently pointed out to the housing inquiry, the General Needs index of the Department of Environment scored Leicester by far the highest in need terms within the East Midlands region, as did the Housing Corporations Housing Needs index.

All the surveys indicated that highly localized pockets of deprivation existed in Leicester within the inner city wards, and many of these coincided with the main areas of immigrant, and particularly Asian, settlement. Professor Jarman, in a study using eight criteria of social deprivation, calculated that Wycliffe Ward was one of the fifty most deprived wards in the country. Take the Belgrave Ward as another example, surveyed in 1981–4: in this district one third of houses had no inside toilet, a quarter no wash basin, a fifth no bath or hot water, and most of the houses were in a state of disrepair having been built in the last century. The area suffered from overcrowding and 64 per cent of the residents had Asian backgrounds. It was not so much overcrowding that presented the main problem (although 2.1 per cent of household heads in the inner area fell into this category in 1981 compared with 1.5 per cent in the city as a whole) as the condition of the housing and lack of amenities.

The concentration of immigrant settlement in the older districts of the city reflected the chain migration and restricted spatial movements of immigrant settlers. In the 1950s and 1960s particularly there was a preponderance of unskilled and semi-skilled household heads among the new settlers that restricted housing choice. But in addition there seemed to have been cultural preferences for locations near existing areas of immigrant settlement and for private sector housing. The low level of participation of Asians in the public housing sector was most marked. In 1981 this was no more than 9 per cent in council tenancies as against 31.1 per cent of the city population as a whole. An in-house review of the Council of the initial results of an ethnic monitoring programme in 1983 pointed out that Asian applicants also waited longer for rehousing and were more likely to refuse the property offered. The review explained the low level of participation in council housing in terms of a cultural preference for housing near to the central areas of settlement and the need for larger properties, especially among the East African and Ugandan Asians. Large properties were in short supply. In 1987, four or more bed houses accounted for only 2.6 per cent of the housing stock in the city, and the council properties were mainly located in the peripheral estates. It has also been suggested in an academic survey of 1987 that other factors may have come into play, such as the adverse reputation that some council estates had for racial harassment. However, the Council was not content merely with offering housing accommodation or seeking to rehouse: it adopted a policy and an action programme aimed at dealing with racial abuse in rehousing areas.

The housing enquiry recognized that Leicester had developed a sophisticated approach towards dealing with the poor conditions of older inner city housing. The programme approved in 1976 sought to provide a co-ordinated framework to relieve housing and related social stress, and to make housing and environmental improvements in the older parts of the city. Initially it was intended to survey all properties by 1991, but expenditure cuts disrupted the full implementation of this programme. Moreover in the early 1980s conflicts arose over the need for demolition in some HHAs, as for example the Grand Union area, where Asians lived as owner-occupiers. The chairman of the Housing Committee was an advocate of more demolition in a gradual renewal policy, but this ran up against strong resident opposition especially among Asian owner-occupiers, which had

An adventure playground in the Highfields area, 1980s

political implications for a Labour Party dependent on Asian votes from inner city wards. There may well have been a clash of values and perceptions on this issue as between Council politicians and officials and resident groups.

The community strength of these inner-city neighbourhoods had implications also for the idea of community development work which came to the fore in council policy during the 1980s. Community work in a broad sense was not a new idea in Leicester, which had a long tradition of providing resources for neighbourhood organizations. The principle of community work was an integral part also of the community college, a concept adopted by Leicester schools after the 1974 reorganization. The intention was not only to refocus adult educational, youth and cultural provision, as it did, but, in the words of the County Director of Education in the 1970s, to provide centres 'where the social conscience of the community can be expressed and enlarged'. In practice, the role of colleges in community development work suffered from education cuts and a lack of clear direction. More generally, in the mid-1980s there was criticism of the confusion surrounding the concept of community development and the extent to which council officers were seriously engaged in it. Over half of those identified as community workers were employed in the voluntary sector. A related theme emerging in the 1980s was the issue of consultation and participation in the government-inspired Inner City programme, a subject that was debated in conferences organized by the Leicester

The resources centre of the Wycliffe Society for the Blind

Council for Voluntary Services. These conferences played a part in helping the council devise ways of trying to overcome tensions between officials and neighbourhood groups.

From the late 1980s there was an acceleration in the support given to existing community organizations, particularly within the immigrant communities, and in the promotion of new self-help neighbourhood projects to which the Council offers advice and assistance. Work with disadvantaged groups to secure resources or get policies changed has benefited from the adoption by the Council of an equal opportunities policy. Some of the initiatives taken have received national attention, as has the Council's multi-racial and anti-racist policies and the experience of multi-racial education in schools such as Judgemeadow.

In the 1930s Dr Millard drew a distinction between the bricks and mortar and the flesh and blood aspects of housing policy. The latter clearly have become of increasing importance in recent years, and with this the tendency to complacency that could be detected in the 1950s has evaporated as the Council has had to confront new challenges and try to re-appraise the role of municipal action in the community life of the city.

Further Reading

The main primary sources for the information in this chapter are the minutes and reports of the relevant council committees. A particularly valuable and convenient source for health and housing is the annual reports of the Medical Officer of Health to 1974. In addition selected use was made of reports in the *Leicester Mercury*, especially for the account of the debate about comprehensive education. The health history of the city in the twentieth century has received very little attention, except for the history of hospital provision; hence the following guide to secondary sources relates mainly to education and housing.

Bamford, Sheila, *Leicester Local Authority Housing: ideologies, successes and failures behind the provision of working class houses in a local context, 1923–30* (1970)

Cliffe, David, *Community Work in Leicester* (1986)

Goodchild, R., and Multon, R., *Development and the Landowner* (1985), chapter 6: 'Leicester – an expanding city'

Hutchinson, E., *Community Education in Leicestershire* (1980)

Leicester City Council Planning, *The Future of Inner Leicester: inner Leicester district plan* (1975)

Leicester City Council/Leicestershire County Council, *Survey of Leicester 1983* (1983)

Leicester Council for Voluntary Service, *Inner City Partnership and Whose Inner City? Reports of Conferences* (1979)

Leicester Inner Area programme, *Reports* (Various)

Leicester Shelter Group, *Reports* (Various)

Mander, John, *Leicester Schools 1944–74* (1980)

Rimmington, Gerald T., *The Education of maladjusted children in Leicester, 1892–1974* (1985)

Rimmington, Gerald T., *The Comprehensive School Issue in Leicester, 1945–1974, and other essays* (1984)

Rutt, C. R., (Chairman), *Inquiry into Leicestershire Housing* (1986)

Westwood, Sallie and Hoffman, Dalla, *Asian women: education and social change* (1979)

Chapter Five

ORGANIZATIONAL AND ASSOCIATIONAL LIFE

O rganizations, clubs and societies have, since the nineteenth century, become an increasingly important part of modern life. They act as bridges within and between communities, behaving as expressions of identity and need across a range of areas of interest. This chapter will consider how the organizational and associational life of Leicester has grown over the twentieth century – sometimes echoing national trends, sometimes diverging from them.

Broadly speaking the nature of these developments might be examined through three periods of evolution. The first of these stretched to the 1930s and essentially represented a hangover of Victorian attitudes and sensibilities. In this period private organizations dispensed aid and attention, often from above, down to deserving causes which of necessity had to be distinguished from the undeserving. But the Victorian period also fostered other forms of associational life based around church, chapel, club and workplace, which attempted to recreate community relations in an era that feared the breakdown of these vital links between individuals and groups. The second period, which stretches roughly from the late 1930s to the 1970s, could be characterized as the age of welfarism. In this period many of the functions performed by charities were increasingly seen to be legitimate areas for initiatives from both local and central government. During this era the role of these organizations was seen as auxiliary, as a method of supplementing basic provision and demand in a range of areas. Moreover the change to supplementing need allowed the work of these organizations and the self-help ethic to spread into new areas of cultural and associational life based around hobbies and interests. The last phase of this history covers the period since the 1960s, in which new needs have been met through a combined approach that has used a mixture of local and central government intervention leavened with the participation of a number of interest groups. These exist to either highlight individual needs or to act as implementers of these grant aided initiatives. This last phase has also been, in part, ushered in by the diversification of these needs reflected by the change in the City's ethnic composition since the Second World War.

The Legacy of Victorian Self-help

Like most cities of the Victorian period Leicester's social and cultural life revolved around membership and identification with religious organizations, societies and clubs. This was, to an extent, influenced by Leicester's nonconformist past, which had greatly influenced development in this area. As a result of the 1851 religious census, the shock discovery that only half of the population attended church or chapel prompted many religious bodies to take action. Though attendance figures were higher in Leicester than in most cities the Anglican Church in Leicester undertook an ambitious programme of church building in the latter half of the nineteenth century, seeking to make good its deficiencies which had been cruelly exposed by Victorian urbanization. New churches like St Matthew's (opened in 1867), St Paul's (1871), St Peter's (1874) were all responses to the fear that the Church was losing popularity. These were followed by a plethora of church consecrations at the end of the century which fortified the religious presence not simply in the centre of town but also in the newer suburbs. Thus St James's (Aylestone Park), St Thomas's (South Wigston) and the Church of the Martyrs on the Westcotes Estate were all products of this ethos. A different response was provided by the decision of the Leicester Association for Church Extension to

Interior of Leicester's Temperance Hall, converted to a cinema during the First World War

Scouts and Boys Brigade troops were an important part of early Leicester organizational life

earmark money for the purpose of the construction of churches within the city. The Anglican Church in particular responded to the problems of city congregations by both enriching the stipends of existing ministers and by building rooms and halls where it was felt that this kind of venture would have more success. This was occasionally seen as a springboard for a more permanent building and congregation. An example of this was the mission established in New Humberstone in 1881 that eventually resulted in the consecration of St Barnabas's church in 1885.

Many of the nonconformist sects also adopted a similar approach. The Leicester Baptists had their own extension scheme which sought to redistribute its resources to account for the changing city. The city centre Harvey Lane Baptist chapel, for example, was replaced in 1903 by the newly opened Robert Hall Memorial church on Narborough Road. Mission halls were also a feature of the nonconformist response with the Revd Hugh Price Hughes responsible for establishing a number of Methodist Mission Halls in the Leicester at the end of the last century.

Charity

Some churches and chapels worked hard to extend their appeal through the increased provision of clubs and societies based around leisure and entertainments such as concerts, sports and cycling. More material needs were served by the vast resources ploughed into Sunday schools, benefit and sick clubs, blanket societies and other forms of self-help. Most churches and chapels provided a number of these as methods of helping their congregations and remaining 'in touch' with their needs and aspirations. This model was so pervasive that even the Humberstone Gate-based Leicester Secular Society provided a Sunday School, a Sick club, a benevolent fund and employed a visiting nurse to look after ageing members during the Edwardian years. Most of these initiatives were founded upon the creed of self-help. In this respect the onus was on the individual to belong to an organization like a church, chapel, friendly society or benefit club, and such membership was almost a confirmation of working-class respectability. This state of affairs was largely confirmed by middle class opinion upon the nature of society and the role of charity. While the honest and deserving who had either fallen on hard times or had provided for themselves while in employment required assistance it was equally plain that the idle and feckless did not. Much of this ideology emerged in Leicester through the operation of the local branch of the Charity Organization Society.

The COS had been founded in 1869 with an express aim to discriminate between the deserving and undeserving poor, 'to distinguish the proper objects for the exercise of their benevolence'. Almost from the outset the respectability of those involved in overseeing its operation was emphasized. The society aimed at consulting at least one representative from each charitable organization of the area and these links were often personal as much as organizational. Thus the earliest committee included many who had been prime movers in earlier charity work, such as David Vaughan, Joseph Dare, seven members of the Ellis family and two of the Gimson family. Though the aim of the organization was charitable it nonetheless provided the opportunity for 'important' work for the concerned members of the upper middle class of the town. In this respect the early century interest in philanthropy was a method by which the leading members of the city maintained contact with each other and with 'Greater Leicester'.

One principal aim of the COS was the suppression of begging – an almost constant cause for complaint in the period leading up to the First World War. Leicester householders were given tickets bearing the society's name, which, when asked for help, were to be given to street beggars instead of money. This was intended to bring the vagrant poor into the COS and its sphere of operations; wherever possible the applicant was to be referred to a local charity. The intention was to restore respectable status to those who had lost it temporarily, generally by re-equipping them with the means of returning to employment. In a similar way the COS also instructed its officers when dealing with the sick to only aid those whose condition was curable. As such it was a celebration of the Victorian virtues of self-help with the COS seeing itself as 'an ambulance on the fiercely stricken field of modern industrial competition; it picks up the wounded and, if possible, heals them and sets them on their legs again'. Thus the main area of work of the COS remained combating the one social evil it squarely recognized – unemployment. During the Edwardian period it hired mangles and sewing machines as a response to obvious trade fluctuations in the town. This was preferred to financial help that might have disrupted what was perceived to be the legitimate operation of the labour market.

Victorian philanthropy in action: an old people's tea, 1900

This combination of concerned middle-class philanthropy coupled with material aid was also evident within the associational life of religious nonconformity within Leicester. The Bishop Street Methodist chapel also ran its own benevolent society in the years running up to 1914 that provided relief for what it called the 'afflicted' poor. Though the relief was not restricted by denomination recipients were visited in their homes, largely by the female members of the congregation, and were provided with religious instruction alongside material relief. The middle classes also organized themselves, however, to combat other evils that afflicted the wider social and material fabric of Leicester.

Civic Organizations

The Leicester Kyrle Society was typical of the organizations that survived into twentieth-century Leicester with a nineteenth-century approach and mentality. Founded in 1880 as a local response to a national concern voiced by Octavia Hill, the society was a mixture of philanthropic organization, expression of civic pride and leisure outlet for the middle classes. Many of its local membership were members of the city's controlling élite with representatives from the Paget, Gee, Stead and Gimson families, all of whom were encouraged to employ their artistic and organizational skills for the benefit of the community. One noted local artist, Edith Gittins, served on the governing council of the society and many of her paintings were donated to local organizations. The society's intention was to provide the 'refining and cheering influences of natural and artistic beauty into the homes and resorts of the poor of Leicester'. This was sought through an extensive programme of visits, concerts and the presentation of paintings and furnishings to local voluntary organizations and hospitals, with the express aim of brightening up these environments.

By the turn of the century the Kyrle Society had twenty years of philanthropic work behind it in the area of town and environmental improvement. By the Edwardian years it was providing considerable unofficial support for Corporation attempts at town improvement. Flowers and pictures were donated to Board schools and children were encouraged to gain a respect for the countryside through organized visits to parks and open spaces. These activities were supplemented until the First World War by the distribution of seeds to school children and essay competitions on town improvement. The society also appointed itself as a watchdog over Leicester's urban development. In the early years of the century it argued strongly for the provision of litter bins and a programme of tree planting and preservation that would enhance areas such as New Walk and the Newarke houses area. Similarly the Society was instrumental in safeguarding local open spaces for the people of Leicester, involving itself in the improvement scheme to beautify the castle bank of the river Soar in 1918, the castle grounds improvement scheme of 1926 and the purchase of Swithland wood as a public park in the same year. However, many of the motives behind these actions expressed an ambiguous attitude towards city life; while it sought the improvement of the town it also expressed concern at what were seen as worrying trends of twentieth-century urban life which pre-date the growth of 'green' issues. The expansion of new patterns of leisure and consumption were considered to be potentially divisive and detrimental to the environment. Indeed at the end of the First World War the society was simultaneously engaged on a war against litter, battling against what it considered to be unsightly advertising, while hoping that post-war prosperity would see 'extra income spent in beautifying homes and home surroundings'.

Throughout the 1920s the Kyrle Society sought to advise the corporation about local improvements, urging for trees, lampposts, park furniture and other amenities to be an essential part of local provision. Interest in many of these concerns prompted some members to become interested in the by now burgeoning town planning movement. Throughout the 1920s the society maintained this interest and took a major part in motivating opinion in this area. In 1928 it organized a civic amenities association containing members of the Leicestershire Archaeological

A Friendly Society photographed outside Leicester Town Hall, 1920s

Society, Literary and Philosophical Society, Leicester Rotary Club and the Leicester Society of Architects. This organization was intended to provide expert opinion on matters of city conservation and development. In the same year the Kyrle Society merged with the newly formed Leicester Civic Society. As more of this conservation and preservation work came into the orbit of local authorities the Civic Society came to represent the promotion of civic and local pride rather than the more heavy hand of late Victorian philanthropy.

Co-operation and Self-help

Alongside this ideal of help from above there was nonetheless an equally strong tradition of respectable working-class self help within the city. Leicester was the only provincial city to support a Secular Society with any degree of success and this was largely due to its ability to attract a skilled working-class membership that valued self help in areas such as education, welfare and leisure. This presence within the labour force survived later in Leicester than in many other towns, which replaced handwork with machinery at an earlier stage. Such artisan pride created a culture that made independence and self organization a virtue. Though the religious and cultural aspects of this independence were increasingly found to be surviving rather than flourishing, there was a constant demand for activities that had more obviously material aims in view. One such activity was the cultivation of allotments, which grew considerably as an organized pastime in the early years of the century.

Allotments in the Stocking Farm area, pictured in 1960

The Small Holdings and Allotments Act of 1908 gave a new impetus to the provision of allotments in the borough. The Act enabled the Borough Council to raise loans for the purpose, according to demand, and the demand proved to be quite considerable. Over 100 applications were received by April that year, the great majority for allotments of up to an acre in area, but among them more than thirty for smallholdings with a combined area of almost 500 acres. Demand for the latter was met in part by leasing some 200 acres at Stocking Farm from the Earl of Dysart, most given over to smallholdings of between 3.5 and 37.5 acres, but a proportion devoted to satisfying the 'numerous' applications for allotments that the Council was now receiving. For instance, the Council turned over part of its own land on the Old Belgrave Sewage Farm to the purpose, while in North Evington a sizeable rented plot was supplemented in 1913 by the purchase of nearly 30 acres between Coleman Road and the Great Northern railway line. Land was also set aside for allotments on the new municipal housing estates of the 1920s and 1930s – at Braunstone, for example, and on the smaller Kirby Estate at Knighton Fields.

The land was normally leased *en bloc* to Allotment Societies, which divided it into holdings and let them in turn to '*bona fide* working men . . . at a rental sufficient to cover all expenses'. Most such societies had the legal status of a friendly society, with powers to buy, sell and rent land, and erect buildings on it. New applicants were normally required to satisfy the committee of their 'respectability and fitness' before being admitted. Local councillors commonly acted as trustees of the societies, and in due course the Small Holdings and Allotments Sub-Committee also co-opted a small number of members 'experienced in the management and cultivation of allotment gardens, and representative of the interests of occupiers' in the city.

Rents varied according to the quality of the land – from around £2 to £5 10s an acre per annum in 1909 – and any profits had to be applied to the aims of the societies. Though they were encouraged in part as a diversion from drinking, gambling and other 'demoralizing' pursuits, 'the promotion of agriculture and horticulture' was their prime objective, and here the 'spirit of competition' was accorded a central role, encouraged by horticultural shows and contests offering cash or other prizes. Members were also required to lay out their allotments and provide a water supply at their own expense, but by buying in bulk, most societies were also able to keep down the cost of seed and fertilizer. The total annual outlay would have been within the reach of most working-class families with a regular income, and – weather permitting – would be more than repaid by a plentiful supply of fresh foodstuffs.

Similar concerns with individual improvement allied to the provision of cheap and reliable produce was part of the mission of the Co-Operative Society and Leicester was, during the years spanning the end of the last century, the centre of one of the most successful branches of the co-operative movement. Though the provision of cheap and reliable goods backed up by profit redistribution in the form of dividends was the primary concern of this self-help activity some of its members had more ambitious plans. The boot and shoe industry was recognized as being subject to fluctuating periods of boom and recession. In an attempt to offset this trend workers at the Anchor Boot and Shoe works entered into an industrial co-partnership, which effectively meant they pooled their money to have a share in the business. It was an instant success, quickly outgrowing the first factory in Causeway Lane and enabling the enterprise to move to a rented factory in North Evington. The factory in Asfordby Street, like all industrial co-partnerships, had an Education Room which was well used for a variety of activities. The records show that Ramsay Macdonald, Philip Snowden, Professor Timson and Henry Vivian were among early lecturers. The subjects varied from 'Roses and their Culture' through 'London and its People' to 'Co-operation and the Housing of the People' and 'The Garden City – A Solution to the Housing Problem'. Lectures were not the only way to stimulate the workers. Classes were also organized and the most important were those on the history and principles of Co-operation. These were organized in conjunction with the Co-operative Union and the first teacher was Amos Mann, who was succeeded by J.S. Wilford, a former student from the class. To supplement the classes on Co-operation there were classes on industrial history, since the students did not want to know only about the winning of battles. Amos Mann tells us, in his *Industrial Democracy*, that 'this study of industrial history revealed to the mind of the student the real causes of wars'. There were also classes on citizenship as a way of fitting workers for public services, as well as an ambulance class, a physical culture class and whist club. At the same time a considerable library was established.

All this Co-operative activity, backed by political discussion, led to consideration of the founding of a Co-operative village. In the first place it was hoped to have the factory as the centre of such a village, so that there might be a genuine Co-operative community, but this raised problems enough for the idea to be abandoned. However, a start was made in 1902 when forty-five Anchor workers held a meeting and began to save small sums. Henry Vivian, who lectured on housing at the Anchor in 1902, gave a lot of encouragement. The Anchor workers, who, as Co-operators, wanted equality of society not so much by levelling down as by levelling up, had an ambition to achieve by collective effort advantages and improvement in their material condition. If the rich could have 'a house in its own grounds surrounded by trees, shrubs, flowers, gardens, lawns and open spaces', why should the workers not also have some of these advantages? An estate committee was set up at a meeting held on 29 September 1903 with the task of selecting a site for the Estate. Ideally it was to be in the city, but the cost of land prohibited this idea. The committee looked at sites in South Knighton, plots on the corner of Welford Road and Seven Bridge Lane, and at Scraptoft. Eventually the site chosen was at Humberstone and the Estate, when built, was in a pleasant rural belt with spring water. There were gas mains nearby but no storm or sewage drains. In October 1907 a presentation was held at Humberstone and the *Leicester Mercury* reported that Henry Vivian presided over the proceedings held in connection with the Co-partnership Tenants Housing Movement. Among those present were Alderman Edward Wood (Mayor of Leicester), the Revd R.P. Manvill, Dr C.K. Millard, Councillors Burrows, Taylor and Mann from Leicester and Councillor J.S. Nettlefold (Chairman of Birmingham Housing Committee). Sir Edward Wood expressed his hopes that the 'day was not far distant when they could see artisans' dwellings in Leicester with a good plot of land attached to them'.

All this was a prelude to the building of the Garden Suburb. Cost was once more a factor and it was decided to use direct labour. George Hern was appointed general manager and he designed the houses in a layout originally devised by Parker and Unwin, chief designers of Letchworth Garden City. The first two cottages were occupied by October 1908, opened by Sir John and Lady Rolleston, and the occasion was commemorated by a plaque unveiled by Dr C.K. Millard (Leicester's medical officer of health). The cottages cost £450 the pair to build and the rent was 6s 6d and this included 400 square yards of land for each cottage. The development of the estate was to be on the same generous lines. The gable cottages covered with roughcast all had individual features and gardens with shrubs and trees. To quote Ernest Mee: 'I would like to stress that we were the first in Leicester to have a bathroom, all to ourselves, in a working-class semi-detached house. Not like the streets in Leicester, we had water in the kitchen and a lavatory all to ourselves.' The comparison was to the courts in the middle of the town with families sharing two or three lavatories among twenty or more people.

Factory Life and Culture

Though this mode of self-help associational life clustered around the home and the neighbourhood, there were also powerful elements of it present in the workplace. One area that exhibited this very strongly was the hosiery trade, and the factory culture of the female workers within this trade was a vibrant feature of the city throughout the twentieth century. In 1915 the programme for the National Co-operative Congress, which was held that year in Leicester, described the women of Leicester in glowing terms: 'They are clever and industrious, and cheerfully shoulder the work of a home and the work in the family as their allotted task. . . . Most return after marriage, often because of economic pressure, but often because they get there some kind of social life, pleasant occupation and cheerful company. "It's too dozy at home", they declare.'

This tradition of women, single and married, working in the city's industries had become established early in the nineteenth century. When the industry moved into the factories towards the end of the second half of the century the need for female workers increased relative to men. Between 1851 and 1901 the proportion of women in the hosiery industry rose from 42 to 68 per cent. The boot and shoe industry, which joined hosiery as a major employer in Leicester, also drew heavily on women's labour. In 1891 the census indicated that the proportion of women who

The workplace as community for working women

were in paid employment in Leicester was 48 per cent, high above the national average of 34 per cent.

'Many women who went out to work made their homes more comfortable than those who did not.' Although they obviously faced problems about childcare and housework responsibilities, they apparently solved them either by tremendous feats of time management and efficiency (rushing from the factory to cook dinner) or by employing friends, family or child-minders to care for the young ones. Such women were more intelligent, lively and responsible than non-working wives, in contrast to the conventional Victorian morality, which suggested that families were more comfortable where the wife was a full-time housewife.

It is not surprising that employers have faced problems of labour shortage and turnover since conditions of work in hosiery factories can be hard, a fact that often escaped the notice of the early observers who spoke so warmly of the Leicester tradition. Beatrice Webb was one such who reported favourably on the 'contented, happy faces, bright appearances and friendly manners' of the women in the Leicester Co-operative factory that she visited at the turn of the century. However, this was meant to be a model factory and another report contrasted the 'merry faces' of its young women workers with 'the dull visage and languid body of so many found in closely packed and hard-driven factories, where machines take precedence of flesh and blood'. Employers in the industry have always been able to find some women who will tolerate such poor conditions and the low wages that often accompany them, particularly in times of economic recession and unemployment. One woman explained why in simple but telling words: 'My answer from experience is that bread and butter is nice, but with a bit of jam on it tastes much better. A new pair of football boots for Johnny gives one a sense of pride instead of him wearing his more fortunate mates' leave-offs.'

Because of this strong sense of family commitment and a desire to make the family standard of living that little bit better, Leicester women through the nineteenth and twentieth centuries were persuaded by employers to work for wages that men refused to accept. 'Although not very well recompensed for their expertise and effort, women have gained other rewards from factory work, particularly from the companionship and sociability that have long been another reason given for going out to work. Judging from accounts of everyday life in Leicester factories, two contradictory pictures emerge. On the one hand factories are described as harsh places, noisy and physically unpleasant, with strict control by supervisors and managers, with the female factory workers portrayed as rough and tough, if goodhearted. The other contrasting picture is of cosy friendly places with a strong family atmosphere, strong links between owners and workers, and docile submissive women too frightened of losing their jobs to make trouble.

Some evidence certainly suggests that a rough and robust factory culture developed, especially in the early part of the century. In some factories gin and rum were rumoured to be consumed on the premises. In one factory where beer was banned, ingenious systems of ropes and pulleys were designed to smuggle it into the factory! Sexual innuendo, horseplay and flirtation enlivened the daily routine. In Paton and Baldwins factory in the 1900s, the head warehouseman was said to keep assignments with women workers in a materials bin! In the same factory at Christmas in 1933 there was a bet that no man would walk through all the departments during the last hour before knocking-off time. The foolhardy who attempted it ended up trouserless. Observers were impressed by the appearance of the Leicester factory girls: 'The personal taste of Leicester young women in dress strikes the visitor forcibly. . . . beautifully clothed in quiet colours, their dresses simply and tastefully made and their millinery expensive but not gaudy, with handsome footwear. . . .'

An interest in fashion is still one of the reasons why young women enter these industries. Another visitor considered that it would be difficult to find 'a more respectably dressed set of operatives'. But their behaviour was not always so respectable. The young women of Picks factory, 'squabbling and chattering like a flock of starlings', spent their lunch hour in the street outside the factory where they 'kicked up their heels to the band organ and jostled pedestrians'. The records of the Leicester Hosiery Union describe incidents where women were dismissed for swearing and fighting. Although factory discipline was harsh in the early twentieth century, with fines for bad work, singing, chatting and arriving late, groups of women sometimes stood up against domineering behaviour by male foremen and managers. The union records note a number of cases where such confrontations led to threats of strikes. In another case the women rounded on a young workman who was harassing them. Female solidarity was reasonably strong and the cases suggest that women were much happier with a female supervisor in charge of them than a man. Not all factory life was unpleasant and riddled with conflict. Women workers looking back also remember good times, friendship, joking, sing-songs and 'fatups', when sausage rolls and cream buns were shared among them. Some of the more enlightened and progressive employers were themselves eager to encourage the social side of factory life, believing it would help workers to become attached to the firm and thus solve the problems of labour shortage and turnover. Corah's, for example, has provided its workers over the years with a stream of social and welfare benefits: a dispensary, dental and manicure facilities, sports clubs, a pensioners 'Evergreen Club', retirement homes (funded jointly by company and employees) holiday schemes, annual balls and dinners.

By all these activities, shrewd employers hoped to develop a sense of the factory family, believing, probably correctly, that family loyalties were most important in their women workers' lives. Corah's works magazine *Encore News* reflected this in the snapshots it gave of employees' family lives, such as 'Mabel Garrett. . . . very much a family woman. . . . her home is her hobby, she takes a keen interest in this and her family'. With few exceptions, the married women operatives' interests were centred on the home rather than on the factory. They derived their status, satisfactions and security from their homes, and it was there that their organizing abilities were used. For them, work was primarily a means of performing their home-making function more effectively. Employers were therefore able to convey their concern for their employees' well-being by taking an interest in family matters: 'Walk through a factory with the head of it and notice how he addresses all and sundry by their Christian names, and makes familiar enquiries as to a mother's health or the progress of a wife with a new baby. . . . the value of such personal relationships needs no labouring.'

The sense of family connections, at home and work, was also strengthened by the system of recruitment common in many Leicester factories, whereby women 'spoke for' jobs for their children and relatives: at J.B. Pick's 'until 1940 a mother would bring her daughter to work in the factory where she had been happy and she in turn would bring her own'. This, of course, was one way to help build up the core of long-serving workers firms found so desirable. Picks estimated that in the 1950s the members of their 25 Club could form a queue stretching half-way down Wellington Street. In fact, in many factories this custom persisted after the war, and numerous factory publications give details of long-serving families, one even totting up an incredible 377 years between them.

Life was hard for starters, who were teased, especially over sexual matters. Old hands would frequently take over the best work if the youngster was allotted it. But happy moments were also recalled and two of the women showed how they had responded to the personal involvement of their employers: 'The owner of the factory, a fine looking gentleman, would visit us once a week and everywhere had to be cleaned; his wife came too, we loved to see her. She would smile and talk to us as she moved down the alleys.' 'Our boss was a real gentleman. In the summer time he would come round the factory, and all the shafting would be stopped and he used to take about thirty-six girls to his big house and garden and we would go picking fruit; it was marvellous, very, very happy hours.'

This same contradictory mixture of women's responses can be found when looking at women's involvement in the trade unions in Leicester. From the nineteenth century, trade union officers tended to see women as 'problem' members, accusing them of apathy and of being unwilling to stand up against their employers or to engage in industrial disputes. They blamed the women for their own lack of representation on union committees. On the other hand, the Leicester Hosiery Union records show that women, when involved in disputes, could often become very militant. Two young women, Nellie and Ivy White, aged nineteen and sixteen, led a fight against what the union called the 'Russian Tyranny' of one factory, Buchlers, in 1910, after being dismissed for joining. In the same way, in the shoe industry a breakaway all-female union was formed in 1911 by Lizzie Willson, in protest against the sexism of the men and their failure to deal with women's interests. One has some sympathy with the girls of the Co-op factory who, in 1905, complained that they hadn't joined the union because they hadn't been 'asked properly'. However, despite the frequent complaints that the union did not cater for women members, from early in the twentieth century there was a grudging realization among the men that something had to be done to get the women more involved. Dances and socials were arranged for women members, a women's committee was formed in 1930 and a women's organizer (Mrs Bird) appointed four years later.

Returning to work after marriage is nothing new to Leicester women who have managed for decades to juggle the competing demands of work and families, 'cheerfully shouldering' what has indeed been at times a heavy double burden; work in hosiery and shoe factories is hard-paced, pressurized and not always carried out in congenial conditions. The women are spirited, tough and competent and have made surprisingly little fuss about the hardness of their lives, although, at times, they have demonstrated considerable militancy. Their lives were perfectly summed up by a team of researchers who studied unemployment in Leicester in the 1930s: 'The Leicester woman is a strong, independent, and often very capable type, but her interests are not primarily in the home. She is driven by the pressure of work. She has no leisure. She was fitted into an industrial mould at the age of fourteen. . . . Her social outlook is necessarily conditioned by the advantages and disadvantages of these experiences.'

The Age of Welfarism

One result of the First World War was an increasingly heightened realization of the need for forms of planning and state intervention in a whole host of areas. Though much of the ideological impetus behind this came from central government its ripples were felt locally very early on.

In some respects the Leicester branch of the COS felt the tide turning as early as 1908 when the introduction of old age pensions started to undermine the ideas that influenced their work. COS ideology was under attack by the Labour movement and social scientists, who increasingly argued for state intervention. The society was aware of the problem and produced counter propaganda, though it was plain that the COS approach merely provided short term palliatives for deeply rooted problems that afflicted all. The failure of the COS response is graphically demonstrated by its inability to distinguish, on its own terms, the deserving from the undeserving. While more and more sought aid, fewer and fewer were turned away.

Despite this the COS actively resisted the advance of the welfare state in all its spheres before 1914, refusing to be responsive to any changing perception of social need. Indeed it still worked hard to support local private ex-servicemen's charities such as the Airman's Family Association and Sir Jonathan North's Discharged Servicemen's Charity. Nonetheless the reliance on case work and the eventual employment of a professional worker was a form of progress that took the charity concept further towards the professionalization of social work. This was fully realized when Mayor Hincks visited the United States to discover the extent of state involvement in this area, which was considerably greater than private initiatives. The first professional social worker arrived in Leicester in 1934 having been trained at the University of Nottingham's department of social studies. In spite of this development the COS still claimed this was rather a vindication of their 'casework' approach. Nonetheless the agency refused to admit that it had been superseded and, while refusing to apply for state funding, it increasingly became an advisory body dispensing information on state benefits to all where it had once dispensed medicine and tickets to the deserving. The Bishop Street Methodist Benevolent Society similarly found itself an irrelevance in the post-First World War world and was wound up in 1917. This was seen by its historian B.J. Biggs as a direct result of the developing concept of a welfare state.

It would, however, be wrong to suggest that the work of charities and the charity ethos was undermined completely during the middle years of this century. Many well established charitable organizations such as Wyggeston's hospital continued to provide accommodation and pensions, so that this particular charity remains one of the largest to still be operating in the latter half of the twentieth century. Despite this it would still be appropriate to suggest local and national intervention by the state was becoming important in areas which had previously been the preserve of private initiative. This had two major repercussions: the first was a recognition of the importance of public policy and the benefits of a state and city wide approach. The second was a realization that the more obviously social side of associational life could flourish once the burdens of provision in other, more obviously welfare orientated, areas were removed. A recognition that this era of 'charity and philanthropy from above' had passed was implicit in the decision of the Kyrle Society to merge with an organization whose very name echoed the changing emphasis – the Leicester Civic Society. Though the Civic Society continued its work into the 1930s it was increasingly responding to developments rather than initiating them. In 1938 for example the society could only 'welcome the interest shown in national parks by the ministry of health' and further urged that a national authority should oversee its provision. Though the Second World War obviously overshadowed the operation of the Civic Society, the heightened levels of state intervention and its promise of further inroads in the post-war world effectively spelled the death of this society.

One further arena within which this new 'civic' approach was discussed was the Leicestershire Literary and Philosophical Society. Though it had been in existence since the 1830s, providing a programme of literary, scientific and historical lectures, it had always maintained an interest in contemporary developments in economics, industry and social change. For many years its committee work had been the preserve of Leicester's ruling families – members of the Gee, Gimson, Ellis, Picton and Paget families had all been past president. Many such as Margaret Gimson had also taken part in the work of organizations such as the COS. Though it continued to operate in its customary manner one unforeseen part of its role in the post-First World War period was as a rapid education for many of Leicester's elite involved in the burgeoning levels of local responsibility. Thus the work of archaeological and botany sections was supplemented by lectures on matters of town planning as well as state and local developments within technical education. Leicester's Medical

Officer of Health, Dr Killick Millard, also raised health matters in relation to important contemporary population and Malthusian birth control policies. Though it was an important forum for ideas its pivotal role as the medium of knowledge and ideas was increasingly overshadowed by the growth of University College (later Leicester University) – an institution that had its basis in a combination of both national and local aspirations. When the Philosophical Society celebrated its centenary in 1934 its president Colin Ellis hoped that the society would raise taste and cherish beauty in an age in which 'this had been lacking in public affairs as in domestic life'. Moreover his hopes for the society's future were decidedly defensive, suggesting that it should 'be an influence towards guarding and increasing the amenities of Leicester'.

With the growth of civic and national provision of welfare needs it was possible for the leisure aspects of associational life to grow in importance. An example of this new emphasis is provided by the Leicester Personal Health Association. On the face of it this society's history covers the period from the embryonic growth of state intervention to the marginalization of private initiatives containing a blend of old and new emphases. The association's intention was to provide education and some entertainment upon health matters to a predominantly middle-class audience who would be 'in some position' to spread the message of cleanliness and rudimentary preventive medicine. Lectures were arranged on subjects such as childcare, yoga and elements of astrology. The association also regularly visited a number of canteens at local sites such as the Leicester branch of Boots the Chemist and the works canteen of Imperial Typewriters to be appraised of modern food preparation methods. All of these were designed to simply impart information rather than effect changes in current health practices. The Leicester Association was linked informally to a national network of health associations, thirty of which exhibited at a health exhibition at Loughborough Town Hall in 1932. In this respect the interest in health was marginalized from real social concerns and became a truly associational activity based around visits, whist drives and fundraising activities, to provide comforts and entertainments to enhance existing provision. The appeal of fundraising, frequent outings and organizing teas was considerable and this organization must stand as representative of many similar 'friends'-type organizations that operated throughout the city and the county, providing constant help and support to worthy causes.

Working Men's Clubs

The working-class taste for an associational leisure culture was provided by some of the sports and leisure pursuits mentioned elsewhere, either as spectators or as participants. More vibrant still than this attachment to sport was the enduring attachment to clubs and societies linked to work or occupational status. The first Working Men's Club in Leicester was established in 1881 in a converted shop in Belgrave Gate, and in 1888 moved into purpose-built premises in New Bond Street, designed by the local architect Arthur Wakerley. Known simply as the Working

The City of Leicester Working Men's Club,
pictured in the mid-1960s

Men's Club, it later became the Borough of Leicester WMC and, later still, reflecting Leicester's changed civic status, the City of Leicester WMC. In 1899 it had around 1,800 members, paying an entrance fee of 4s, and a monthly subscription of 6d. In the meantime more WMCs had been founded, some of them more enduring than others. The Manchester Unity of Oddfellows Club in Humberstone Gate – commonly known as the 'Manny' – and the Nottingham Imperial Oddfellows Club in Chapel Yard, Gallowtree Gate – the 'Notts' – were both established in 1895, and by 1899 catered between them for over 1,000 members of registered friendly societies. New clubs were also built beyond the town centre in expanding residential areas: the North Evington in 1893, for instance; the Belgrave and District in the following year; and the Spinney Hill and Newfoundpool (non-political) WMCs in 1897. Like the Aylestone and District WMC, which moved into a substantial new building on Saffron Lane in 1903, most began their existence in very modest premises – in converted houses or, in the case of the Aylestone itself, in a small wooden building formerly used as a temperance meeting place.

If working men's clubs were originally conceived as 'the strongest counteraction to the Public House, the desire for social enjoyment and the love of excitement are the impulses that habitually drive the working classes to visit the beer shop', the expansion of the movement in the later nineteenth century and beyond was in fact financed largely by profits from the sale of alcohol. This being so, any significant reduction in revenue from this source could jeopardize their existence. It also made them a natural target for temperance campaigners, who might also be able to exert some significant influence over legislative controls. Thus, when the production of beer was reduced under the Temporary Restrictions Act early in the First World

War, members of the national Working Men's Club and Institute Union were urged to oppose any 'order of a character which is unnecessary or tyrannical, or not dictated by public necessity but by teetotal fanaticism as many undoubtedly are. . . . You should at once (not next week, but at once!) write to your MP . . .'.

In the early 1930s the CIU waged a strenuous campaign against the Beer Tax and Club Tax. 'It is not equality to tax the workers, the principal consumers of beer, out of all proportion to their means and then to impose a heavy additional burden . . .', its Executive wrote of the former: 'Assuming the fairness of the pre-war tax of 7s 9d, how can the present tax of nearly fifteen times that amount be justified!' The CIU President, Robert Richardson, himself a Member of Parliament, described the tax as 'vicious' and 'immoral' – all the more so because in turn it increased the rate of the Club Tax itself. This was based on the wholesale cost of beer plus excise duty, and 'is believed to be the sole instance in British taxation of taxing a tax. . . . The amount of Club Tax is insignificant in comparison with the national revenue, and as a simple measure of justice . . . my Executive ask that it may be repealed.'

It was not, in fact, abolished until 1960, and coupled with the high rate of unemployment in many areas at this time, these taxes strained their resources to such an extent that in 1932, 63 per cent of a sample of almost 2,500 affiliated clubs were operating at a loss. Almost eighty had been wound up over the same period, and 'before long, hundreds will collapse unless some relief is forthcoming. . . . Some of these clubs in danger of closing have taken decades to build up. They are the result of years of work and sacrifice. . . . The breaking up of these clubs is a tragedy,

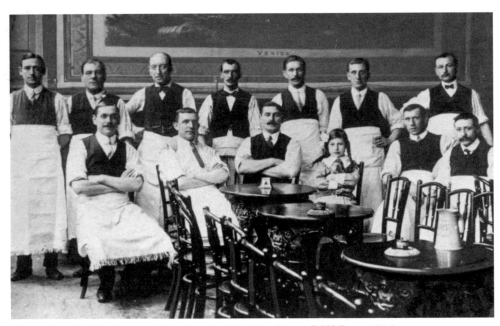

Stewards at the Humberstone Gate branch of the Manchester Oddfellows, 1914

a grievous loss to the people of the district who thus lose their opportunities for association and friendship with their fellow men.'

The clubs themselves remained a true reflection of their title, organized by and for working men. 'Lady guests may be admitted by invitation tickets on such occasions as the Committee may think fit, and on the personal application of a member,' as the rules of the City of Leicester said in 1934, and although women were later admitted more freely, they were not permitted to become members in their own right. However, the inter-war depression and the financial distress suffered by many families had given a new impetus to the WMC's aim of providing 'the means of social intercourse, mutual helpfulness, mental and moral improvement, rational recreation and the other advantages of a club'. In Leicester, as elsewhere, several existing clubs moved to larger premises, and a number of new clubs were founded. Among the latter were the Saffron Lane WMC and the Braunstone and District WMC, serving the residents of two new municipal housing estates; among the former, the North Evington WMC, whose imposing new building in Green Lane Road was one of the several designed for easy conversion into a cinema should the financial climate cause them to be sold.

'Leicester is a Club Town, with nothing mean and shoddy,' wrote the CIU Assistant Secretary, R.S. Chapman, in 1929. 'Its Club Houses are the largest and best I have seen anywhere.' They might be, as another CIU official said in the same year, 'hostages to fortune and the permanence of the movement . . .' but 'Ambition, though a sin in angels, was a virtue among workers', and 'In the architecture and furniture of the clubs were reflected the high ideals of club life. . . . Their outward appearance should be the sign of their inward grace.' High standards of conduct were, in fact, expected within their walls. A new member had to be proposed and seconded by two existing members 'able from personal knowledge to vouch for his respectability and fitness to be a member', and 'gambling, drunkenness, bad language or other misconduct' were strictly prohibited. In addition to the sick clubs, which were a feature of the clubs, most WMCs also contributed regularly to hospitals, convalescent homes and 'any other charitable or providence institution' as their means permitted. Sick club subscriptions normally enabled members to receive medical care or other assistance when needed, and their widespread cancellation was one 'heartbreaking economy' demanded in the early 1930s. By then, however, WMCs had already moved some distance from their early objective of 'promoting education by the establishment of lectures, classes, examinations and scholarships'. Secondary education and expanding provision for adult education were of some influence here, but less important, it seems likely, than the changing tastes of working men themselves. Alongside its lecture and news rooms, in 1899 the New Bond Street WMC was offering skittles, bagatelle, billiards and chess, while concerts were staged at both the 'Manny' and the 'Notts' two or three times a week. Ten years later, the Borough of Leicester, as it had now become, had added gymnastics and French classes, a brass band, debating society, and cycle and air-gun clubs to the list, and the 'Manny', prompted perhaps by growing tensions between the European powers, now boasted its own miniature rifle range.

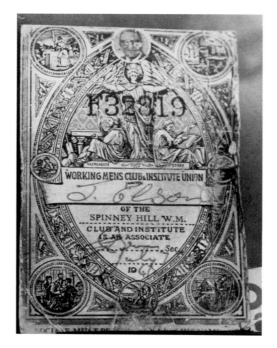

*Spinney Hill Working Men's Club
membership card, 1960s*

In the period following the Second World War new clubs were once again established to serve new housing estates, among them the Eyres Monsell WMC and the Humberstone WMC at Thurnby Lodge, which later became the Scraptoft Valley WMC. Others, like the Braunstone Victoria and West End WMCs, were established by and for ex-Servicemen. By the 1950s, however, as rising real incomes brought a wider range of leisure activities within the reach of working-class families, and television began to offer a home-based counter-attraction, many WMCs found themselves under financial pressure once again. A past president of King Richard's Road recalled that, when he first became a member in the mid-1950s, club officials were providing newspapers from their own pockets, some breweries were insisting on cash on delivery, and the concert room was unused for a time because the club could not afford to hire entertainers.

Salvation came in 1957 through legislation permitting the playing of tombola for cash prizes. At KRR the first house initially paid *2s 6d* for a line and *10s* for a full house. The game was played with re-usable cards, and the numbers covered with counters – or bottle tops, as an alternative. Further legislation in 1965 enabled the clubs to install fruit machines or 'one-armed bandits', and between them these two forms of entertainment continue to provide them with the bulk of their income. Nevertheless, said one official of a local club in the late 1970s, 'I can never accept the widely held view that the Working Men's Club is merely a place for booze and bingo. The basic things are already supplied, of course – a good pint of beer, facilities for sports and live entertainments in good surroundings. These are not to be sneezed at. People who work hard all week are entitled to relax in whatever manner they wish. Clubs provide a kind of friendly umbrella where people can shelter from the storms of life. . . .'

Adult Education in the Community

Though the leisure aspects of working-class associational life were dominating consumption patterns and choices during the middle years of this century, educational developments within the same circles were also of increased significance. In this respect the concern for education and the resources poured into it almost came to replace the earlier fields of philanthropy and material self-help in the search for associational life with a wider social purpose. In this respect community education, which had begun in the last years of the nineteenth century, took on a new significance as its value was recognized by state approval and eventually by state funding. The leading institution in this area was the Workers' Educational Association, which flourished in Leicester.

The Workers' Educational Association, an independent and voluntary adult education association, had been founded nationally in 1903, and in 1908 the decision was made at a meeting in the Trade Hall to establish a branch in Leicester. The strong adult education tradition already established at the Vaughan Working Men's College, adult schools and through University Extension classes eagerly embraced the idea of the tutorial class promoted by the WEA. The aim of such a class was to provide a course that was intensive but accessible to students with a limited education. The majority of students were weekly wage earners whose education had ceased at thirteen or fourteen. Up to thirty people would undertake to attend a two hour class once a week for twenty-four weeks each year and produce written work as required by the tutor. Eventually it was hoped that a proportion of students would progress to study at Oxford University. The tutor was usually appointed with the consent of both the students and the university (the first university to do this in Leicester being Oxford). The same scrutiny of tutors was applied to preparatory classes and the first class proposed by the Leicester branch was Industrial History. Classes took place in a variety of locations, largely through the goodwill of other bodies. Sources of funding for payment of tutors and accommodation were as varied as they are today. Students paid a fee of 1s for this first class and enrolment seems to have been between thirty and forty. In addition, the Board of Education generally would make a grant to cover about half of the tutor's fees and travelling expenses, and the Local Education Authority in this first instance allowed the WEA free accommodation and made a grant of £8 towards the expenses of providing the class.

The preparatory course was followed in 1909 by an advanced course in Industrial History. Alongside this the branch ran a preparatory class on Social Teachers in Literature in co-operation with the University of Cambridge, as well as a series of popular lectures, paid for largely by affiliated societies. The success of the three year tutorial class was evident from student demands that it should be extended, and it proceeded to a fourth year. At its conclusion the branch reported that 'the discipline of systematic study, the development of the power of self expression, the gaining of a wider and more sympathetic outlook on life, the widening of the mental horizon, the learning to respect the opinion of others, have been the most important results, and these are the things the WEA exists to help people achieve'.

In the years immediately following the First World War the branch developed its work in Leicester to the point that it was holding three or four tutorial classes a year, an equal number of preparatory or one year classes in places such as Desford, Glenfield, Wigston, Fleckney and Barwell. The establishment of the first adult education regulations of the Board of Education in 1924, created a so-called Responsible Body, which could receive grant aid from the Board towards the cost of providing classes. This was to begin a process of considerable change for the Leicester branch. Universities became responsible bodies for the provision of tutorial and preparatory tutorial classes and the WEA districts for the provision of elementary classes. However, the East Midlands District handed over its responsible body function to the university, which undertook the financing of all the teaching work undertaken through the WEA in the extramural area of Nottingham.

At a meeting held in 1919 the Leicester Branch Executive Committee welcomed 'the gift of the Old Asylum to Leicester as a University College', and there began an interesting relationship between the WEA and the university that continues to this day. In 1926 the Vaughan College building was accepted by University College to serve as the headquarters and main centre for a Department of Extra-Mural Studies, the decision for University College to enter the field of adult education having been taken in consultation with the Branch and District WEA, and with the consent of the University College of Nottingham. From 1929 University College, Leicester, assumed responsibility for the provision of all WEA classes in the City, and the branch and its classes finally had premises of their own. Before long the WEA – in the words of Professor A.J. Allaway, a former Vaughan Professor of Education – 'had literally captured the College', partly because its secretary occupied a key position within the institution, and partly because the extramural students had been well organized under the WEA banner. Indeed, no other branch of the WEA in the country except London was as prosperous. Interestingly enough Professor Allaway, on his appointment, was informed by F.L. Attenborough, Principal of University College, that one of his first duties would be to recapture 'the Vaughan' for University College!

The advent of the Second World War brought about changes to the WEA that the First had not. Three year courses were totally impractical as was serious private study, and tutorial and other long classes disappeared from the branch programme to be replaced by short and weekend courses, without the requirements of written work. Despite this there was a considerable increase in provision and in the last year of the war 126 classes were held with 2,555 enrolments. The post-war years saw a number of changes. Though tutorial and sessional classes were restored, the branch

The old Vaughan College, Great Central Street

promoted on its own responsibility a number of classes and weekend schools, and the Department, through the Board of Extramural Studies, provided several special classes and courses. However, there had also been a considerable qualitative change in the audience for adult education. The students had become mostly salary earners who had received at least a grammar school education. Further changes took place in 1951–7 when it was decided that the branch and department be administered separately, and that an extension committee and a joint committee with the WEA and a Board of Adult Education be established. This meant in practice that the WEA branch now had a limited partnership with the university's Department of Adult Education, had direct responsibility for programme planning and recruitment, and had effectively lost its tutorial classes.

The branch had pursued aims initiated nearly seventy years before with the stress on liberal academic education. Up to this point the branch had been controlled largely by one man, Frederick T. Watson, who joined the WEA soon after the branch was formed and was treasurer and secretary for many years until his death in 1989. Fred Watson became involved in the WEA during the First World War, when he was imprisoned as a conscientious objector. He joined the Blackburn branch and then moved to Leicester. During his long life Fred Watson had been an active supporter of working-class movements in Leicester and, as well as being a City councillor, he had also chaired the Education Committee for some eleven years. He felt that the WEA had not changed essentially since it was formed, except for a tendency for it to become more academic, and that it continued to provide an effective stepping stone for people who have not done well at school to gain education and, in his own words, 'to become responsible citizens who will take an interest in the affairs of the city in which they live'.

In 1977, the appointment of Terry Mahoney as tutor organizer was a turning point for Leicester's adult class programme. Terry Mahoney's interest in priority groups, and the fact that he was a member of a working party assessing education in the inner city, encouraged him to pursue the idea of establishing an inner city adult education project similar to that established by Ashcroft and Jackson in Liverpool. The West End of Leicester was chosen as a suitable area because the two local centres offering classes – the Fosse and Westcotes School – were to be closed, and there would be no facilities for adult education or community centres in the West End. Despite opposition from some district members of the WEA, a grant was obtained to purchase a three-storey terraced house along the Hinckley Road, which opened in 1980. In the first instance a community worker was appointed to run the project, as that expertise was felt to be necessary for the project's development. To begin with a small number of classes were run at the centre but, in recent years, the project has flourished, attracting community groups and establishing courses at a variety of venues in the West End including Shaftesbury Junior School, the neighbourhood centres, libraries and temples. Students now attend an extremely varied programme of classes, many aimed at helping people with everyday problems. As in Leicester, courses are instigated by the branch and by the Development Officer. Funding for this project now comes from a variety of organizations, but mainly the WEA District, Leicester City and County Councils.

The Age of Joint Initiatives

By the 1990s this sort of joint co-operation between the public and the private through a variety of responsible bodies has become an essential part of organizational and associational provision. This two-handed approach has recognized that provision from above is not always desirable and that initiatives generated by, and for, the community are often those best qualified to satisfy desire and need. One particular area of response that has emphasized the necessity of this approach has been the very different experiences, problems and possibilities brought to Leicester by the numerous ethnic communities that have chosen it as their home. The arrival of these communities has necessitated a rethink of the nature of community services, which have had to review and update themselves to remain relevant.

At the beginning of the twentieth century the closely packed terraced house districts of Highfields, Belgrave and the West End were home to individuals and families from every county in England and Wales, with the north of England particularly well represented, attracted by the thriving hosiery, boot and shoe and engineering industries. The opportunity to get steady work also drew migrants from further afield with the census of 1911 recording 1,059 people born in

Scotland and 886 in Ireland. There was also a small number of foreigners, the census of that year reported 445 non-British nationals resident in the city. The process of integrating the constant flow of newcomers with those born and bred in Leicester took place, with working-class districts literally overflowing with people and offering every type of shop, service and community activity.

The Impact of Ethnic Diversity

To gain some appreciation of the intensity of urban living in the early years of the present century it should be noted that the overwhelming majority of Leicester's 211,579 residents lived within the area bounded on the west by Fosse Road, on the north-east by Gipsy Lane, on the south-east by East Park Road, on the south by Avenue Road and Knighton Fields Road. Compare this with the 270,600 enumerated in the 1991 census who live within a city area that extends north to Beaumont Leys, east to Thurnby Lodge, south to Eyres Monsell and west to Braunstone and New Parks. Rented accommodation, either the whole of a two-up two-down terraced house or part of one, brought families and individuals into such close contact with each other that an intense community spirit developed, which helped them enjoy the good times and survive the all too common bad times. Newcomers would often move in with relatives, or friends from 'back home', until they found their feet, but in the case of the English these clusters were seldom large enough to be recognized beyond the streets and households directly involved.

In the case of the Scots and Irish much more 'high profile' communities emerged to which new arrivals would automatically gravitate. The Irish established themselves in the Highfields area and through their churches, church activities, clubs and pubs created a point-of-contact and entry into the city's economy and society. This 'presence' attracted a steady flow of Irish (Eire) to Leicester, which reached its peak in the 1950s when Leicester's industries were crying out for unskilled labour. From a maximum of around 4,500 in the early 1960s, not only has the community declined to around 3,500, through death and return migration, but it is also no longer so highly concentrated within Highfields. This has been due to families moving out to peripheral council estates or to own homes in other parts of the city.

Between 1901 and 1951 Leicester's population increased by 73,602 to 285,181, mainly through natural increase supplemented by the continued flow of migrants from elsewhere in the UK and Eire. Apart from the latter group, as has already been described, the social structure of the city did not have any strongly identifiable 'regional' component. Indeed the inter-war housing policies of slum clearance and council house development were tending to break up any such groupings by reducing household densities within the inner city and moving families out to the suburbs. This was the situation at the outbreak of the Second World War, during and after which Leicester became the destination for a succession of migrations by individuals and families from Europe, the Caribbean, Asia and Africa, which have been instrumental in Leicester's emergence as one of Britain's truly multi-cultural cities.

The first steps in this process were taken as early as the last century. A small Jewish community first emerged in Leicester in the middle of the nineteenth century and by 1875 it was a fully organized congregation, recognized by national Jewish organizations and, locally, by the town itself. One of its leading figures was Israel Hart, who founded the major tailoring firm of Hart and Levy, which attracted a small number of Jews from elsewhere in Britain. One important group of new members came from immigrants fleeing from poverty and persecution in Russia, and by 1897–8 the congregation had grown to the point where they had been able to build a new synagogue in the Highfields area. The ability to build, as distinct from converting an existing building, was almost unique in the Midlands, and is a testimony of the vitality of this group. Equally significant was the election of Israel Hart to the mayoralty of Leicester on four occasions. Indeed this community during its first century was to provide three mayors or lord mayors for Leicester.

The First World War brought a number of new members to the congregation, but the largest increase came with the arrival of German Jewish refugees before 1939 and with the wartime rationalization of the textile trades. This brought a number of leading manufacturers from London and, together with evacuation, led to the congregation trebling in size. The end of the war led to many returning to London but the congregation was still larger than it had been earlier, and the growth of the university remained one significant feature in its continuing strength. The original community had concentrated in the Highfields area where the synagogue was built. This was as much for religious reasons as for any other. But as the 'popular' urban area moved out to the south-east and the Highfields area changed its character, many in the community followed the trend so that there was no longer any significant area of settlement.

The political upheaval, social dislocation and economic devastation of Eastern Europe and the Soviet Union brought about by the Second World War left many people, particularly the young men who had been in the forces, with no homes to return to. The rise of Nazism in Germany had already resulted in an exodus of Jews and others not willing to live under such a regime. The wartime devastation suffered by Germany also prompted others to leave and build new lives in Britain. Leicester offered an attractive destination for a small number of these migrants, 724 by 1951 (Table One, p. 186), through its established Jewish community and the availability of work in its thriving industries. A striking feature of this migration was the fact that females outnumbered males by two to one. These newcomers did not gather together in any particular areas; indeed the reverse was the case, as they were quite dispersed both spatially and socially throughout the city.

The fact that Polish soldiers, sailors and airmen came under general British command during the Second World War forged strong links of comradeship and familiarity, which were to be of great significance to many young Polish men and women when their country became a Soviet satellite state after the war. Many decided to start new lives in Britain. Leicester, like most cities in the UK, was the destination for part of this settlement; 1,003 people born in Poland were enumerated in the 1951 census (Table One). However, because of the buoyancy of its economy and the vibrancy of the Polish community the city continued to attract migrants from elsewhere in Britain throughout the 1950s, resulting in a community of 1,509 by 1961. The first arrivals came under the most adverse of circumstances since, despite having helped win the war, they found themselves refugees with little or no money and in many cases only a smattering of English. It was therefore not surprising that they gravitated to a part of the city where cheap rented accommodation, often digs with English families or shared by several single Polish men, was most readily available, and which was close to factories offering a range of jobs. Highfields was the chosen area and within a few years a thriving Polish community had been established there. The unequal gender balance of the migrant community, more than two males to every female, meant that many men married English girls, but there was a steady movement of Polish-born women to the city that went some way towards redressing this imbalance. The strong sense of national identity and the desire to maintain and develop Polish culture and traditions bound the community together very closely and much has been done to pass these on to its children. The 'Polish' church, on the corner of Dale Street and Melbourne Road, and its adjoining hall has served as the focus of the community. Over the years the Polish Saturday School, established in 1954, has taught the Polish language to GCSE and 'A' level and offered courses on the history and geography of the country. The Ex-Combatants Association on University Road was a focal point for the community for many years, but as the number of servicemen surviving has dwindled its role has been somewhat diminished. The ageing of the Polish-born population is reflected in the opening of a Day Centre in the church hall in 1990 at which members can meet friends, have traditional meals, hear talks and watch films. The community continues to thrive, but is now much less clustered as the original residents and new arrivals have moved to houses throughout the city. As is almost inevitable with a community that has not received a continuous flow of new migrants it is likely that a viable Polish community in Leicester will be difficult to sustain for many more years.

At the end of the Second World War people from Estonia, Lithuania, Latvia, the Ukraine and many other countries and states in Eastern Europe and Russia who had been forcibly moved to Germany found themselves abandoned and stateless. In addition there were many soldiers, particularly Ukrainians, who had been prisoners of war who were in a similar situation. Those who could not accept communism had no desire to return to their homelands and some came to Britain to build new lives. The 1951 census enumerated 1,029 people born in the USSR, mainly Ukrainians, in the city. The older terraced house areas offered rented accommodation that was within their price range and this accounts for the emergence of the Ukrainian community in the West End. The nature of the migration meant that some of the men were separated from wives and families, and since males outnumbered females by two to one many single men married local girls. A close-knit community emerged, which first worshipped in St Peter's church on King Richard's Road and met in the community hall established on Westcotes Drive in 1958. Ten years later the community had saved enough to buy its own church, on the corner of Hinckley Road and Fosse Road South. Meanwhile the Orthodox Ukrainians, who had first held services at St Michael's church on Melton Road, had moved to All Martyrs' church on Westcotes Drive. The churches and community centre provided meeting places for interest groups which, along with a Saturday School, were instrumental in preserving and developing Ukrainian culture and traditions. The involvement of first and second generation 'Leicester Ukrainians' in these activities and clubs has done much to offset the inevitable consequences of the ageing of the original migrants. However, as with the Poles, it seems likely that with the passage of time the Ukrainian community will merge with the wider community, but its culture and traditions will be preserved in the history of settlement in Leicester.

Italian prisoners of war had been held in prison camps in rural Leicestershire until 1945 and of those who decided to stay on in Britain a number moved into the city. The immediate post-war years also witnessed the arrival of women from Italy to take up jobs in private households and in local industries. The 1951 census records 163 people born in Italy and resident in Leicester, but as a result of agreements between the British and Italian governments during the 1950s this number had increased to 660 by 1971 (Table One). This migration involved equal numbers of men and women since Leicester offered good job opportunities for both sexes. Immigration from Italy ceased in the 1960s, which meant that although they chose to live in Highfields the number involved was never large enough to generate the intensity of community activity found in the Polish and Ukrainian communities. A priest comes from Nottingham to say mass in Italian, and on a city-wide scale there is a Dante Alighieri society. The ageing and dispersal of the Italian group has resulted in its merging with the community at large to a greater extent than has as yet occurred in the other European communities.

Table One: Leicester – Population born in selected European Countries

	1951	1961	1971	1981
POLAND	1,003	1,509	1,505	1,172
USSR	1,029	918	825	679
GERMANY	724	722	700	756
ITALY	163	455	660	528

Source: UK Census

The post-war boom of the 1940s and '50s gave rise to severe labour shortages, particularly in the service sector and those industries heavily dependent on semi-

Table Two: Leicester's New Commonwealth Population

1951	1,500
1961	4,624
1971	26,419
1981	59,709
1983	68,822
1991*	90,000+

* Estimate
Sources: UK Census; Survey of Leicester 1983

skilled workers. To meet the demand a number of major employers which included London Transport and the newly created National Health Service embarked on an active recruitment campaign throughout the Caribbean. High unemployment and overpopulation in most of the islands ensured the enthusiastic take-up of the jobs being offered, stimulating an upsurge in emigration to Britain. As with most other migrants the Afro-Caribbeans headed for the larger cities, particularly those that offered good job opportunities. Leicester met both of these requirements and received a steady flow of new arrivals throughout the 1950s and '60s. The Afro-Caribbean community presently numbers 5,084, of whom 2,530 were born in the Caribbean. Although this was a voluntary migration and they did speak the language, most had no experience of urban living, few had skills relevant to the jobs for which they were applying, and they came with little or no money. It was therefore not surprising that they gravitated to the inner city where the cheapest houses were to be found and near to the widest range of potential employers. When they arrived the central area redevelopment programme being actively implemented by the City Council meant that terraced houses were readily available on very cheap short term rentals as former residents were rehoused on local authority estates. Taking advantage of this niche in the housing market a substantial Afro-Caribbean community came into being in the St Peter's area of Highfields. The subsequent clearance of part of this area resulted in the rehousing of many Afro-Caribbean families on council estates throughout the city. However, the St Peter's cluster survived when clearance was discontinued and when members of this community were offered houses in the flats built to replace the cleared terraced streets. The evangelical churches on London Road and St Peter's Road are important foci for the community, as are the social and sports clubs that have been established in the

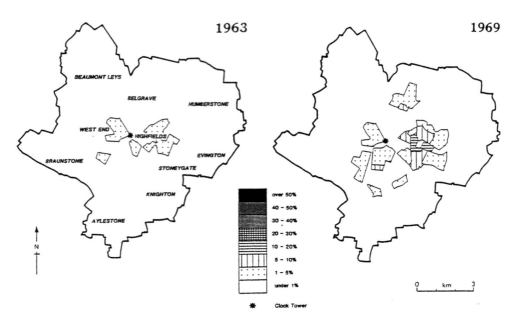

Asian settlement in Leicester, 1963 (left) and 1969 (right)

area. The high level of unemployment experienced by all sections of this community, but especially by the young, has resulted in the establishment of a number of central and local government supported community agencies and organizations, such as the Highfields Induction and Training Scheme and the Highfields Community Coaching Project, which have done a great deal to foster community activities, investment and involvement. The growth of a number of Afro-Caribbean owned businesses, flourishing youth clubs, and sports teams that are prominent in the city's football and cricket leagues and basketball programmes, reflect the existence of a vibrant community that is actively extending its range of cultural, social and sporting activities.

Long-established links between Britain and the Indian subcontinent had resulted in an ebb and flow of migrants throughout the twentieth century. The 1951 census found that 624 people born in India, or what was to become Pakistan, were resident in Leicester. As the demand for unskilled labour grew during the 1950s this information was transmitted back to the subcontinent along with details of wage levels, living costs and conditions. This information was undoubtedly accompanied by offers of a place to live and help in getting a job. When these were received in rural Gujerat and the Punjab, where unemployment was very high and opportunities for economic and social advancement almost non-existent, it was not too surprising that the process of chain migration was initiated. This has been a dominant theme among Leicester's Asian migrations ever since, resulting in the spectacular growth of the community. Bearing in mind the magnitude of this migration decision, especially for people with no money, limited familiarity with the language and few relevant skills, it is not surprising that it was overwhelmingly undertaken by lone males. Many left wives and families behind, others were young single men, and most viewed the migration as a temporary one, which would enable them to amass sufficient savings to allow them to return home with enhanced economic and social status. On arriving in Leicester they naturally formed very close knit groups in order to preserve key elements of their cultural identity. To maximize their ability to save, these groups established a series of lodging houses along the main roads in both the Highfields and Narborough Road areas of the city. With the passage of time it became evident that the remittances sent home were not going to be sufficient to significantly improve the family's long term economic and social standing back home. This realization resulted in a change in the nature of the migration, as husbands decided that they wanted their wives and children to join them and many single men went home, got married, and returned with their wives. The flow of migrants increased year on year as information about job opportunities spread throughout Gujerat and Punjab. It reached a peak in 1962 as a result of the UK government's intention to introduce restrictive immigration laws.

The family reunion phase initiated an important change in housing requirements since the lodging house accommodation was no longer appropriate. Coming as it did in the early 1960s this coincided with the City Council's plans to redevelop large parts of Highfields. The availability of a plentiful supply of cheap rented accommodation attracted Asian families to the area, and within a few years a substantial community had been established. The opportunity to rent and then buy homes close to other Asian families was particularly important for the womenfolk who naturally wanted the support and company of other Asian women, as many spoke little or no English. The numeric dominance of Asian families on groups of adjacent streets also fulfilled the community's desire for a return to traditional social and cultural lifestyles. This desire was strongest in the Muslim community because of its special religious requirements and the intense social interaction within the group. The existence of complex networks of kin and friendship links within the Asian community resulted in different groups establishing their own residential clusters. Within Highfields this accounts for the concentration of Muslims around the mosque on St Peter's Road, the much larger Hindu community in the area north to Spinney Hill Park and the Sikh community to the east and north of the park. The precise size of the Asian community has always been difficult to establish because ethnicity was not included in the census until that undertaken in 1991. Best estimates suggested that there were 20,190 people in the Asian community by 1971, almost all of whom were living in Highfields. As the number of households increased so did the range of cultural, social and service facilities located within the area.

In addition to the mosque, several Hindu and Sikh temples were established, along with meeting places for different cultural and interest groups. However, the ownership and nature of the shops and services is perhaps the most striking manifestation of the emergent community. Most of the shops along Evington Road and East Park Road, together with the corner shops scattered throughout the area, were taken over by Asians and a great variety of specialist food and clothing stores were established to meet the particular needs of the Asian community. This process intensified within the established areas and spread outwards during the 1970s and '80s. Initially growth was north to Uppingham Road, but as families became more prosperous they moved eastward into the semi-detached and detached houses on both sides of Evington Road.

In the late 1960s Leicester was the main destination for Asian families being displaced from East Africa as a consequence of persecution, in the case of Uganda, and the process of Africanization of business and public services in Kenya, Malawi and Tanzania. Between 1968 and 1978 it is estimated that in excess of 20,000 East African Asians arrived. They were attracted by the presence of an active Asian community, the city's excellent record in race relations and its reputation as a prosperous business centre. This unique combination provided an almost ideal migrational context for this professional and entrepreneurial group. The East African refugees differed from the earlier Asian groups who had settled in the city. In addition to their strong trading, business and professional backgrounds and good knowledge of English, they were fortunate to come as complete families, often

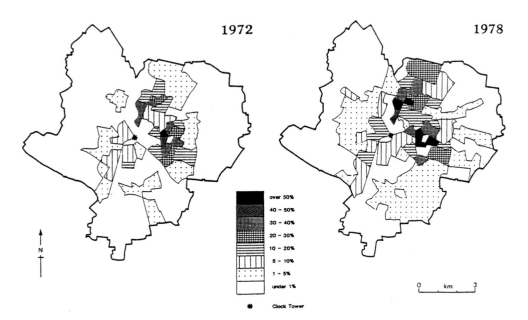

Asian settlement in Leicester, 1972 (left) and 1978 (right)

including ageing parents and relatives, and many were able to bring some, or all, of their savings. The availability of capital was to be of great importance in the development of new communities in the city. After what was often a very brief stay with relatives or friends in Highfields they wanted to purchase homes of their own. As the flow of houses on to the market in the Highfields area was not sufficient to meet the demand the East African families began to look elsewhere in the city. In Belgrave they found an area that was experiencing a loss of households as a consequence of rehousing and the ageing process. They moved in as a replacement population and quickly established an incipient community to which many new arrivals moved directly. By 1978 Belgrave had emerged as a flourishing community. The arrival of East African families also added a suburban dimension to the city's Asian community as families purchased houses on new estates being developed at Rushey Mead.

In 1983 Leicester's Asian population was found to be 63,186 and is now estimated to be over 90,000. Striking though the numbers are, the intensity of community life that developed in this area is of much greater significance. Hindu temples have been established throughout the area, there is a very active community centre and a variety of social and sporting clubs have been opened. Melton Road has emerged as one of the most striking retail and service thoroughfares in Britain. The opportunity to buy almost any conceivable type of Asian food, household furnishing, item of clothing or piece of jewellery, or to do business in an Asian bank, finance, estate or travel agency has made this street the focus not only of Leicester's Asian communities, but also for others throughout the Midlands. Alongside these highly visible components is the equally important, but rightly private, intense family and social interaction, which is a feature and strength of Belgrave and Leicester's Asian community.

Each successive wave of new arrivals has made its own unique contribution to the city we know today. The passage of time means that communities come and go, but their memory lives on through the institutions, businesses, history and geography they created. The multitude of English migrants who came to the city in the nineteenth century, and their descendants, created the present society and urban structure to which successive migrant communities have made their own distinctive contribution. The Irish and Scots, although no longer as numerous as in the past, have left a legacy of churches and societies. The European groups, on the other hand, continue as significant, if ageing, communities each with its own local area, institutions and cultural events. This contrasts with the large size and comparative youthfulness of the Asian communities. These groups have revitalized what were decaying inner city housing areas through their investment in the properties, intensive social interaction, taking over shops and businesses and establishing temples, mosques and community centres. Leicester has been fortunate to have received these repeated injections of 'new blood', which have revitalized its social and economic well-being. More importantly it has shown that this can be done in a spirit of harmony, that is most clearly reflected in the ease with which traditional and new religious and secular festivals are celebrated throughout the city.

Immigrant cultures in Leicester: performers in Leicester Arts Festival, 1978

Though the twentieth-century interest in leisure pursuits catalogued in another chapter has doubtless had its effect upon associational life and its related organizations, some aspects of community remain surprisingly durable. The sense of community that clusters around the workplace is increasingly under question as the average size of enterprise shrinks, but nonetheless represents a shared experience common to many in Leicester's staple industries throughout most of the twentieth century. Similarly the arrival of a succession of immigrant groups has regenerated certain inner city areas, has revitalized community life, and has stimulated interest and the application of resources to a range of problems – for the benefit of the whole local community. Though the charity style provision of the Victorian era has been substantially superseded by state intervention, its work in marginal areas remains important. This is increasingly seen, in a number of political quarters, as a way ahead and contains within it a deeper questioning of these state operated agencies. However, this ideological approach has also been balanced by these agencies becoming increasingly willing to consult communities about policy and provision through development and improvement schemes, community programmes, educational initiatives, as well as arts and health provision. Perhaps only with the passage of time and a renewed historical perspective will it be possible to assess how successful this process has been.

Further Reading

Allaway, A.J., *Vaughan College, Leicester 1862–1962* (1962)

Allaway, A.J., *Challenge and Response: WEA East Midlands District 1919–1969* (1969)

Bryant, M.T., *A way to God: a study of some of the beliefs and practices of Hindus in Leicester and Leicestershire* (1983)

Harding, Brian, *The good old days? 1881–1981: one hundred years of Working Men's Clubs in Leicester* (1985)

Maret, Valerie, *Immigrants settling in the city* (1989)

Mowatt, C.L., *The Charity Organization Society 1869–1913, its ideas and work* (1961)

Silverman, H.A., *The Vaughan College, Leicester: its history and future* (1930)

University of Leicester, Department of Geography, *Ethnic minorities in Leicester: a select bibliography*

Chapter Six

LEISURE AND CONSUMPTION

The history of leisure and consumption, perhaps more than most areas, reflects the changes that the twentieth century has brought to Leicester. At the turn of this century the growth of factory production and its effects of regularizing work and leisure patterns was still a comparatively recent phenomenon. The availability of regular leisure time to many groups of workers was important since it provided the impetus to the development of 'gate-money' sports such as football, cricket and rugby union. A century-wide perspective reveals a number of contrasts; the turn of the century witnessed leisure emerging as a self-generated cottage industry, whereas by the 1990s it has grown into a multi-million pound concern which is a vital part of both national and local economies. Leisure is particularly useful as a sensitive barometer to a number of social and economic developments. It often responds quickly to changes in economic prosperity as it is generally the last area to benefit from increases in disposable income. Similarly leisure time offered individuals choices which had not been available to earlier generations, and their response reflects attempts to carve out class, religious, racial, age and gender identities.

Edwardian Leisure

The leisure landscape of Edwardian Leicester was similar to that which had predominated in the late nineteenth century. The tension between old and new was emphasized by the growth of more modern entertainments such as football, rugby and other sports taking place alongside the continuing popularity of church- and chapel-based leisure. Though the Saturday half holiday came early to Leicester as a consequence of changing working practices in the hosiery trade, most factories and workshops were still working a fifty-plus hour week until they were altered after the First World War.

Leicester's tradition of nonconformity was an important factor in the survival of church- and chapel-based leisure initiatives. Most religious organizations had been spurred into action by the effects of suburbanization, which had depleted congregations in the centre of the city since the late nineteenth century. From the 1890s onwards most had done much to increase their appeal, either through making their services more accessible or through the development of recreational activities such as cycling and sports clubs, sewing circles, Men's and Women's Associations and educational classes. However it must also be remembered that alongside these developments the churches and chapels retained importance as places of worship. One of the most successful chapels in the first years of this century was the evangelical style Melbourne Hall which attracted considerable congregations throughout the Edwardian period. All of these attractions were, by the start of the century, increasingly geared to gaining the attention of age, gender and class specific groups. One of these forms of leisure which was pioneered by religious organizations and provided an outlet for many varied skills was the organization of bazaars. These fundraising occasions were grand affairs, which were built around a theme often employing expensive and elaborate sets and costumes, making them a popular form of entertainment. Attempts to capture the interest of youth were also important. Most churches and chapels had branches of the Boy Scouts or Boys Brigade as well as sports clubs. These were quite successful since they provided sporting activity that was not otherwise available, bearing in mind the organization and resources required for team games. While these activities were seen by church and chapel to have a moral and recreational value in themselves, they were also regarded as alternatives to the public house and other forms of diversion.

Works teams were frequent contributors to sport in Leicester. This is the Wolsey's ladies hockey team, 1926

The Old White Hart, in the Wharf Street area – later demolished to make way for the St Matthew's Estate

During the early years of this century the public house itself was the traditional centre for working-class leisure, and held a more important place in the community than it perhaps does today. In the absence of both home comforts and opportunities for cheap leisure the pub became a natural resort for many in search of conviviality and hospitality. The actual popularity of these pubs and drink in general is difficult to assess beyond the rather untidy figures for drunkenness, which only give a picture of over-indulgence. Figures for drunkenness in Leicester indicate that it was no worse or better than many other cities, but its frequency diminished considerably from the First World War onwards.

Though the effects of the public house quite often manifested themselves in the police courts they were also the centre for a community street culture which took in many illegal and semi-legal practices. Evidence for Leicester pubs indicate that they were centres for everything from organized betting and gambling through to the staging of unlicensed boxing matches, a particular feature of pubs in Wharf Street. As such they continued in operation in the twentieth century largely unhindered. Their eventual decline was more attributable to longer term changes in public taste than to the effectiveness of policing or the action of local authority.

Street Culture

One spin-off from this vibrant pub culture, the so called 'Sunday night parade', was cause for considerable concern well into the 1930s. This arose out of the large number of young people of both sexes who chose Sunday evening to congregate on and mill about the streets. The nature of the working week and the stringent limitations placed upon Sunday entertainment concentrated the problem on this day. These youthful activities stood in marked contrast to the more conventional forms of Sunday entertainment, such as the family walk and the Sunday concert, pursuits which were the very embodiment of respectability. A picture emerges of youths striving to emulate those whom they saw as 'slick' adults, and who flouted conventional standards. During the 1930s the *Leicester Mercury* was full of complaints from victims of this phenomenon. One letter written in 1933 drew attention to what it characterized as 'the growing menace in the Leicester market of youths, girls and boys, running like mad every Sunday evening around the covered stalls'. Though this 'parade' was represented by the *Mercury* and its correspondents as a social problem there were also more sympathetic views expressed. The Secretary of the YMCA was 'disturbed by the plight of Leicester boys who waste their leisure hours lounging in the street and meeting their companions around a street lamp'. Others laid some of the blame on overcrowded homes, which forced the Sunday night youth into the street, the public house or the working man's club.

The Chief Constable of Leicestershire was concerned with the 'Sunday night parade' as a public order problem. In 1930 he expressed the view that something was needed 'to take young people at a loose end, off the streets on Sunday nights'. However, the majority of the Leicester Council were not convinced and in April 1933, apparently largely on religious grounds, a resolution favouring Sunday cinema opening was defeated. Whatever the intentions of this proposal it stood more chance of transferring and containing rowdiness than it had of ending it. In 1930 the *Mercury* commented that rowdyism during concerts at De Montfort Hall produced a regular flood of complaints, while local cinemas similarly hinted that maintaining order in their establishments was no easy task.

Though much pressure to regularize forms of leisure and behaviour had come from official bodies like the watch committee, the corporation, local sabbatarian pressure groups and the media there was a more important factor at work. A clue to this is contained in the number of convictions for drunkenness in Leicester for the early century. This indicates that the pre-1914 period bears close resemblance to the late nineteenth century, which was the heyday of this offence. The dramatic fall in convictions in the immediate post-First World War period suggests that Leicester was starting to conform to a more modern pattern where over-indulgence was increasingly the exception. The factor that was of supreme importance for this change was the rising expectations induced by a growth in real incomes and the effects of this on home comforts and perceptions of living standards in general. This was also happening while a recognizably modern working week was coming to Leicester's major industries. The advent of the Saturday half holiday finally made the sports of football, cricket and rugby union a regular activity and persuaded many that they could actually be going concerns.

The Development of Spectator or 'Gate-money' Sports

The link between what might be termed the old and the new world of leisure is emphasized by the fact that many of what became Leicester's nationally known sports teams started life in the late nineteenth century as offshoots of other organizations. Leicester Tigers Rugby Club was founded, for example, by ex-army officers who saw it as a natural progression to take the Leicester regiment's nickname into the sporting sphere. The rugby club, with its high cost of subscription, emphasized its exclusive nature – with players only being granted their playing expenses as late as 1898. Leicester City Football Club took its lead from the religious organizations that had promoted many sporting teams in the city. The club began in 1884 as Leicester Fosse FC, founded by a group of youths, mainly Old Wyggestonians, who were members of the same Bible class. Leicestershire County Cricket Club similarly had its roots firmly in county society, and it was dependent on patronage from this source more than any other sports club. Several county families have been represented within the club throughout the early twentieth century, either by service as players or as committee members. These include the Hazelrigg, and the De Lisles as well as members of the Everard and Ruddle brewing families. Though members of the county gentry could be relied upon in earlier years to provide players and much needed patronage for the cricket club, their ability to do so for this and all other sports declined sharply as the century progressed.

Lapel badge for Leicester Fosse, 1901–2

Early Professionalism in Rugby and Cricket

Very quickly the formation of a major sports club brought with it a number of other imperatives. Both the football club and the cricket club were rapidly under pressure to provide play of a high standard and to contemplate entering the professional sphere. In the 1888 season Leicester City FC took the first momentous step towards professionalism when a player called Harry Webb was signed for a half a crown a week. The club's historian Noel Tarbottom noted that Webb's arrival was an early sign of the diverging interests of the playing and non-playing members of the club. On balance the former were presumably more committed to playing football, while the latter were perhaps becoming increasingly concerned with achievement and the quality of performance. The year 1891 was something of a watershed for Leicester Fosse. Not only did they move to Filbert Street, Leicester City's present ground, but they also gained entry to the Midland League.

The early years of the 'Tigers' suggest that the task of cultivating interest in the game of rugby itself was of primary importance before more ambitious club developments like those of the football club could be contemplated. Many changes in the rules were introduced during this period to encourage skill, and in some cases appear to have been aimed at whetting the appetite of the paying public. Already by the 1890s the practice of hacking had been abolished, and was closely followed by a reduction in the number of players from twenty to fifteen, suggesting a crucial phase in the development of rugby union into a handling game from its ramshackle footballing origins. Some tactical changes were inspired by the touring New Zealand 'All Blacks' who brought the virtues of support play and quick passing to a previously static game. After an initial season playing at Belgrave cricket and cycle ground the rugby club made a conscious decision to play its games in Victoria Park, where a larger, non-paying audience could be expected. By 1888, when it returned to the Belgrave ground, it took a large number of paying customers with it, as well as a growing fixture list that included regular derbies with Moseley, Northampton and Coventry. The club finally felt secure enough in 1892 to move to a permanent home, initially obtaining a ten year lease on the land from the City Corporation. By the closing years of the nineteenth century the club was making an impression throughout the region with an increasingly impressive fixture list, as well as having been finalists in the Midlands Cup two years running.

The County Cricket Club underwent similar rapid development in the closing years of the last century. Leicestershire became a first class county in 1895, also taking out a lease on its Aylestone Road ground offered by Leicester Corporation; this was extended to 21 years at £200 per annum in 1899. The acquisition of this new ground combined with the recent elevation to first class status awoke considerable public interest in the first seasons of the new century. Despite early promise the county were unable to deliver consistent results, though the performance in 1904 was noteworthy since the team rivalled the major counties of Yorkshire and Lancashire before finally finishing seventh.

As all three clubs entered the new century the enhanced status that they had gained within national leagues and structures seemed to offer a bright future for them both as successful clubs and as successful businesses. However, all three quickly realized that these new forms of existence brought responsibilities and commitments that were sometimes hard to reconcile with one another. Financial stability often varied with the popular pressure from fans, which generally aimed at improving the performance of the team on the field of play. So often these two aims could appear to be incompatible, leading to a dramatic polarization of views about how Leicester's sporting clubs were run and whether they were there for the benefit of fans or merely for committees and Boards of Directors.

Professional Football

The pressures making for professionalism within Leicester City Football Club, for example, were very powerful. The ambitions of the membership which first stimulated this process also led the club, when faced by financial crisis, to press ahead rather than contemplate a return to the shallows of the Association game. In 1894 these same pressures also drove the club to apply successfully for membership of the second division of the Football League. At the same time, the constraints of organizational and financial viability began to have consequences for the balance of power within the club. Members were cautioned when electing committee members 'to temper any democratic impulses by remembering that committee men would be required to provide a guarantee to the bank'. These signs of splits within the club are further confirmed by the emergence of an 'us' and 'them' divide, which surfaced in a series of letters to the correspondence column of the *Mercury*. In 1897 the club was registered as a limited liability company and the increasing dominance of financial matters clearly irritated a section of the club's ordinary supporters. During this period their dissatisfaction was born out of frustrated aspirations rather than abject failure since, in the first three years under the new administration, the team finished seventh, third and fifth in the second division. Paradoxically, it was only when the Board considered the club to be more secure financially and, therefore, felt able to turn its attention to team building that a long decline set in. Having acquired an 'expensive team', the club began the 1900–1 season with high hopes. However, the competition proved to be stronger than anticipated, because by January the team found itself struggling in the lower reaches of the second division. Continued criticism of the board provoked a director, a Mr Curtis, to state bluntly that if the crowd 'want[ed] football next season it had to be paid for and the directors could not advance any more money'.

In April 1901 at another public meeting, George Johnson, the club secretary, adopted a more conciliatory tone. He said that the 'directors wished to know where they stood. If the members will inform them what sort of team they would like, the directors will try and fulfill their wishes.' Numerous public meetings seem to have done little to curb the criticism of the Board. One contributor to the correspondence column of the *Mercury* urged fellow supporters to apply for a share, so that the Board would 'have to acknowledge us'. In the 1901–2 season, the unresolved financial crisis led the Board to opt for a 'cheap team', unfortunately with predictable consequences, resulting in the Board's eventual decision to enact a clean sweep of the team. Clearly this inherently unstable policy could not even guarantee second division status, let alone allow the entertainment of thoughts of promotion. Any remaining doubts on this score were finally put to rest at the end of the 1903–4 season when Leicester Fosse had to apply for re-election to the second division. The *Mercury*, for the moment conveniently forgetting its role in generating the optimism that had been dashed, remarked: 'Time after time we have been buoyed up by the hope that, at last, the committee have secured a really strong team and just as often we have found that as soon as the talented ones have breathed Leicester air they have become as ineffective as their predecessors and even more disappointing.'

In the wake of this crisis, further attempts were made by the club to raise public money. A supporters' fund was established with the promise that the proceeds would be left under the sole control of a Supporters Executive Committee. However, within three months the fund had folded and, in a clear attempt to conceal its failure, it was said to have been replaced by the Million Farthing Fund. From the depths of having to apply for re-election in 1904, there occurred a steady improvement in the club's league position. The improved form attracted larger crowds, and the increased takings more or less freed the club from debt. The improvement continued and the following season proved to be the most successful in the history of Leicester Fosse, the club winning promotion to the first division of the Football League. However, at a public meeting in May 1908 the chairman, Mr Squires, dispelled the promotion euphoria by pointing out that to compete successfully at the higher level meant that the club required an injection of £5,000. He proposed that £1,500 of that sum should be raised by a share issue. The immediate response was poor, with only eighty to ninety of the shares taken up by the assembled supporters.

Leicester Fosse's first taste of first division football quickly turned sour. By as early as December 1909 relegation beckoned and, inevitably, the criticism began to flow. In the face of this kind of hostility Johnson renewed the invitation to supporters to become shareholders. Such an offer was not to the liking of at least one supporter and in the course of delivering his response he may well have articulated the views of many ordinary fans: 'The object of management is to provide good-class football for its patrons who pay the recognized charge. While the club is carried on as a business, the customers as spectators, are only responsible for the charge made at the gate; the management and shareholders must do the financing.'

Amid such acrimony the club was relegated, with inevitable financial consequences. Under this ominous cloud, a meeting consisting of shareholders and ticket-holders agreed to pay an extra admission charge for three matches. Moreover, a subsequent meeting of supporters from the Popular Side and the Spion Kop not only agreed to pay an extra 3*d* on Christmas Day, they insisted on doing the same for the Boxing Day match. The *Mercury* was quite uplifted, writing: 'Never before has there been such gratifying unity between management and supporters.' This, however, was the only optimistic moment in a long period of uncertainty.

Pre-First World War Developments

Declining performances after the hope generated by enhanced status was also apparent at the County Cricket Club. Though occasional seasons in the early years showed that the county could compete on level terms with the bigger counties, such as 1912 when Kent, Surrey, Lancashire and Yorkshire were all beaten, the years leading up to the First World War were generally characterized by under-achievement. Alongside this the finances caused concern, since despite strenuous attempts to promote membership the club ran a deficit of £1,500 in the same year as such comparative success was achieved on the field.

The organizational demands of county cricket placed considerable strains upon the Leicestershire club, and indeed these were to do so down to the middle of this century and beyond. As a county Leicestershire did not enjoy the advantages for cricket possessed by other counties. Its small size limited its catchment area for players in the early years of the century, when the necessary qualifications to play for a particular county were considerably more stringent than today. Thus Leicestershire County Cricket Club was forced to rely on the limited local talent available. In the last years of the nineteenth century players were found from the village cricket enclaves of Earl Shilton, Barlestone, Ratby, Mountsorrel, Birstall and Carlton Curlieu as well as the city of Leicester itself. Similarly the county also made much of its connections with local schools and colleges. The most notable of these was Uppingham School, which produced a number of players for the first eleven. This connection was to be continued in later years when the school produced a string of players for the county into the 1980s, as well as providing teaching and coaching employment out of season for several players. In later years when regulations were relaxed the county found itself in perennial competition with four neighbouring counties for both players and supporters. Similarly, the lack of a strong established local league structure like those in Derbyshire, Yorkshire and Lancashire also proved a long term handicap. Perhaps as a consequence of these disadvantages the county husbanded its resources more intelligently than other counties, frequently enacting game orientated innovations to survive.

Though the struggles of the cricket club were more often than not attempts to survive in an unhelpful climate, Leicester Rugby Club was able to be in the forefront of changes that were professionalizing both the provision and the consumption of gate-money sports. The growth of the Tigers into a club of national prominence was in a large part due to the efforts of the Leicester printer and stationer Tom Crumbie. Crumbie was the club's secretary in the years which straddled the turn of the century and his reforms were designed to ensure the

Leicester Tigers Rugby Club 1919–20 (Tom Crumbie is seated on the extreme right)

success of the Tigers beyond the local area. The scope of the club's aspirations is demonstrated by the discontinuation of its A and B teams and the transformation of the club into an invitation side, which brought in talent from beyond the confines of Leicester. Though the resulting financial savings were distributed to other local clubs, the net result was probably a lowering of the competitive horizons of rugby throughout the rest of the county as the Tigers 'collared' the local market. Nonetheless there is no doubt that this decision ensured the quality of the game practised at Welford Road. The success of this policy was evident since the team's efforts were appreciated by average crowds of between 5,000 and 8,000 in the Edwardian period, and these reached a pre-First World War peak of 10,000 in 1913.

The onset of hostilities in 1914 provided a break in the development of Leicester's premier sports clubs, with the suspension of sporting activities and the requisitioning of many facilities by the armed forces. The years that immediately followed the war saw a considerable boom in crowd attendances which had been facilitated by pent up demand and by reductions in working hours for many workers that followed shortly after in 1919. When competitive sport resumed the cricket club picked up where it had left off, fielding almost the same side that had competed in 1914. As with many other sports including football and rugby union, the game of cricket went through something of a boom in the years immediately following the First World War. In 1921 upwards of 12,000 came to the first day of the county match with the touring Australian team and the club made a profit of £2,000 on the year. However, the cricket club found stability harder to come by than the other two premier sports clubs. Leicestershire owed thanks to Leicester City Football Club for raising £1,000 from a match with Airdrieonians to service the debt accumulated during the financially disastrous 1924 season. This was to be followed by a similar charitable act eight years later when the rugby club raised £1,500 for the county from a match between Leicestershire and an East Midlands XV.

The rugby club itself was, however, enjoying a level of popularity that enabled those in charge to invest in a wide range of resources inspired by the new agenda that the status of gate-money sport brought with it. The Tigers were, for example, the first club to introduce forms of rudimentary protection for the playing surface when sand was laid on the pitch to avoid a money-spinning encounter with Coventry being postponed. Similarly, developments to the ground were a matter of priority once a high profile provincial status for the club became a desirable goal. In the first ten years of the century the club spent liberally on seating capacity, turnstiles and a press box. A club house followed in 1909, which provided much needed changing and entertainment facilities previously provided by a nearby hotel.

Other improvements to the ground followed, and in 1919 a large stand (later named after Tom Crumbie) was erected on the cattle market side of the road. This stand and the work carried out during the previous twenty years brought the total ground capacity to over 40,000 spectators. The opening of this stand by the president of the Rugby Football Union, W.E. Presscott, in 1920 was in some respects a further chapter in the RFU's recognition of Leicester as a provincial rugby centre. This had been developing from the first years of the century, with Leicester hosting an impressive array of major fixtures including the second ever North versus South match and an England versus Ireland international. The financial importance of these games was not lost on the club, emphasized by the profit of £700 from the latter fixture. In addition to this the arrival of a regular Boxing Day fixture against the Barbarians, the most famous invitation team in the country, further served to indicate Leicester's arrival as a major club.

The Era of Supporters' Clubs, 1920–39

The renewed and significantly increased interest in the fortunes of the city's major sports clubs in the inter-war period was viewed with considerable optimism by the officials of the clubs concerned. This is hardly surprising since it offered some hope of security in both sporting and financial contexts. However, it is important to note that the increasing role of spectators in providing these forms of security for the clubs concerned also had its price. Supporters and regular spectators increasingly saw their regular attendance as a form of participation that should be acknowledged by clubs and their officials. This became an increasingly articulate voice in the shape of supporters' clubs or 'friends' of the sporting club concerned. All felt they had a right to representation within 'their' club, which had been earned through vocal and financial support.

Thus the period after the First World War brought a considerable qualitative change in the relationship between the Board and the supporters of Leicester City Football Club. The Board became distinctly less communicative and more distant. In 1924 one correspondent to the *Leicester Mercury* wrote: 'at Filbert Street there is autocratic rule in the relationship of the directorate and the spectators. Surely we supporters are entitled to some say in the government of the game we support?'. Certainly there were strong authoritarian tendencies running through the development of the club and its relationship with the supporters. Throughout, these tendencies were firmly tied to the general commitment to maintain the club's Football League status. However, there is little doubt that these conditions suited the preferences of the Board, as men of business, to run their own affairs. Yet in the pre-1914 period, it seems that the resources of these men of business were not sufficient to enable them to bear the accumulating deficit generated by the regular seasonal shortfall in gate receipts. As is generally the case today, attendance was a particularly sensitive barometer of the team's performance. If the team's prospects were in decline after Christmas, so too was the crowd.

The consistent failure of the Board to communicate its intentions rekindled an idea first proposed in 1921, namely that a supporters' club should be established. Initially this suggestion had been presented in the mildest of terms, although by 1923 some supporters were getting rather more bullish in their demands and felt that such a club should be represented on the Board. But as has so often been the case, these calls for greater participation subsided when the fortunes of the club improved. In the 1924–5 season, Leicester City won promotion to the first division of the Football League. The demands for greater supporter involvement in the affairs of the club only re-emerged in the early 1930s when fears of relegation began to mount, culminating in the club being relegated at the end of the 1936–7 season. However, notwithstanding the fact that Leicester City regained first division status the following season, supporter criticism soon began to sharpen. By 1939 even the *Leicester Mercury*'s establishment orientated sports columnist Simon Dee was beginning to warm to the idea of a supporters' club. For its part the Board showed no signs of even contemplating the prospect. Yet magically, a few months later, the Board publicly reversed the élitist stance it had maintained for almost two decades, welcoming the prospect with seemingly unbridled enthusiasm. A meeting was called and the membership quickly grew to some three hundred, though the momentum evaporated rapidly. Not surprisingly the news that the club was encountering difficulties was speedily overtaken by the news that its activities were to be suspended for the duration of the war.

The history of the attempts to voice concerns regarding the running of the rugby club in some respect echoes that of the football club, where increasingly vocal opinion became a focus for discontent that was taken seriously only when gate receipts were threatened. In 1925 *The Times* declared that the Leicester ground was the best in England after Twickenham. Though this enhanced prestige was desirable there was a price to be paid locally. The club was almost constantly in debt during the inter-war period and the creation of an invitation team almost certainly raised expectations, which the club at times found it difficult to sustain. In the same year as *The Times* had complimented the club there were complaints that the teams fielded were of variable quality, with recruits from local teams used as makeweights when international players were unavailable. During the same period there resurfaced the often voiced complaint that the club's invitation policy led to the neglect of both local rugby and local talent, which also suffered from the withdrawal of financial support in the wake of the Leicester club's own problems.

This discontent was only of real importance when it was harnessed in the shape of a supporters' club, which became a reality for the Tigers in 1934. Once again the concept of a supporters' club was, in the eyes of administrators, a means of ensuring commitment and income. Thus a supporters' club was consciously seen as a fund raising body to assist the financing of a club policy already in place. The supporters' club staged its first function, a 'Tigers' Night' at the Palais de Danse, on 8 December 1934, and this set the agenda for the direction of its subsequent efforts – organizing fêtes, dances and other social functions. In this respect the almost defensive role of the supporters' club reflected the inter-war marginalization of the sport itself, which was losing its mass audience to football and other pursuits. The necessity for this defensive role, coupled with the absence of a league structure with its attendant promotion and relegation issues, served to inhibit the growth of expectation, making the rugby supporters' club a thoroughly different animal to that generated by the football club.

Despite this there were still grumblings in the years leading up to the Second World War concerning erratic team performance and the need to ensure a steady stream of new recruits. It is also perhaps of no coincidence that many of these complaints were followed by concerns expressed in the *Mercury* regarding falling gates. In 1936 the *Mercury* appeared to recognize this, when it asked what the Tigers would give today for one of their early century attendances in excess of 16,000. In response to the problem the club made attempts to raise money, which included the introduction of match programmes, the letting of the ground for professional boxing and an abortive attempt to introduce greyhound racing! Meanwhile on the pitch the tension for the Leicester club between promoting local rugby in the county and rejuvenating its status as a gate-money attraction was brought into sharp relief by the suggestion that gates would increase if the Tigers relinquished some of their local fixtures in favour of games against the more famous Welsh clubs. These measures were forced on the club by the harsh realities of the 1920s, which saw members' subscriptions fall by over £7,000 in ten years while crowds never repeated their pre-war level. When this decline is put in the context of the resources that had been put into the club, and the ground in particular, the situation appeared serious.

For Leicestershire County Cricket Club the 1930s were the crucial decade for the development of club/supporter relations. This period witnessed a string of mediocre team performances set against the backdrop of dwindling finances. Though the county finished a respectable sixth in the championship table in 1935 it incurred a debt of £5,000 which, if it had not been cleared by appealing to local cricket enthusiasts, would have led the county into a potentially disastrous merger with Lincolnshire. As with the other two major sports clubs of Leicester a period of great financial need brought forth the suggestion that a supporters' club be formed. This was instigated by a minor club official, Captain C.E. Loseby, who saw it as a fund raising initiative, and its history of organized donation bears comparison with the rugby supporters' club. While this new innovation promised much, the performances of the team on the field still left a lot to be desired, and the decade closed in 1939 with the county occupying last place in the County Championship.

In some senses the Second World War rescued Leicester's premier clubs from a vicious circle of dwindling financial resources, leading to polices that had a detrimental effect on team performances. The storms that the inter-war economy weathered certainly left sports clubs increasingly in competition with one another. Both the reliance on gate money and the demands of a professionalized approach added to these problems by also encouraging supporter participation. If this could be regulated by the club itself it was welcome, but it equally provided a variety of platforms for potential discontent.

The Post-War Boom: Benefits and Costs

Though the immediate post-war period witnessed a boom in the popularity of all gate-money sports the optimism that this created was to to offer these clubs no respite from the pressures they had experienced in the pre-war period. Once more supporters and club members began to demand a greater voice in a variety of matters that affected their clubs. The Leicester City Supporters Club re-emerged in 1946 and immediately sought external recognition by affiliating to the National Federation of Football Club Supporters. Despite this the Board of Directors remained hostile to the very idea of such a club and its outsider status was highlighted when it failed to gain any preferential treatment in the allocation of tickets. Any remaining hopes that the supporters' club may have harboured about its imminent acceptance by the Board must surely have been crushed in 1948 when the chairman, Mr Pallett, expressed the view that: 'the Football Club was a public limited company and the shareholders put a board of directors in charge. All of you running your own business would not want somebody else to tell you how to do it.'

Undaunted, the supporters' club continued with its policy of uncritical loyalty. While this strategy did not reap any immediate rewards, by 1954 the chairman Len Shipman and the manager Norman Bullock had begun attending the annual dinner of the supporters' club. However, even in 1957 an official of the supporters club could report that it had still 'not been recognized by the powers-that-be at Filbert Street'. It suffices to say that while over the 1960s, 1970s and 1980s the football club has increasingly accommodated the supporters' club in what amounted to a *de facto* recognition, it did not formally recognize the supporters' club until 27 November 1990.

The enforced inactivity of the war years left the rugby club nearly £2,000 in debt, while it also reclaimed a ground that had been damaged, requiring a public subscription to put matters right. Though the club went through a brief post-war boom, which offered an opportunity for rugby union to re-establish itself as a popular spectator sport, it still maintained older attitudes that served to separate the club from its patrons and must ultimately have limited its appeal. Though spectator accommodation was impressive by national standards there was little attempt to integrate the paying public into the club. In a manner that echoed the sport's public school origins, refreshments were not provided for spectators and the comparatively sparse social life was maintained for players only, with wives excluded until 8 p.m. Though a bar with a more relaxed policy was eventually introduced, the post-war boom in attendances had evaporated by then. By the early 1950s it was clear that rugby was once again losing out to other sports and leisure pursuits. In the 1949–50 season for example the home crowd was never above 10,000, with the exception of the money-spinning Barbarians fixture. Stringent economies rapidly became necessary, which brought into sharp relief the still unresolved tensions between those who saw Leicester Tigers as a prestige club with traditions, not unlike those of the Barbarians, and those who urged the adoption of a more modern outlook that would produce success on the field and bring back the crowds. Among new fundraising initiatives new reforms banished forever the invitation club ethos that had characterized the early years of the century, and this break was confirmed by the insistence of the reformers that the whole committee should support the new direction. Though much of this remedial action had positive effects, encouraging a stabilization of support for the club, the committee still had trouble in the 1960s in raising funds for improvements to the clubhouse.

When cricket resumed in 1945 there was considerable damage to the pitch and buildings on the Aylestone Road ground, which led the Corporation Education Committee to offer the county the use of the Grace Road ground. The offer was graciously received, and the county settled into its new home as a second boom period descended on county cricket and other pastimes as a leisure hungry audience flocked back to the turnstiles. Though the county only finished fourteenth in the championship in 1947 this performance was nonetheless watched by record attendances. The following year saw 16,000 turn out on the Saturday to see the county take on the Australians. One consequence of the post-war boom was a concerted attempt by the cricket club to extend its appeal within the county. Thus in the years following the war the cricket club staged regular games in Ashby and Hinckley. More fleeting appearances at Barwell, Melton Mowbray, Coalville and Loughborough were all attempts to draw on the resources of what was always one of the smaller counties involved in first class cricket. Both Ashby and Hinckley staged cricket weeks in the early 1950s, which were the nearest the county could provide to the lucrative festival weeks that Yorkshire, Lancashire and other major counties had long since instituted. Generally speaking they did not have the impact that was hoped and the use of grounds out in the county began to dwindle from the 1960s and 1970s onwards as they became increasingly uneconomic.

Leicester's Premier Clubs and Mass Leisure

In an earlier attempt to keep the club afloat a winter football competition was launched, which followed an earlier precedent set by Worcestershire County Cricket Club. Almost inevitably the re-establishment of the supporters' club came back on to the agenda, and it was once again considered as a method of organizing and administering the football competition. By the end of 1953 the supporters were able to give the club more than £20,000, with the weekly contributions collected by an army of agents rewarded by honorary membership of the county club. Other attempts to establish a regular source of revenue for the county club were the brainchild of Mike Turner, a former county player who became the club's youngest ever secretary in 1961 at the age of twenty-five. Turner was responsible for the introduction of the Midland counties knock-out cup, which brought the concept of one day, limited overs cricket to a wider public. This eventually became the first national knock-out competition in the shape of the Gillette Cup, intended to provide a sorely needed injection of cash, which once again became a problem for the club. The subsequent retirement from playing duties of Charles Palmer, one of the county's most influential figures, served to confirm the impression that the county was swimming against the tide in the late 1950s.

The next decade began in the same dispiriting manner, with the club finishing bottom of the county championship in two of the first three years with no sign of it becoming financially solvent. It was in this atmosphere that Mike Turner conceived the idea of one day, limited overs cricket as a possible solution. The explanation for this innovation was simple. Audiences for the three day format had been falling for some time so that one day cricket was seen as an important source of extra revenue, which fitted in with the constraints of modern mass leisure patterns and the public taste for a completed game with the certainty of a result. The concept began as a Midland Counties only knock-out competition but within a year it had become national. Though the introduction of this competition was a brave move its format also relied on some degree of success for it to deliver the extra, hoped for revenue. Unfortunately for Leicestershire the team's performance in the early years of the Gillette Cup was not impressive. In a further attempt to boost revenue the county was the first to introduce Sunday play in the county championship in 1966, though it initially did little for the club's finances since the close season saw a deficit and cutbacks in the playing staff. Though both results and finances improved in 1967 the long term benefits of one day cricket were still seen as the way forward. The introduction of the John Player League and the establishment of regular Sunday cricket was a recognition of this trend and was an essential shot in the arm for all of the smaller, poorer counties.

For Leicestershire the introduction of a second one day competition coincided with the best period of its history. The arrival of Ray Illingworth from Yorkshire, a captain and player of considerable ability, inspired Leicestershire to a series of performances that set new standards in one day and three day competitions. Leicestershire's first success came in the Benson and Hedges Cup, a third one day competition extending the appeal of this form of cricket to a mid-week audience. Illingworth led the county to two victories in this competition in 1972 and again in 1975, as well as the John Player Sunday League championship in 1974. However, the county championship was still the major prize and this found its way to Grace Road for the first time in 1975, which was also the first year that the county succeeded in defeating the Australian touring team. The county's achievement was recognized by both the City and the County councils, and was commemorated by a civic reception and the naming of some roads on the Rowlatts Hill estate after players from the championship winning side. In the wake of its success this period also saw the recognition by both City and County council of the county cricket club as a civic amenity, and accordingly it was granted £5,000 per year as a recognition of its role in encouraging cricket development in schools. The late 1970s also saw the county extend its facilities for the development of local cricket. A new trophy, the County Cup, was instituted and it has remained sponsored by local companies

The finalists in the Young Muslims' Cricket Tournament, 1989

with the final played at Grace Road. Similarly the club has also hosted women's matches at both its headquarters and at the miners' ground in Coalville, which staged a match between East Midlands Women's Cricket Association and an Australian women's touring side in 1976.

From the early 1950s changes have been underway that have combined to undermine the insularity and exclusivity of the Boards and committees of all of Leicester's major sporting clubs. In short these clubs are faced with a struggle for survival in a more competitive world in which potential audiences have fragmented in response to a variety of alternative pastimes. In response to these combined pressures the more powerful clubs have sought to ensure that the resources available to major clubs, ranging from supporters to star players, have been increasingly redistributed in their favour. In addition to this, football clubs like Leicester City have been forced into relationships with external organizations. Such clubs are also heavily dependent on the police to maintain order, and the increased involvement of the Football Trust has given it a correspondingly important voice in club affairs. The role of local authorities in the granting of ground safety certificates has made football clubs become more professional in their approach to providing for fans and selling spectator sport as an end product. Finally television, with its own agenda, has now become the single most important influence on the modern game of football, and this is fast becoming true of rugby union as well. The growth of a premier league structure is the culmination of these pressures and supporter groups are likely to press for a meaningful say in the way in which their football club is run. These pressures for professionalization have also had their effect on Leicester Rugby Club, which made considerable progress throughout the twentieth century with a largely unaltered amateur ethos. The jealously guarded status of major provincial club meant that it was in a prime position to take advantage of the onset of professionalization, winning the John Player cup competition on three occasions in the late 1970s. There is no doubt that the arrival of national competitions, like the John Player Cup and the establishment of the Courage League, have altered the climate for rugby union considerably. Once these competitions brought with them considerably higher gates than the ordinary 'club' games the pressure to succeed at the highest level has been enhanced, with the price of failure being costly. Success itself brought rewards through the turnstiles, as well as ensuring the ability of clubs like Leicester City and Leicester Tigers to draw on a shrinking pool of quality players. The increased demands of faster games on the players themselves has increased the pressure to professionalize all sports. With clubs adopting shirt sponsorship and players demanding an increasing share of the income they generate, cricket, football and rugby union are facing dramatic changes in the years that will close the century. While Leicester Rugby Club has entered the arena of league and cup competitions at a comparatively high level, bringing an enhanced share of national and local interest, should this situation be reversed then it may find itself fulfilling the demands of the casual and armchair supporter as professional football has increasingly had to do.

Both choices contain an element of risk since the commitment to the television agenda has not always been a recipe for success. In the early 1990s even the appeal of the Sunday form of cricket appears to be under threat as widespread television coverage has ceased and crowds have fallen. It has also become clear that the enthusiasm of the players for one day cricket has been exposed to be a myth. This, alongside the greater physical demands of the modern game, has been laid bare in *Eight Days a Week,* a factual account of the 1988 season written by Leicestershire's former fast bowler and now broadcaster Jonathan Agnew. Despite this revelation observers might be forgiven for asking what motivates decisions at the highest level of modern gate-money sports, since the 1993 cricket season has seen a lengthening of Sunday play and the introduction of coloured balls and clothing meant to appeal to a generation more at home in the television age. However, the machinery to capitalize on the renewed interest such developments might provide is in some senses already in place. The county's own development programme in local schools, currently operated by Laurie Potter (a member of the first team), has been a positive response to the perception in the 1980s that cricket has vanished from the school curriculum. In this respect the future lies in harnessing the interest and talent of the next generation of potential players and supporters. While traditional avenues of support will need to be reinforced new markets will have to be developed. In a Leicester context it is noticeable that the ethnic minority communities remain under-represented as supporters of the City's major sports clubs.

Leicestershire County Cricket Club's coaching scheme in action

The concessions that all clubs have to make to public taste, articulated through the turnstiles, may at last see a final untangling of the relations between clubs and their supporters. Under these conditions supporters' organizations may well be able to acquire a growing influence in the affairs of their clubs. In both instances the clubs themselves will be faced with the perennial criticism of supporters voiced through an increasing variety of media such as the fanzine, a subcultural product of the 1980s. These publications, such as Leicester City's *The Fox,* have an increasingly important role in stimulating both loyalty and criticism in an age that otherwise threatens to produce purely armchair interest in sport.

Music Hall and Theatre

At the beginning of the twentieth century Leicester had five professional theatres, all in close proximity in the area of Horsefair Street, Hotel Street, Silver and Wharf Streets and Belgrave Gate. Each venue provided a different type of fare so that the tastes of all were catered for, while the town was well served by good tram and train services, which brought in people from the county. The course of the twentieth century has seen these institutions go through many changes, which have themselves reflected the inconstant nature of public taste and the increasing need to make theatres successful businesses.

The oldest building was the Theatre Royal in Horsefair Street, backing on to the market-place, which dated from 1836; though by 1901 the interior had been altered many times. Here were performed comedies, tragedies and the 'blood and thunder' melodramas that were extremely popular with the audiences. The more bloodcurdling and exciting the plays were the better the patrons liked them, especially those who sat up in the 'Gods'. The very titles indicate what the contents must have been: *Twixt Good and Evil, The Penalty of Crime, Greed for Gold* and *Mysteries of the Thames.* However, although the local papers claimed that audiences were enjoying their evening entertainments, business cannot have been good. The Theatre Royal Minute Book in the Edwardian period shows that the lessee of the theatre was often in arrears with the rent, and was permitted to reduce the prices of the dress circle from 3s to 2s. The late payment and reduction of prices were no doubt due to the considerable amount of unemployment in the town at that time. By January 1906 the lease was transferred to Milton Bode and Edward Compton, the proprietors of several other theatres, including the Northampton Opera House, now the Repertory Theatre.

The local papers did not carry regular advertisements from 1906 to 1924, but the few surviving advertisements show that weekly touring companies occupied the boards, giving plays of all types. In 1914 the Theatre Royal moved to twice nightly performances with a matinée on Thursdays, which was early closing day in the town. By this time, however, falling attendances were caused by extra war work in the textile industry, which coincided with an increased difficulty experienced by theatre managements in booking good companies during the conflict. The inter-war period saw the introduction of companies who stayed for a short season, so enabling the management to save on moving actors and scenery. In 1925 Fred Clement's Company of Skegness Entertainers performed for eight weeks with a constantly changing programme. No doubt many people had seen the Entertainers at Skegness, the perennially popular seaside resort for Leicester inhabitants. Revues took over the stage from 1927–33, when the theatre closed, to be reopened in 1934 when repertory companies, with a new play each week, became the order of the day. The names of these companies and their players are still remembered with affection by Leicester people: the Terence Byron Company, the Edward Nelson Players, the Regency Players, the Saxon Players, the Leicester Repertory Company, to name some of them.

At the beginning of the Second World War the times for the rise and fall of the curtain were strictly controlled by Parliament. This ensured that times were staggered so that large numbers of people did not come out on to the streets at the same time. After the air raids in Leicester, performances at the Royal were given at 3.45 p.m. and 6 p.m., with the last buses leaving the town centre at 9 p.m. Audiences were good since many firms were evacuated to the city and the workers needed entertainment and relaxation. When the Royal, a Grade 2 listed building, closed in May 1949, a committee of influential citizens attempted to gain civic support for it, but without success. Even when the Local Government Act of 1948 allowed local authorities to raise a 6*d* rate for public entertainment, Leicester City Council dragged its feet. The theatre was eventually sold to a Birmingham syndicate and reopened for fortnightly repertory by Derek Salberg and Basil Thomas. The company stayed until July 1950, but there was insufficient support. The companies that followed reverted to weekly changes of programme but they had to battle against the rising popularity of television, and in June 1956 the theatre closed. Eventually the Leicester Permanent Building Society purchased the property and the demolition men moved in.

The Royal Opera House occupied a site that ran through from Silver Street to Cank Street. The frontage of red brick and white stone was built in the Queen Anne style, and the *Leicester Journal* of 15 June 1877 stated that it was 'in excellent harmony with the general characteristics of public buildings in Leicester – simple and unostentatious and . . . of an eminent substantial appearance'. As befitting an opera house great attention had been paid to the acoustics of the auditorium, which seated 2,350 people. By 1900 the theatre had become a favourite venue, particularly with patrons who preferred a 'higher class' of entertainment than that provided by the Royal. The audience could enjoy Frank Benson's Shakespearean Company and, Mr D'Oyley Carte's Opera Company, performing Gilbert and Sullivan, when every performance was sure of a full house. In 1903 Henry Irving appeared and all the reserved seats were taken before the curtain rose on the first night. Pantomimes were staged every year with elaborate transformation scenes, and a performance was always given at the Poor House. The plays of George Bernard Shaw were always popular, and the same was true of the performances given for a week, every year, by the Leicester Amateur Dramatic and Musical Society. The Opera House prospered with its varied programme of opera, musical comedy and drama until the summer of 1932 when a season of variety was presented. This was followed in October by *The Good Companions*, brought at 'a cost of several hundred pounds'. It was a big production with '16 scenes', and forty local people were employed as extras. This was in addition to the local employment that was always generated by the theatres, for dressers, ushers, stage hands, box office staff and cleaners. As at the Royal, however, bookings of good companies became difficult when television started. The theatre struggled on until 1953 when it closed. In 1959 it was bought by Samuel Locker, who had been concerned with the purchase of the Royal. He reopened with a pantomime, but no redecoration had been done to repair the ravages of closure, and when the curtain fell on 11 June 1960 it was not to rise again. The theatre was immediately demolished and replaced by the Malcolm Arcade.

In 1901 the McNaghten circuit took over the Prince of Wales Theatre, which was on the corner of Belgrave Gate and Wilton Street, renaming it The Pavilion. Programmes of variety, revues and plays were staged, and an episode of a film, which always ended in a cliff-hanger, was shown. Many famous artistes appeared there – Lily Langtry, Gracie Fields, Bud Flanagan and Rob Wilton among them. A repertory company was booked in 1929, playing twice nightly, with a Thursday matinée, and performing two plays each week. The company, originally booked for three weeks, stayed for eighteen months and would have continued, but the theatre was doomed by a road widening scheme. On 6 December 1930 the last house was packed, and 'there was scarcely a dry eye' as the final curtain fell and the 'Old Pav' was pulled down.

Pavilion Theatre, c. 1930

Concert Night

It is possible to see the tendency towards more professional and commercial administration of premises through the rapid changes that occurred even in forms of entertainment that sprang from a relatively spontaneous pub culture. Music halls developed from the 'free and easy', more often known as the 'free and boozy', concerts in public houses. The popularity of this type of entertainment led to part of several premises being converted into concert halls with a stage. The body of the hall was generally furnished with tables and chairs or benches, and a bar from which patrons were served during the performance. The Gladstone Hotel and Concert Hall on the corner of Gladstone Street and Wharf Street was such a venue, seating 500 people and with an admission charge of 3*d*. By 1901 it had been rebuilt inside as a theatre and renamed the Royal Empire Palace of Varieties. In addition to turns, the patrons could watch films and newsreels on the American Bioscope. In 1921 after a further name change to the Hippodrome films took over competely, until it closed in the later 1930s. Now only the exterior remains as a reminder of its earlier life.

The jewel in the crown of Leicester music halls was the Palace Theatre of Varieties, situated in Belgrave Gate where Argos now stands. Designed by Frank Matcham for Oswald Stoll it opened in 1901. It was a comfortable house, beautifully decorated, with a colour scheme of copper, gold and blue, and carpeted throughout. Variety stars such as Marie Lloyd, George Formby, Harry Champion, Charlie Chaplin, Harry Lauder and Little Tich topped the bill. Stoll was determined to continue to provide top class entertainment when the First World War started, even though the introduction of Entertainment Tax in 1917 caused a rise in prices as, of course, it did for the other theatres. The reviews indicate that houses were

Interior of the Palace Theatre in its heyday

good, but a comment suggests that it was 'only the young and frivolous who can find much time to attend temples of drama. If that is so, and the shortening of work hours brings an older class of patrons into the dramatic market, it may be that the new industrial development will prove a good thing for the stage.' The house turned to films in 1931 and remained as a cinema, with the exception of a production of the ice show, *St Moritz*, until 1946, when variety returned. At first houses were good but the audiences soon dwindled, and by 1956 nude shows were presented, but even these failed to fill the house. The management said in 1958, before it eventually closed, that it had cost over £50,000 to keep the theatre running during the last five years.

For 160 years Leicester had supported entertainment in purpose-built theatres: by 1960 the only theatre still in existence was the Little Theatre, Dover Street. Developed within the shell of a chapel and opened in 1930, it was the home of the enthusiastic players who formed the Leicester Drama Society. The LDS became one of the leading amateur theatres in the country, and despite a disastrous fire in 1955 that necessitated rebuilding, the society continues to provide live drama of the highest standards. Faced with the possible eclipse of drama in the city the Leicester Theatre Committee continued working towards the re-establishment of professional theatre. This was ultimately a recognition that the provision of live theatre in the city was a civic amenity rather than simply a market-led leisure industry. Proposals were made to adapt existing buildings, but these schemes fell through. Despite this the committee made valiant efforts to bring live drama to the city, inviting Stephen Joseph's company to Vaughan College in 1958, when full houses watched Margaret Rawlings in *Phedre*. Joseph's company paid a return visit, with new programmes, and performed in the halls of Wyggeston Girls', Wycliffe School and the College of Art. Another innovation was the Century, a mobile theatre made up of trailers, which formed an auditorium for 225 people when joined together. The committee brought this theatre to the city, set it up in De Montfort Square, and it played for a month in 1959.

By this time it was realized that more permanent provision should be made for a theatre, and a site was earmarked in the new Haymarket development. To provide for the interim the Council and a Theatre Trust built the Phoenix, which seated 274 and had an open stage. It was received with enthusiasm, playing to 90 per cent capacity in its first season. The intention was that this theatre should close when the Haymarket was up and running, However, when this occurred in 1973 there was an outcry from the faithful Phoenix audiences that resulted in Phoenix Arts Ltd being set up, which now runs the theatre under the auspices of the Council and De Montfort University. Rebuilding of the foyer and the siting of a piazza facing Newarke Street has recently created a pleasant enclave where all forms of the arts are catered for.

Leicester Haymarket under construction, 1973

Opened in 1973 as a fully equipped professional civic theatre, supported by the City and County Councils, and an Arts Council grant, the Haymarket is now recognized as one of the leading provincial playhouses in the country. In the main house and the studio all types of plays have been produced, while musicals are always popular, and opportunities for children to perform are provided by the Haymarket Young People's Theatre. Many of the shows have transferred to London, bringing in very welcome royalties, for in common with most theatres financial problems have loomed large, though artistically the theatre has gone from strength to strength. In an article about the Llyubimov production of *Hamlet*, the *Stage and Television Today* of 2 November 1989 wrote: 'It carries the torch for the Haymarket around the world, making the company cultural ambassadors for the UK, and trail blazers for developing international partnership in our theatre.'

Though Leicester has been a centre of mass entertainment the experiences of the city's main sporting clubs, theatres and cinemas has indicated that the potential audience for these attractions has been more or less shrinking during the course of the century. Though two post-war booms injected degrees of optimism they were both ultimately short-lived. In the earlier half of the century the pattern of leisure and consumption outside the home was increasingly being eroded by improvements in both the level of real income and the facilities offered by modern housing. In the latter half of the century the magnitude of this change grew in importance as the number of amusements both inside and outside the home multiplied. Increasingly it was the emerging possibility of domestic leisure that was to have the greatest impact. Though this trend had been visible in the 1930s it was greatly accelerated by the changes that the Second World War brought.

Leisure during the Second World War

Leisure played a crucially important part in the lives of people living in Leicester during the Second World War. It provided an outlet for those living under the stress of wartime conditions and gave relaxation to those employed for long hours on essential war work. On 3 September 1939, at the onset of hostilities, places of entertainment attracting large crowds were closed down. The government order was issued to prevent mass casualties in the event of enemy bombing. These closures created an outcry, however, resulting in the re-opening of cinemas, theatres, football grounds and so on in neutral reception areas, like Leicester, only six days later. The war had a devastating effect on sport both in Leicester and on a national level, causing many cancellations in the sporting calendar. Teams were depleted as young, healthy players were often either the first to volunteer or were called up for active service. Facilities were also rapidly commandeered – in 1940 all city swimming baths, with the exception of Vestry Street, were used for civil defence training. Granby Halls was used as an Ambulance Station, while Victoria Park was dug up and used for allotment plots.

As outdoor sport declined in wartime Britain, indoor entertainment flourished. In

1940 the BBC introduced a new wireless Forces Programme, concentrating on light hearted entertainment appealing to a mass audience. Variety shows, dance-band music and sport were in sharp contrast to the traditional stuffy and often highbrow Home Service. People in wartime Leicester could laugh along with Tommy Handley in the phenomenally popular *ITMA* ('It's That Man Again'). In the same year *Workers' Playtime* was introduced, a twice weekly variety programme broadcast from factory canteens. Audiences were treated to talented performers, such as Elsie and Doris Waters, Flanagan and Allen, and George Formby. However, not all listeners appreciated this type of entertainment. A letter to the *Leicester Evening Mail* of 6 August 1942 protested 'against the growing tendency to introduce vulgarity into BBC Programmes'. When employed for long hours in war work at the Standard Telephone & Cables factory at Aylestone, a young worker recalled *Worker's Playtime* coming to her factory a couple of times: 'I didn't think it was anything outstanding, not at the time; I think it was the big factories who had the main *Workers' Playtime* with all the top stars. . . . One of the things I do remember when we were on day work was what we called *Morning Star*, from seven until quarter-past seven in the morning, which was all the top line singers . . . on the whole the BBC didn't play an awful lot of pop music, as they call it now, in them days.' Radio news, especially the 9 p.m. bulletin, understandably attracted the largest adult audience, eager for up-to-date information. A young wartime wife and mother remembers listening with regularity to the news and hearing the speeches of Churchill and Chamberlain. *The Brains Trust*, with experts answering and debating listeners' questions both serious and 'quirky', at its peak attracted listening audiences of 10–11 million each week. Its appeal resulted in local 'Brains Trust' panels being set up in areas all over Britain. In Leicester in 1942 a 'War Works Brains Trust' was advertised as a daily attraction at the Bell Hotel Ballroom.

Reading was a popular leisure activity during the war. Books were borrowed from public libraries or exchanged and loaned by family and friends. In addition to national newspapers, Leicester people had a choice of two local issues: the *Leicester Evening Mail* and the *Leicester Mercury*. The woman on the 'Home Front' enjoyed magazines like *Woman, Woman's Own* and the *Woman's Weekly* for fiction, fashion, beauty and for recipes and knitting patterns. The *Leicester Evening Mail* ran a regular daily feature, 'World of Women', which covered, among other things, women's war-time activities, charity events, cookery, household hints, children's issues and sport. Pre-war leisure sometimes became necessary work: the 'Dig For Victory' campaign encouraged the British people to become more self-sufficient in the growing of essential food. In August 1940 the *Leicester Mercury* demonstrated considerable local pride in reporting Leicester's 8,000 allotment plots. Travelling in and around the city was made difficult with the rationing of petrol, and the governmental campaigns asking 'Is Your Journey Really Necessary?' added further pressure. Buses to the outskirts of town were often full and the bicycle became an essential means of transport for work and for leisure. A cycle into the countryside was a popular activity, as was a ride out to Bradgate Park.

The cinema during the war was immensely popular: 'We liked light hearted films like Bing Crosby in *The Road to Singapore*, anything that wasn't too serious.' Musicals were the particular favourite of a young war worker, especially those with popular stars like Fred Astaire and Ginger Rogers. Because of travelling restrictions and blackouts another war worker, like many other Leicester people, went mainly to cinemas near her home, on and around the Narborough Road. This area was well endowed with cinemas, but it was the Roxy or Olympia she used regularly. When she visited the city centre cinemas it was usually either the City or the Odeon for the Saturday afternoon matinée. 'We used to like the Odeon because it was new, there was the organ coming up out of the pit playing music . . . the decor was quite nice . . . there were lovely silk curtains.' She recalled a cinema on High Street 'which was called the "flea-pit" . . . it was a bit crummy . . . if you told anybody you'd been there they didn't think much to it. It was like saying you'd been to a shady dive.'

There was an arts revival in Britain as individual performers and companies escaping the London blitz toured the provinces. In Leicester the Sadlers Wells Opera & Orchestra performed Rigoletto, La Traviata and Madame Butterfly over a

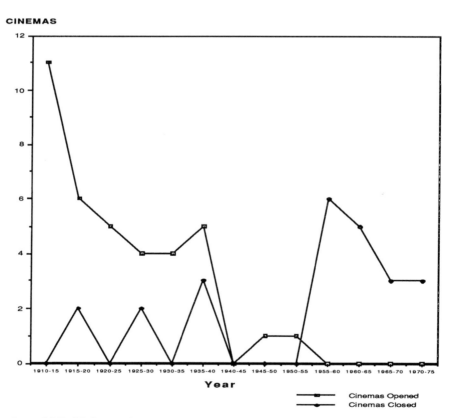

CINEMAS

The rise and fall of Leicester cinema

two day period at the Opera House in December 1942. In August 1942 both the Hallé Orchestra and the London Philharmonic Orchestra performed at De Montfort Hall, both conducted by Dr Malcolm Sargent. Richard Tauber made a personal visit to the Opera House as Schubert in *Blossom Time*.

Dancing was another favourite pastime during the war years. The palm-courted 'Palais de Danse' on Humberstone Gate had 'two bands on a Saturday night: one at the top and one at the bottom'. Like the Palais, the De Montfort Hall had its own residential band, The Metrognomes Dance Band, spot prizes, a licensed buffet and lighting effects added further attractions. The Joe Loss Orchestra and vocalists appeared for the first time in Leicester, at the De Montfort Hall on 8 August 1943; tickets cost 5*s*. Leicester people often used their local dance halls. An Aylestone girl danced at the local Working Men's Club while a South Wigston girl recalls dancing in the soldiers' gym at the barracks, and 'we used to have a little hop at St Thomas's Hall, every so often'.

There was, though, some dissatisfaction with Leicester's pub life during this period:

'We used to catch the bus, a crowd of us, over to Mountsorrel, and then we used to go to the dance there, or in the pub for a drink and then we used to walk all the way to Sileby to catch the train back to Leicester. Because there were nothing in Leicester on Saturday nights, apart from the dance halls; the pubs had no music, nothing like that . . . it was the Leicester Watch Committee, the deadest people on Earth, and you can print that, they really thought they were dictators. You couldn't do this on a Sunday and you couldn't do that. The working men's clubs had music, but of course you had to be licensed. But we used to go to another place in town called the "Hat and Beaver", I mean, that weren't legal, we used to have music in a room at the back, anybody who could play the piano used to get on the piano and we had a good old sing-song.'

The presence of the American GIs around Leicester was acknowledged with mixed feelings. For some they brought life and bustle to an otherwise quiet town. 'A lot of girls got carried away with them. . . . I didn't think a lot to them, to tell you the truth. . . . They were spoiling for a fight all the while our men and them; you couldn't blame our men because our women were falling over them.'

Summertime to many Leicester people meant holiday-time even during the war: 'We went to Blackpool; you could only go on certain parts of the beach. We had a week's holiday there, about six of us from work.' Nearby countryside was also a popular place, 'because you didn't have a lot of money to go away, or go far. We used to go in and around Matlock in Derbyshire; we've had lots of holidays round there.' With little motor traffic about, children in wartime Leicester could play safely in the street. Traditional games like hide-and-seek, tick and skipping were often played. One mother would take her children for walks in Abbey Park, and let them run around on the grass. In summertime there was a children's paddling pool,

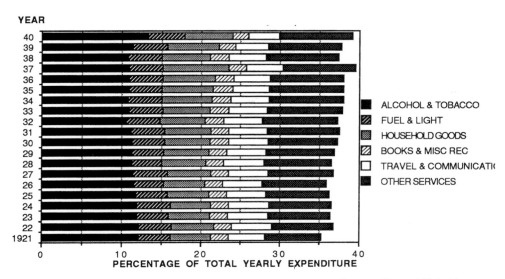

YEAR

PERCENTAGE OF TOTAL YEARLY EXPENDITURE

- ALCOHOL & TOBACCO
- FUEL & LIGHT
- HOUSEHOLD GOODS
- BOOKS & MISC REC
- TRAVEL & COMMUNICATI(
- OTHER SERVICES

Consumer expenditure at current prices as a percentage of total yearly expenditure, 1921–40

swimming and sunbathing at the Lido near Humberstone Car Terminus with 'half a million gallons of pure water'. For some, because of rationing, there was the almost obsessive pursuit of sweet things: 'I missed sweets, I've always had a sweet tooth . . . we made toffee out of treacle or Lyles Golden Syrup . . . you got a concoction which was a bit like Crunchie bars.' In times of happiness and celebration, leisure became more spontaneous: 'My cousin got married on VE day; she didn't know it

VE day celebrations took many forms in Leicester

was going to be VE day, of course . . . afterwards we all trooped into Leicester and danced round the Clock Tower. There were folks rushing up, everybody kissing each other. They were doing the conga round the Clock Tower – it was all boarded up, most of it was – folks were singing. . . . I remember a sailor kissing me . . . everybody was out of their minds, they just couldn't believe it.'

Post-War Leisure and Consumption

Increased living standards, particularly from the 1950s onwards, enabled the growth and development of a number of hobbies and pastimes that competed with the more traditional ones. Part of Britain's export-led revival in the years immediately following the war was based upon the production of consumer goods, many of them related to the leisure market. It should be remembered that new industries began to take shape since these goods had to be produced as well as consumed. One area that was represented in Leicester and grew in importance was the photographic industry. Leicester's associations with the printing trade made it a natural focus for the development of this post-Second World War consumer industry, when firms such as Reid and Sigrist and Rank, Taylor & Hobson became important players. Reid and Sigrist had only recently relocated to Leicester from bomb damaged London, benefiting from wartime industrial policies. One branch of the wartime Special Operations Executive was engaged in 'liberating' patents from German factories and distributing them to British and American companies. At least one patent from the Leica factory came to Reid and Sigrist, and the Leicester firm spent considerable

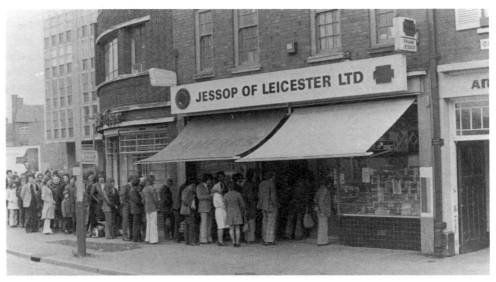

Customers queue outside the original Jessop's camera shop upon the abolition of purchase tax, April 1973

time and research developing a 35-mm rangefinder camera to supply the needs of British industry and capture post-war markets. One further advantage that Leicester had as a centre of camera production was the existence of a firm supplying very high quality lenses – Taylor, Taylor & Hobson. In the period immediately preceding the war the firm was renowned for its movie camera lenses, which were used in Hollywood studios, beating off the German competition. This lead in the movie industry was maintained by the firm's design team, which solved the technical problems associated with the technicolour film medium and the later developments of cinemascope and Vista Vision. Thus by the mid-1950s Rank, Taylor & Hobson estimated that they were supplying over 80 per cent of feature film camera lenses. Unfortunately the precision and quality of Taylor, Taylor & Hobson products never made a lasting impression on the increasingly important consumer volume market. Cheaper and cosmetically superior competition from Germany and, increasingly, Japan made the Leicester firm concentrate on the precision market, and it was later to become a part of the Rank organization.

From the late 1960s Leicester's expertise in the area of photography shifted into the realm of retailing, a trend that was indicative of the failure of the manufacturing side to compete. The firm of Jessop's began trading in a small shop near the Newarke in 1930 and many citizens of Leicester must have obtained their first camera from these premises. The rise of Jessop's coincided with a dramatic increase in sales of domestic photographic equipment in the mid-1960s and with the abolition of price maintenance within the industry. Very quickly Jessop's became a major company in the world of mail order retailing – on the back of bulk buying practices, competitive prices and a vigorous advertising campaign. Leicester was regarded and is still regarded as the prime site for such an operation because of its central location, with good road and rail communications. In 1978 Jessops moved to larger premises on the Hinckley road, which remain the largest single photographic retail store in Europe. By the 1990s the firm possesses over forty branches nationwide and is the biggest photographic retailing chain in Europe, employing over 600 staff. Although Leicester is acknowledged as the British centre of photographic retailing, the cameras and lenses that sit on the shelves of its shops are made in Japan, Taiwan or Hong Kong when once they would have been made in England, perhaps even in Leicester.

In the post-war world the centre of leisure significantly shifted into the home rather than the sports arena, pub or theatre. Radio had brought the war as well as national entertainers into the homes of millions. Similarly radio coverage of sporting events, begun in the pre-war period, increased in the years afterwards and created an audience for national culture, sport and current affairs. This trend was consolidated with the gradual arrival of television, which broadcast from a national perspective and sought to present a picture of a 'national' culture to which all in Britain subscribed without reservation. This was as true of television as it was of radio, which, even in its popular music broadcasting, was still based on a national network and image. The sheer dominance of the BBC in this area in part led to the popularity of pirate radio stations such as Radio Caroline in the early 1960s. This in

A queue at the Clock Tower for racing editions of the local papers, 1955

turn precipitated the rethink of the nature of popular broadcasting, which brought Radio One on to the scene. The examination of broadcasting needs and priorities also highlighted the need for a more local approach in future developments.

It was in this climate that the concept of local radio was born, with Leicester chosen as the pilot area for this experiment. The choice of Leicester was perhaps influenced by a long-running belief among marketing men that the Midlands, being neither north nor south, represents ideal territory for the test-marketing of any new product. However it may also have been influenced by the fact that Leicester, as the *Radio Times* supplement launching the station declared, was not only 'a great sporting city', but was also increasingly host to a considerable variety of interest groups and audiences with differing needs. The station was eventually launched on 8 November 1967 with a brief to provide public service broadcasting, to be achieved in consultation with voluntary local organizations in order to reflect the diversity of individuals through programmes for the old, the young, housewives and other interest groups. Most importantly of all the station intended to promote an awareness of issues and activities within the locality: 'It will make listeners aware as never before of what is happening in the factories and shops – and of firms' achievements and activities, from the factory floor to the boardroom.' Though coverage of Leicester's commercial activities has been important it has been in the area of community service broadcasting that the station has achieved its most notable successes. In its own celebration of ten years of broadcasting, Radio Leicester emphasized its ability to help during times of emergency such as the severe floods of July 1968, with appeals for blankets and accommodation for those rendered temporarily homeless. Similarly it pointed to the advantages that

Ethnic minority sport – Kabadi tournament

community groups had gained from advertising events on the station. Last of all the station's own initiatives in raising funds for various charities were also seen to be of considerable importance.

One area in which the programming of Radio Leicester has been particularly successful has been its provision of programmes for the Asian communities. This was pioneered by the programmes *Milan* and the *Six O'Clock Show*, which presented a mixture of entertainment and information regarding local news and facilities. A survey conducted in 1978 by the Commission for Racial Equality discovered just how successful Radio Leicester had been in reaching the Asian communities. The survey discovered that whereas 63 per cent of English speaking Asians regularly listened to Radio Leicester, 84 per cent of those who spoke Gujarati were regular listeners, as were 86 per cent of Punjabi speakers and 87 per cent of those speaking other Asian languages. Though the Commission's report was appreciative of the efforts of the BBC it nonetheless suggested that ethnic minority broadcasting was still considered a comparatively low priority. This was in truth a symptom of a wider belief that broadcasting should be made even more accessible. This clamour for community television channels, reinforced by the diversification of broadcasting through commercial radio, Channel Four, satellite television and even the impact of the cornershop video store, is itself part of a disintegration of the cultural monopoly previously held by the BBC. As the 1990s progress the trend towards more community based broadcasting will accelerate, as has been demonstrated by the recent interest of a number of communications companies in establishing in Leicester a locally based cable television network.

Though it is possible to exaggerate the scope of changes in the history of leisure and consumption in Leicester, we can at least identify some trends that have been at work over the period. The early part of the century witnessed a more neighbourhood based approach to leisure represented in the local institutions of the pub, cinema and local sports clubs. The inter-war period saw the appeal of major sports clubs in particular go into a decline that coincided with both the heightened search for national status and the failure to admit the paying public to active participation in 'their' clubs. Increasingly popular leisure pursuits such as radio and television required less commitment from individuals and eroded the audience for theatre, cinema and spectator sports since they offered either viable alternatives or even coverage of the events themselves. These leisure pursuits were increasingly found in the home, which itself had become a more comfortable environment as the century progressed. The impact of the BBC's broadcasting policies was to create a national culture which effectively undermined the regional identity of much regional leisure. Though it remains to be seen what will be said of the last years of the century it is likely that community/neighbourhood conceptions of leisure will be seen to have made a resurgence.

The first step towards this process has been the increased identification of indiv-

Coaches line the A47 to take Leicester holidaymakers to Skegness in the 1970s

idual need by a number of voluntary and statutory organizations, which has influenced the producers and providers of leisure opportunities. Similarly there has been an increased awareness among consumers of leisure that they have an ability to influence those who control and regulate leisure opportunities. Thus the period between the 1970s and 1990s has seen everything from the emergence of the Campaign for Real Ale to the development of a football fanzine culture, which argues for greater individual and community participation as the way forward for football and perhaps, indirectly, all leisure pursuits.

Further Reading

Carswell, Jeanne, Johnson, Rachel, and Kirrane, Siobhan, *Ours to Defend . . . : Leicestershire People Remember World War Two*

Crump, Jeremy, 'Amusements of the People: the provision of recreation in Leicester, 1850–1914', PhD thesis, University of Warwick (1985)

Gimson, J.R., *Leicester Ivanhoe Cricket Club* (1923)

Graham, John, *Before my time: The Story of the Leicester Drama Society* (1983)

Leacroft, Helen and Richard, *The Theatre in Leicestershire: A History of Entertainment* (1986)

Leicester University School of Education Library, Oral History Archive:
  I Remember Leicester . . . Cinema (1985)
  I Remember Leicester . . . Theatre (1985)
  I Remember Leicester . . . Music Hall (1985)

Murphy, Patrick, Dunning, Eric, and Williams, John, *House of Cards: The development of Leicester City Members plan* (1985)

Smith, David, *Of Fossils and Foxes: The Official History of Leicester City Football Club (1989)*

Snow, E.E., *Leicestershire Cricket 1949–1977* (1977)

INDEX